S0-AYZ-531

The Lord Is On Your Side

The Lord Is On Your Side

By Jim And Tammy Bakker

Edited By Mary McLendon

PTL Television Network
Charlotte, NC 28279

All scriptures in King James Version
unless otherwise noted.

Editorial Journalist: Anton Marco
Cover Design: Jerry DeCeglio
Photos By: Ken Kandle, Greg Davis, Eddie Holder,
Neil Howell, Phil Egert
Typography: Donnie Beck, Jacqueline Olsen
Inside Design & Layout: Jerry Dunning, Jerry DeCeglio,
Frank Clark, Donna Frierson

© 1980 by
Heritage Village Church and Missionary Fellowship, Inc.
All rights reserved. Printed in the United States.

First Edition-December 1980

Acknowledgements

A lot of hard work and research has gone on behind the scenes at PTL to make this devotional guide possible. We'd like to take this opportunity to thank our dear friend, Cliff Dudley, for helping us with the final review. Our special thanks also to Dr. Maynard Ketcham, a member of the PTL Board of Elders, for assisting in the editing.

The Publications Department, under the direction of Mary McLendon, and her fine staff, Annette Green, Carolyn Howell, Sylvia McAllister, Anton Marco, Marjorie Richardson, and Jan White, worked countless hours compiling and editing these devotionals from our notes.

We would also like to thank Jacqueline Olsen who volunteered her time to typeset the majority of this book. Her labor of love saved PTL thousands of dollars, and we are deeply grateful to her.

We are grateful to each one for their contributions.

"If it had not been the Lord who was on our side, when men rose up against us, then they had swallowed us up quick, when their wrath was kindled against us: then the waters had overwhelmed us, the stream had gone over our soul . . . Blessed be the Lord who hath not given us as a prey to their teeth. Our soul has escaped as a bird out of the snare of the fowlers: the snare is broken, and we are escaped. Our help is in the name of the Lord, who made heaven and earth."

—Psalm 124:2-8

Dear Friend,

We hope that this devotional guide will bless and inspire you during your quiet time each day.

Both of us have shared many of the experiences, the joys, and the tears that we've encountered in our walk with the Lord. As each trial has passed, we've learned that our trials are *"more precious than of gold."* 1 Peter 1:7

Through it all, we have learned that God is on our side. He loves us, and He loves you. He wants to meet your need today according to His Word.

We pray that these nuggets of truth from the Word, and the experiences and revelations we have shared together in this book, will minister to you and your family.

You, our friend and partner in sharing the Gospel, are in our prayers each day at PTL. We love you with all our hearts and pray God's best for you in 1981.

Remember, there is always someone to talk and pray with according to Matthew 18:19 *"Again I say unto you, that if two of you shall agree on earth as touching anything that they shall ask, it shall be done for them of my father which is in heaven."* Call the prayer counselors at PTL any time at 704-554-6080.

God loves you! And we do, too!

Love,

Jim + Tammy

Jim & Tammy

The Lord Is On Your Side!

"The Lord is on my side; I will not fear: what can man do unto me?"

— *Psalm 118:6*

The Lord is on your side! This is what God's Word is saying to you and me today. Did you know that's in the Bible? I was talking to Oral Roberts one day, and he said, "Jim, is that true? You know, everybody's always said you've got to be on the Lord's side."

Well, that's true. You'd better choose whose side you're going to be on today. We must be on the Lord's side. And the Bible says that He is on our side!

As I searched the Bible, I learned that God is even on the side of the sinner! Now, that is hard for a lot of people to believe. People think that God is some big, old, grey-bearded man up there with a huge club to knock them in the head. But I want you to know that God loved you enough to save you, even as a sinner. He's not going to just come and throw you out of His hand because you might have had a bad day. He is on your side!

Now, you could choose to serve the devil, but I want you to know that if you're on the devil's side, he's not on your side — because he's going to kill you. He's going to give you drugs and alcohol and promise you a high, and he's going to give you the lowest low that you've ever had. Everything he gives has a hangover, and the lowest one is hell. You'd better stick with God — He's on your side with "life more abundantly."

You may be going through the biggest problem or struggle in your life right now. And you may say, "Jim, I don't feel like God is on my side." Yes, He is! I've got news for you — He'll bring you through deep waters. He'll turn that trial into gold bricks. Just keep trusting Him. "If God be for us, who can be against us?" (Romans 8:31) God is on your side today. Follow Him, and you'll start putting the devil on the run!

Doing And Trusting

"Loving God means doing what He tells us to do, and really, that isn't hard at all ... by trusting Christ ..."

— *1 John 5:3-4 (LB)*

It seems like almost every day, someone will come up to me and say, "Jim, if you don't do this, you're going to be in trouble." Fifteen minutes later, somebody else will say just the opposite. Then another person will come along and advise me to do nothing. But I've found a solution to this head-spinning dilemma: I stand on God's Word. I do what He tells me to do. I keep my eyes on Him for guidance and advice.

An Eastern king was contemplating his son's ability to succeed him as ruler of his domain. He devised a shrewd test for the young man. He filled a large shell with oil and told his son, "Take this and run through the city. If you can do this without spilling a drop, I'll know you are fit to rule."

The young man ran through the city and spilled not a drop. His father asked, "Son, how did you accomplish this feat? Did not the marketplace, the sights, and the crowds of people distract you?" "No," the son replied, "I did not notice the marketplace, sights, or crowds. I kept my eyes on the oil, and not one drop spilled."

And that's the key: The only way you're going to make it through the marketplace of life is to keep your eyes on Jesus Christ. I'm not saying that you should disregard all advice, but that you should weigh it carefully in light of what God's Word and His will revealed through fervent prayer would have you to do.

Jesus, I do love you today. And I know that's more than a feeling, it's doing what you want me to do. I ask you for your clear direction for this day right now — and the determination to follow it faithfully. Let me not look to the right or the left, but straight toward the goal of pleasing you. Amen.

Believe And Ye Shall Have

"Those things that you desire when you pray, believe you receive them and you shall have them."

— Mark 11:24

I remember when we first started building Heritage USA. The land was overgrown and wild. There were no roads to speak of in the whole twelve hundred acre tract, so the only way to get around was by a four-wheel drive jeep.

Many Saturday afternoons, I took Tammy out there in the jeep, and I'd try to tell her what I saw. I had prayed and asked God to let us build this Christian Retreat Center, and I believed it in my heart so deeply that I could see the campsites, the tennis courts, the seminar halls, the chalets . . . I could see the whole thing through my spiritual eyes.

Poor Tammy, all she could see were wild plum thickets, mud holes, and a lot of trees. She must have thought I had lost my mind.   But God tells us, that when we pray, to believe that we receive them. Whatever the desire is in your mind, picture it in faith as you pray, see yourself in that new job, in that new house, with a better marriage relationship, with that health problem all cleared out.

Do you have that pictured in your mind?

Then dwell on it, confident through the Word of God that He will do this thing for you.

It just takes active faith. The Bible says, "Faith without works is dead." When I wanted to see Heritage USA built, I went out there and helped lay out roads and helped clear brush, all the time keeping my mind on the end result, the fulfillment of a dream.

Get ready to receive from God. Believe in your heart, do all you can humanly do, and sit back and watch God work!

The Lord Is On Your Side

"And Jonathan said to the young man that bare his armor, Come, and let us go over unto the garrison of these uncircumcised: it may be that the Lord will work for us: for there is no restraint to the Lord to save by many or by few."
— 1 Samuel 14:6

TAMMY: You know, I really like the story that is told in this scripture. I was talking to some friends about Jonathan one day and it really amazes me how two men could go out and face an entire army. But then, you have to realize that they weren't alone — they had the Lord on their side!

Jonathan was being the strong man and he decided he wanted to find out what the enemy was doing. But you know what happened, don't you? Jonathan and his bodyguard ended up right in the middle of the battle instead of looking on from the side.

Here they were, two men standing right in the middle of the entire Philistine army looking around and trying to figure out what they were going to do next. They talked it over and Jonathan told his bodyguard that he thought they should go across to the heathen and pray that the Lord would perform a miracle for them because it doesn't make any difference to the Lord how many enemy troops there are. They made a commitment to each other to stand together and fight the enemy.

They believed that the Lord was on their side and they could not be defeated. And they were right. They began to fight the enemy and they started falling dead to the left and right of Jonathan and his bodyguard. This scared the army so bad that they retreated and just took off. And, there were Jonathan and his bodyguard standing in the middle grinning and shouting praises to God!

When your troubles seem too huge to tackle, remember that the Lord is on your side and He will help you to overcome them. If one can defeat a thousand, and two can put ten thousand to flight, think what everyone standing together can do!

Tell Somebody About Jesus

"Those who turn many to righteousness will glitter like stars forever."

— Daniel 12:3b

My Grandpa Bakker was an unusual man. He was not well accepted. People really didn't know how to take him.

In all honesty, I really wasn't that fond of Grandpa Bakker. When I was a kid, he would pray so long before a meal the food would get cold. There was always an hour's sing and a whole revival service before we could eat. And you know how kids are.

He used to spend most of his money on Bible tracts, and any time he had a few minutes, he'd be on a street corner somewhere handing them out.

After he died, I went to his house. He lived in an old rustic log cabin up on a hill. I entered the cabin and looked around the front room, and everywhere I looked there were hundreds and hundreds of tracts. Across every chair, in the whole place, there were stacks and stacks of tracts.

I was thinking about him just the other day. He was misunderstood because the only thing really important to him was spreading the Word of the Lord. He didn't have the tool of television like I use today, so he used what he had, and spread tracts everywhere he went.

There is no doubt, in my mind, that old Grandpa Bakker is "glittering like stars" in heaven today, because bringing people to righteousness was his whole life.

Many of us sit back and say to ourselves, "Well, one day I'll start winning souls to the Lord. I'll start witnessing to others at work and in my family."

My friend, it is later than you think. I really feel that Jesus is coming again so soon. And what we are going to do, we must do quickly.

Tell somebody about Jesus today!

Good News!

"And the angel said unto them, fear not: for behold, I bring you good tidings of great joy, which shall be to all people."

— *Luke 2:10*

Don't you just love to tell somebody some good news, like someone's having a baby, or someone's getting married?

Well, that's why I love being the host of the PTL Club. Everyday, I get to tell millions of people across the United States that Jesus loves them. And that's fun!

One of the greatest testimonies that documents that the saving grace of Jesus can be transmitted through the television screen is that of Efrem Zimbalist, Jr.

He is a very well-known Hollywood actor, as you probably know, who found the Lord through Christian television. One night he was unable to sleep. As was his habit, he got up and began playing with the television dial.

That night, instead of the normal fare of old westerns and car salesmen, he chose to watch a Christian program — why? Because he thought it was funny!

Well, God says His Word will not return void. Night after night, Efrem watched until the message finally got through to him. He accepted the Lord as his personal Savior.

Since that time, he has gotten very much involved with Christian television. He is on our Board of Directors, he helps raise funds every year for a station in Clearwater, FL, and he often appears on PTL, the 700 Club, and many other television outreaches.

Because of his Christian outreach and testimony, only the Lord knows how many people have been saved.

God expects us to spread His Good News to all who will hear. That is not just our right and our privilege, it's our responsibility, and we must not forsake it!

Two Houses

"And the rains descended, and the floods came, and the winds blew, and beat upon the house; and it fell: and great was the fall of it."
— *Matthew 7:27*

Jesus was talking here about two kinds of people: the wise and the foolish. He said they were like two houses built on two different foundations — one on a rock, the other on sand.

Every builder knows how important a foundation is to the success of a building job. No house constructed on loose or sandy soil is likely to stand for long. After a while, erosion from water and wind carries the soil away, and the house crumbles. The ideal foundation goes down to bedrock, which doesn't shift with changes in weather. One of the things that makes New York City so conducive to building skyscrapers is that Manhattan Island is mostly solid rock just below its topsoil. Mexico City, on the other hand, has swampy underpinnings, and taller buildings start sinking down into it from the moment they're built.

The two houses Jesus was describing might have been built exactly alike, and by the same builder. The difference in their fate was the strength of their foundation. The two kinds of people this parable illustrates also have similarities: They have both heard Jesus' words. They know what Jesus taught. On the outside, these people may look exactly the same. But Jesus says that one person *puts those sayings into practice,* while the other one doesn't. That's the difference. And when the storms of life come, the person who isn't *doing* what Jesus says to do, isn't going to stand firm.

Do you see that the foundation of Christian living is in the *doing* of God's will, not in the knowing? Are you firmly grounded in *doing* what God's given you to *do?* You can't be on the Solid Rock's foundation until you let Jesus *do* through you His perfect will. Ask Him to give you the opportunity to put the things of God into practice in your life today.

Don't Grieve The Spirit

"And grieve not the Holy Spirit of God . . . ."
— *Ephesians 4:30*

A boy once made a pet of a beautiful dove. With bread crumbs and flower seeds, he coaxed it until it felt safe to perch on his shoulder and eat from his hand every day.

He enjoyed its gentle company for a while, but as boys will, he tired of the dove once the challenge of winning it was gone. Then its affection for him became annoying. One day, when the dove settled on his shoulder, the boy offered it a bit of bread, as usual. But as the bird reached for the treat, the boy suddenly closed his fist tightly.

Startled, the bird fluttered away for a moment, but soon flew back to the boy's shoulder. Again, the boy offered the bread, but again, he snatched it away. This time, the dove flew to a nearby tree limb and sat waiting. The boy tempted it to his shoulder yet once more, only to trick it again. This time, the bird flew away over the treetops, into the distance. Realizing what he had done, the boy quickly ran after it, with bread crumbs in his outstretched hands, but the dove would not return.

This story reminds me of the kind of people who "play" with God. They call upon Him when in trouble. They promise Him all sorts of things and cry, "Oh Lord, how I need you." They hold out "crumbs" of themselves to God. And He responds to them and brings His help and love. But when they're on safe ground again, they slam their hearts' doors, and treat God and His people cruelly, shutting His Holy Spirit out of their lives.

You can't keep "playing games" with God. Yes, He is kind and compassionate. But His Holy Spirit can be grieved, and as Psalm 103:9 says, He will not always strive with us; nor will He keep His anger forever. If you've been toying with God, stop it before it's too late. What a tragedy it might be, to lose forever the gentle presence of the Lord!

Don't Give Up

". . . Arise, take up thy bed and walk."
— Mark 2:9

C. M. Ward tells the story of a man at the age of thirty-nine, who took a daring dive into the icy waters of a lake in Eastern Canada. He came up out of the chilly water with polio.

Just before he had suffered the worse defeat of his political career as he lost his bid for Vice-President of the United States. Both his doctors and his friends thought he was through. They were sure he would remain an invalid for the rest of his life.

However, the man never gave up. He could not accept this terrible fate. He overcame it, and later served as President for four terms — the man, Franklin D. Roosevelt.

Roosevelt could have accepted his friends' diagnosis. But he was a fighter, and he fought with every ounce of energy within him.

No matter what the sickness is, we Christians have something to fight back with — the Word of God. Nothing that Satan can throw at us is as strong and powerful as the Almighty God.

Jesus made the way for our healings. "Surely He hath borne our griefs and carried our sorrows." The word "griefs" is often translated as sickness and disease in the Old Testament. The word "sorrows" is often associated with physical pain.

Our avenue to healing is through faith. If you are in need of a healing in your body today, trust God with the problem. Call PTL or another friend that believes in the power of prayer and have someone agree with you for your healing.

Remember our theme verse at PTL, "And Jesus said unto them, If two of you shall agree on earth as touching anything that they shall ask, it shall be done for them of my Father which is in heaven." Matthew 18:19

Don't give up! Whatever your problem — commit it to God today. Let Him fight your battles!

Count Your Blessings

"I will bless the Lord at all times: his praise shall be continually in my mouth."
— *Psalm 34:1*

As long as I live, I'll never forget my trip to India. It was like a nightmare. A terrible flood had engulfed the country, filth floated on the top of the deep currents, rats scrambled for safety everywhere you looked.

I remember one little girl, she was so tiny and fragile that I wondered how she was even alive. The cold, bitter wind swept over the filthy water, and she leaned up against me for warmth, her only clothing was a thin, dirty diaper.

She had come to the place where Mark Buntain feeds thousands every day with the help of PTL. That day, they couldn't even bake the bread. Shivering in the cold, she held out her hand for a bit of raw dough and a cup of milk.

As tears streamed down my face, I thought, "How blessed we are in America — how very blessed we are!"

Over two-thirds of the world goes to bed hungry every night, yet we have the gall to all but fuss at God because our house isn't fancy enough or we have to eat hamburger instead of steak.

If any country, in this world, should be constantly praising God, it's America. We have food, we have clean water, we have decent shelter, we have warm clothes.

Not all Christians have the freedom to praise God and worship Him in public gatherings like we do in America. I think we often take our many blessings for granted.

Remember the old song, "Count your blessings, name them one by one . . . count your many blessings, see what God has done . . . ." I think we all need to do that — and often, too.

You Can't Out Give God

"Though I appreciate your gifts, what makes me happiest is the well-earned reward you will have because of your kindness . . . They are a sweet smelling sacrifice that pleases God well. And it is He who will supply all your needs from His riches in glory."
— *Philippians 4:17, 18b, 19*

I know how Paul felt as he wrote those words. PTL is built and supported by the freewill love gifts of people in the body of Christ that believe in what we are doing to spread the Gospel.

Though I am forever grateful to these people that send in their gifts to PTL, I know in my heart that God is going to bless them and meet their every need.

Over the years, I have received many letters from critics who attack PTL for raising money over television. They think that we rob little old grandmas of their pension money and the poor old ladies never get anything in return. Hogwash!

Tammy and I know, from experience, what it is like to give out of our need. Many times, God has spoken to us to give away things we felt we needed, and every time, God has returned the blessing, and given us back something even greater.

If you believe in the Bible as the Holy Word of God, you have to believe every word of it as true. This scripture is true. I dare you to try it.

Look around you today. If you have a need, ask God what He would have you give away. It doesn't have to be money. Maybe God would have you give of your time and take care of the neighbors' kids for an afternoon; or maybe the Lord would have you bake a cake for that poor family around the corner.

This I know: You can't out give God!

If You Really Believed It . . .

"For whosoever shall call upon the name of the Lord shall be saved. How then shall they call on Him in whom they have not believed? and how shall they believe in Him of whom they have not heard? and how shall they hear without a preacher?"

— *Romans 10:13-14*

People resent preachers sometimes, but God's chosen preaching as one of the means of bringing people to Himself. People expect preachers to believe with all their hearts in what they are preaching. Perhaps that's why they're so hard on preachers. It's a shame that today there are some men standing in pulpits who don't really believe what they're saying.

There's a story told of a young man who'd been sentenced to die in the electric chair for murder. As is customary, the prison chaplain came into his cell to talk before the young man "walked the last mile."

The young man listened closely as the chaplain spoke about Jesus Christ as the Savior of all men. The minister talked of the eternal life God promised to everyone who believed in Jesus.

The young man, who had been quiet during all this, suddenly shouted in rage, "Stop it! You don't really believe that. If you believed it, you'd be begging me to receive Jesus! You wouldn't be talking to me here, when I'm about to 'fry.' You'd have spoken to me long ago, before I killed. You and all those people in church pews would be on the streets and from house to house and in stores telling everyone you could what you just told me. That's what you would do — if you *really* believed it!"

Do you really believe the message of salvation today? Then share it with another soul, while there's still hope in this world for them.

The International Salvation Test

"Beloved, let us love one another: for love is of God; and everyone that loveth is born of God, and knoweth God; for God is love. In this was manifested the love of God toward us, because that God sent his only begotten Son into the world, that we might live through him."

— *1 John 4:7-9*

There are a lot of tests today on television and in national magazines. There is the National Drivers Test, the National School Test, and many others. Well, I want to give you the International Salvation Test.

The verse above will tell you if you are ready for heaven. If you love, then you are born of God and you know God. Because God is love.

When love dies, there is nothing left. If love dies in a church, the church splits. I've seen it happen. If love dies in a home, the marriage falls apart.

The Bible says that the way to tell if someone has passed from darkness into life is by love. "We know that we have passed from death into life because we love the brethren. He that loveth not his brother abideth in death."

I know that is harsh teaching, but it is straight from the Word of God. We can't go around hating our brother and expect to go to heaven. God says something very powerful about that in 1 John 4:20, "If a man say, I love God, and hateth his brother, he is a liar: for he that loveth not his brother whom he hath seen, how can he love God whom he hath not seen."

We, as Christians, don't have the right to pick and choose who we love. Remember, God sent Jesus to die for us even though we were deep in sin, and the gift of salvation He offers us is free. All we have to do is love.

Little David — and You

"This day will the Lord deliver thee into mine hand, and I will smite thee, and take thine head from thee . . . . "

— 1 Samuel 17:46

This is David talking to Goliath the giant. I bet that giant was looking down and saying, "What a cocky little kid! Who does he think he is?" And he hollered to David, "I'm going to feed you to the birds and the beasts!"

A lot of people may decide that they can do what you're doing a lot better than you can. They can bake a better pie, teach a better Sunday School class, pray better or build a doghouse better. But I've got news for you: Only you can do best what you're doing, because God has got a plan for you.

I used to get discouraged because I thought everybody could preach better than I. Then one day an old preacher said to me, "Jim, Billy Graham may preach better than you, Oral Roberts may preach better than you. But only you can do what you have to do and what God has called you to do. Hey! You are special to God — you're an individual!" I stopped worrying about whether somebody else could do what I was doing better. I concentrated on doing what was there for me to do.

Little David had a chance to fight like a trained warrior. But God had another plan for him. David rejected King Saul's armor, and with the slingshot and stones God put in his hands, he went out and slew that giant.

You may not think that you've got what it takes to do the tasks facing you today. You may think someone else ought to be filling your shoes. But God can use you as He can use nobody else. You may have to face "giants" in your life today. Don't wish for someone else's armor. What you have will do to win the battle — because God in you is greater than your biggest problem. Believe that — and slay that giant!

No Condemnation In God

"There is therefore now no condemnation to them which are in Christ Jesus, who walk not after the flesh, but after the Spirit. For the law of the Spirit of life in Christ Jesus hath made me free from the law of sin and death."

— *Romans 8:1, 2*

When I was in high school, I often worked as a disc jockey at school dances. One night I was disc jockeying at one of these dances, when I looked up to see my father standing in the doorway watching me.

He didn't come inside — he just stood there in the doorway. Neither he nor my mother ever mentioned his coming to the school that evening.

I found out later they had been defending me to church people who had been criticizing me for being a disc jockey at the dances.

That incident in my life has always stuck in my mind, because it reminds me so much of the way Jesus deals with His children.

When He looks in on our lives and sees something He doesn't like, His love for us never varies. He doesn't criticize or condemn us, but just as my parents defended me, Jesus stands before the throne of God, defending us against the accusations of Satan (and church people).

Fortunately for us, His love doesn't depend on our ability to be perfect and worthy of love. The God I serve is a merciful God, quick to forgive and slow to anger at our many falls from the path of His righteousness.

If you've been carrying the burden of guilt from some past sin, then lay that burden at Jesus' feet today. If the most high God isn't condemning you for your mistake, then rejoice and condemn yourself no longer!

Let God Use Your Abilities

"The Lord will perfect that which concerneth me; thy mercy, O Lord, endureth for ever; forsake not the works of thine own hands."
— *Psalms 138:8*

TAMMY: For some reason, some people have the misguided notion that when you become a Christian, you have to give up using all your natural talents and abilities and go to Africa as a missionary, become a minister, or marry one!

Actually, nothing could be further from the truth. Becoming a Christian enhances your natural talents and abilities because when you give them to God, He gives them back doubled and tripled. God wants fulfilled children, so He's at work perfecting and developing *everything* that concerns us.

I have always loved music. I grew up learning the piano from my musical mother. When Jim and I began our ministry, I used my musical ability in our services while Jim preached. But I longed to do more.

I should have known that the God who put musical talent in me would bless it when I put it to use for Him!

First a man walked up to me one Sunday morning after a church service and gave me an expensive accordion. My eyes popped wide open!

I didn't know how to play it, but God took care of that, too! The pastor at our next revival knew how to play the accordion expertly, and he taught me. I sounded like a professional in three weeks.

Don't shy away from using your talents for the Lord, Christians! God will bless them, and develop them in you even further if you'll use them in His work. Today, hand over a talent to God you've shied away from using. Watch Him hand it back to you perfected!

His Unique Creation

"In the beginning, God created the heaven and the earth."

— *Genesis 1:1*

If you don't believe the first verse in the Bible, the rest of it probably won't mean much to you either. If you don't believe in a God who could create the universe, you are not likely to believe that He sent His Son, can work miracles, or do anything else really meaningful in your life.

A lot of people today don't believe that such a living God exists. They explain everything in existence as the result of a slow process that developed matter and life from some ancient atoms. Then they say some slime collected and eventually, animals and man crawled out of it. "From goo to you by way of the zoo," as Harold Hill put it.

A person like this once visited Isaac Newton, the scientist who discovered the Law of Gravity. The visitor looked at a mechanical model of the solar system in Newton's study, and asked, "Who made that model?"

"Nobody," Newton replied.

"What kind of fool do you take me for?" the man shot back angrily, "This is the work of a genius."

Newton reached out to touch a tiny globe. "It is only a poor imitation of a much greater system," he said. "How is it, my friend, that I cannot convince you that this toy didn't have a designer, though you believe the great original has come into being without a designer or maker?"

Everything in nature reveals the hand of a divine Creator. The reason some don't see God in His creation is because sin has made men blind. If men had to admit to a God great enough to create the universe, they'd have to admit that such a God should be worshiped and obeyed. Sinful man wants no boss but himself.

Thank God, He opens our eyes to see the truth of who He is! Thank Him right now for creating you and for making you His child.

God's Prosperity For You

"Beloved, I wish above all things that thou mayest prosper and be in health, even as thy soul prospereth."

— 3 John 2

Some very dear friends of mine and PTL's, the Happy Hunters, gave me the thoughts for today's scripture. When you read this, you must think of this sentence — God's *PROSPERITY* is for you. God's prosperity is for *YOU! GOD'S* prosperity is for you!

Look at those three ways of saying that one little sentence. With the emphasis on a different word each time, you change the meaning of the statement, but when you put them all together you have the answer to prosperity.

God wants YOU to prosper. You must believe that He truly intends for you to reap the benefits here on earth, also, from living for Him. I'm sure, at one time or another, you may have thought about prosperity in terms of money. Well, I have done that, too. But, the thing we have to remember is that there is a tremendous amount about money in God's Word. He is constantly talking about giving it away and that is the secret — GIVING IT AWAY!

God wants you to prosper in every part of your life. He wants your marriage to prosper. He wants your family relationships to prosper. He wants your business relationships to prosper. He wants your church relationships to prosper. He wants your relationships with your children to prosper. He wants your relationships with your employer to prosper. And, He wants your health to prosper.

The secret of living is giving! If you give love, you will get back love. If you give fellowship, you will get back fellowship. If you give time to God, you will get back more time than you know what to do with. And, if you give money to God, you will get back money.

God tells us that we control the amount that we will prosper. Whatever amount we give to God, He uses that same measure to return to us. Begin today to put your trust in God and you will begin to prosper!

First Love

"I know thy works, and thy labor, and thy patience, and how thou canst not bear them that are evil . . . and hast borne, and hast patience and for my name's sake hast labored, and hast not fainted. Nevertheless I have somewhat against thee, because thou hast left thy first love."

— *Revelation 2:2-4*

When we first fall in love with that special person, no task feels like too much trouble when we're doing it for our sweetheart, and no obstacle causing some kind of a problem in our relationship seems too large to overcome. We'll do just about anything to stay close to our loved one, even if that means going out of our way.

One of my staff members and good friend, Phil Egert, used to drive two hundred miles a day — every day — for six months, just to be near the girl who would soon be his wife! That's a lot of miles when you add them up! Of course, if you knew Ruth Egert, a lovely lady who also works for me, Phil's behavior might not seem so odd! But we do seem to go the extra distance when we first fall in love.

I think it's like that when we first meet the Lord, and fall in love with Him. We think about Him all during the day, and we'll go out of our way to make time in our busy day to spend with Him.

We have to be very careful, though, not to let our relationship with the Lord get to be routine after we've walked with Him for awhile. Sometimes, it's easy during a hectic day to let the time we usually spend with God slip right on by without even noticing. No one in any relationship likes to feel they're taken for granted, and I would imagine that God doesn't either.

Today, even if you're exceptionally busy, take the time to fellowship with God — if you'll make the effort you'll be rewarded with that same feeling of love you had in the beginning of your relationship with God.

It Won't Be Long!

"And the God of peace shall bruise Satan under your feet shortly...."
— *Romans 16:20*

Have you ever felt like the devil has stepped all over you? Have you just about had all you can take of Satan's meddlings in your life? Then here's a promise for you!

Do you remember another promise God made, ages before this, at the dawn of human history? It was to the devil, after he'd tempted Adam and Eve into sin: "And I will put enmity between thee and the woman, and between thy seed and her seed; it shall bruise thy head, and thou shalt bruise his heel" (Genesis 3:15). As soon as sin entered the world, God promised that He would send a Deliverer — and that Deliverer would bruise the head of Satan! Praise God, we know who He was — Jesus Christ, who bought our salvation at Calvary!

There, Jesus took away sin, vanquished death, and broke the power of Satan. The Word promises God is going to finish the job! At Jesus' Second Coming, Satan will be bound. After being loosed at the end of a thousand years, he'll be tossed into the lake of fire with his wicked followers to burn forever and ever! That will be a bruising indeed!

But today's promise has a present application, too. For it says that God is going to bruise Satan's head under *our* feet! He's doing that, day by day, as we win victories for Jesus in the now. We may get our heel bruised in the process, but I'd rather have a bruised heel than a crushed head, wouldn't you?

Think of it right now: When you tell a neighbor about Jesus — there goes your foot on the devil's head! When you read your Bible, pray for a friend's healing, visit a lonely shut-in, forgive an enemy, hold on to God's promise to supply your needs, love Jesus today as you've never loved Him before, you are bruising Satan's head. Do the will of God today, and give the devil a whopping headache!

More Than You Can Imagine!

"Now unto Him that is able to do exceeding abundantly above all that we ask or think, according to the power that worketh in us . . . . "
— *Ephesians 3:20*

What a verse! No matter how big you can dream, no matter how huge a blockbuster prayer you can pray, God is able to do exceeding abundantly above that! It sounds like there are no limits to what God can do. Maybe we need to expand the limits of our trust in Him!

God has proven this scripture true in my own life and in the PTL ministry. No matter how big a dream I had, or how wild I let my imagination run, God has outdone me. Sometimes He's even changed my vision because He had some greater blessing than I'd envisioned.

When I first thought about Heritage Hall, the huge "barn" auditorium at Heritage USA, I pictured in my mind a flat, barnlike entrance, and a large stage inside the auditorium.

But Tammy came up with the idea of extending the entrance and decorating it with a stone front. That gave us a bigger "barn," with more room to work with, so we made a beautiful Partner receiving area. The stone front made the auditorium look even better, too.

When we found the stage area wasn't working right, we "stretched" out the back wall and moved the stage back. That gave us a much greater seating capacity than we planned, but God was thinking bigger than we were!

How far does your imagination stretch today? God can take the reality of your dream further than you ever hoped. He may not have in mind for you to build a ministry like PTL. But He can imagine a better dress than you think you can make. He can imagine a growth in your business that you didn't see possible. He can see better school grades than you're getting. If you let Him, He'll do more than you can imagine — if you can imagine that!

Have No Fear

"But the fearful, and unbelieving, and the abominable, and murderers, and whore-mongers, and sorcerers, and idolaters, and all liars, shall have their part in the lake which burneth with fire and brimstone which is the second death."

— *Revelation 21:8*

TAMMY: I don't know how many times I have read this verse and how many sermons I have heard from it, but I never realized that fear was the first on the list. I never understood that the fearful are going to find their place in hell, which is the fire and brimstone and the second death.

Understanding that the fearful are listed with the unbelieving, abominable, murderers, whoremongers, sorcerers, idolaters, and liars took my breath away. The Holy Spirit had opened my eyes to this verse!

But, then I began asking myself, "Why would the fearful be put in the very beginning of this verse by God?" The answer was so simple — fear is the opposite of faith and without faith we can't begin to please Him.

When we have fear, we aren't putting all our trust in God. If you refuse to do something because you are scared of it, you are telling God you don't trust Him. Fear dishonors God and faith honors Him.

Fear is never from God — it is always planted by Satan. Whenever we feel the first tinge of fear enter our minds, we have to instantly remember that it isn't from God. God gave us everything that is the opposite of fear.

You have to cast fear out of your life. With fear present, we can't love and honor Jesus as we should and there is something wrong with our relationship with Him. If you are fearful all the time, you had better check on your relationship with God. Remember — you don't fear someone you trust totally!

Strength From Trials

"These trials are only to test your faith to see whether or not it is strong and pure. It is being tested as fire tests gold . . . ."

— *1 Peter 1:7*

Have you ever wondered why life seems to be one hurdle after another? You've just made the final payment on your car, and the transmission breaks down — and as soon as you fix that the tires need to be replaced. I think that sometimes we look at life's struggles as just a jumble of hardships. We look at them as painful experiences with no worth. But there's a better way to look at these difficulties — and that's as toughening exercises.

A little boy was once collecting cocoons for a science project. One day he noticed some movement in one, and as he watched, he witnessed a miracle. What he thought was a caterpillar struggled mightily, finally broke free, and flew away as a butterfly!

Soon he noticed that same movement in another cocoon, and he decided to help this butterfly get a head start on life. He tore back the outer layer, and sure enough, there was the butterfly. But it just lay there, fluttering its wings, unable to fly as the other had. The little boy had thwarted that struggle of rebirth, and in so doing destroyed the butterfly's chance ever to fly. The butterfly needed that struggle to gain the strength to launch into the air.

Just like the butterfly, God knows you need the inner strength that comes with facing and overcoming your daily challenges with His help. Maybe you're going through a struggle right now. Remember, it's meant to make you tough and strengthen you to stand. If you keep your faith in God and let Him try you and purify you, one day soon you're going to fly away, too — just like that butterfly!

Never Forsaken

". . . For He hath said, I will never leave thee, nor forsake thee."

— Hebrews 13:5

Tammy and I experienced a real joy one day not long ago when our little son, Jamie Charles, came up to Tammy and said, "Mommy, I want to have Jesus in my heart." He had been hearing us talk about Jesus and decided that he wanted Jesus, too.

And he asked, "How does Jesus get into my heart? Does He come in through my tummy button?" Tammy said, "Well, no, all you have to do is ask Jesus to come into your heart." And so he did. He sat down right there and said, "Dear Jesus, come into my heart."

He was real quiet for a moment and then he said, "Mommy, is Jesus in my heart now?" Tammy answered, "Yes, if you've asked Him to come in, He's in your heart." Jamie Charles thought about it for a little while. He didn't say a thing. At last, he looked up and said, "Mommy, I'm going to keep my mouth shut — so Jesus can't get out!"

Now, I think maybe there's a kernel of good advice in that little remark! But seriously, Jesus doesn't leave us so easily. He's promised never to leave us or forsake us.

I feel for people who are afraid that Jesus is going to leave them each time they do the tiniest thing wrong. Some think that after every sin, they have to ask Him into their hearts all over again. Well, you don't have to do that. You would have to totally abandon everything you do or think that has anything to do with God. You'd have to stop loving and serving Him totally and completely immerse yourself in godlessness and sin — you'd have to forsake God to lose Him — He'd never forsake you.

If you have love for Jesus in your heart, if you're trying to do His will, you can rest your soul about His presence in your heart today. Thank Him right now for being there.

The "Detour" Of Criticism

"Sanballat was very angry when he learned
we were rebuilding the wall. He ... insulted us
and mocked us and laughed at us ..."
— Nehemiah 4:1

Every time you attempt to do something well, there's always someone trying to stop or detour you. One of the most effective detours these people put in your way is criticism.

Now, if it's constructive criticism, you can take it and build on it. But if it's destructive, it can tear you down. Either way it can be discouraging, and if you listen to everyone telling you what to do and what not to do, you'll be so confused, you'll do nothing!

A boy and his father were once going to market with their donkey. The father was riding the donkey and the son was leading it along. A man came by and remarked, "How terrible! That man is riding the donkey and making the boy walk!" So the father got off, and the boy climbed on the donkey. They started off, and someone else came by and said, "Shameful! A young boy riding, while the old man has to walk!" So they both mounted the donkey. Soon other people came and said, "Such cruelty! Two people on that poor little donkey!" So they both got off. Finally, a man approached and cried, "Two people walking with a donkey not carrying anything — how stupid!" So the father and son tried to carry the donkey, and they never got to market.

Nehemiah faced criticism when he rebuilt the wall around Jerusalem. But he ignored the criticism, looked to God for guidance, and was successful as a result.

Don't be detoured because somebody says you can't do something or that you're not good enough. You'll never please all the critics. Just remember, you're God's child and you can do all things through Christ. You can be a success in business and you can succeed at home. You can succeed at school. You can succeed — with God!

_____

Work With Your Hands

"And that ye study to be quiet, and to do your own business, and to work with your own hands, as we commanded you."
— *1 Thessalonians 4:11*

There's something very satisfying and relaxing about working with your hands. Employees and Partners sometimes find me working at night at Heritage USA, stocking shelves at the General Store, collecting firewood, or doing some other type of work with my hands.

I imagine some of them say, "Now why in the world is Jim Bakker doing that? He has a lot of people working for him who could do those jobs." But the rhythm of that kind of work has a way of letting your mind flow freely, and I've often done very productive thinking at such times.

The apostle Paul had a lot of responsibilities — preaching, teaching, taking the Gospel to the Gentiles, and establishing churches. Yet he worked with his hands. This highly educated former Pharisee worked as a tentmaker. I imagine he must have been a good one. And it must have added a lot of weight to his witness for Christ to be in business and be known for his fair treatment of customers and good workmanship. Paul knew what he was talking about when he spoke this Scripture.

We can be "quiet" before God in our minds while working busily with our hands. We need the physical labor to help us get rid of some of life's daily tensions.

If you haven't found some quiet and productive thing to do with your hands, I urge you to seek one. It may be gardening, carpentry, needlework, or just redecorating your home. Then, use this time to communicate with God while working with your hands.

Try it today. If you're anything like me, I'm sure the time you'll spend on your new "hobby" will prove most relaxing!

Considering Trials As Joy

"My brethren, count it all joy when ye fall into divers temptations; Knowing this, that the trying of your faith worketh patience. But let patience have her perfect work, that ye may be perfect and entire, wanting nothing."

— *James 1:2-4*

No matter how many trials and tribulations we run into during our lifetime, we must stand firm on our belief in Jesus as our Lord and Savior, for He will help us through all situations. The testing of your faith develops perseverance and then you grow spiritually as well as maturing in your character. You must be mature spiritually as well as mentally to overcome the obstacles Satan puts before you.

Whenever I think of how we must mature as Christians, I remember a story a pastor once told in a youth meeting. He was going on a skiing trip one winter. All the way to the slopes, he only thought about how scared he was of trying skiing. Once he was there, he still couldn't overcome his fear.

Once he was out on the slopes and the instructor told him the basics, he was off on his first attempt down the beginner's slope. At the bottom, he liked it so much he hopped on the ski lift and went straight back to the beginner's slope to try it again. This went on several times and he was having the time of his life.

Soon, the instructor told him it was time he stopped going down the beginner's slope and attempt the intermediate slope. He answered by saying how much he was enjoying skiing here, so why go on to a harder place. The instructor replied, "You must go on to the intermediate slope because you can't grow until you get out of your comfort zone."

This applies to Christians as well. We must get out of our comfort zone and go on to the next level of maturing spiritually and mentally in Jesus.

Idle Words

"But I say unto you, That every idle word that men shall speak, they shall give account thereof in the day of judgment."
— *Matthew 12:36*

The Bible clearly tells us that on Judgment Day, we will have to give an account of every idle word we've ever spoken. When I appeared at the Federal Communications Commission (FCC) hearings in Washington, I think I got a good idea what that day's going to be like!

All the written and taped material the FCC officials compiled made my head spin! They would play a tape or show me a document, that I had supposedly said or written, and I couldn't believe it! Some of the things I had never even seen before. From all the thousands of documents and hours of tapes they had, they wanted to know why I had said or done these things. Some of the comments on the tapes were made on the PTL Club over the past three years or just off the top of my head. They wanted me to give an account for every word and it was very difficult to try to do.

It isn't a pleasant thing to think about, but if you're going to have to do that in Heaven, there are some people in the body of Christ who had better watch out. I tell you, it's going to be rough up there. When I face that Tribunal, I want to be sure that it's all under the Blood!

When Jesus spoke these words, I believe He wasn't just trying to scare people. Everything God does, He does out of love. He gets no joy out of threatening to put someone on the "hot seat." Jesus was trying to get His listeners to look to God and be saved.

When you consider this Scripture, I urge you to let it drive you into the arms of Jesus. I urge you to let it help purge from your lips the things that might be unpleasing to Him. Let it help you learn to think before you speak. Let it be a reason to thank God for your salvation so that for those who love Him, judgment will be unto salvation, rather than to perishing.

Man Plans — God Directs

"A man's heart deviseth his way: but the Lord directeth his steps."

— Proverbs 16:9

All too often, we think we're responsible for orchestrating all the details of our journey through life. If we would put our confidence instead in God who directs our steps, we would walk much more securely.

If God called you to be a missionary to Africa, but the missionary board wasn't listening and missed hearing the Lord call your name, hang onto what God told you anyway. It's not the missionary board that's controlling your future — God is. If He says something is going to happen, then it will!

The great missionary-Apostle Paul never would have been sent out by a mission board. With his reputation as a fierce persecutor of Christians, the board would probably never have even considered his application. They would probably have figured it was all a trap.

In fact, something like that did happen to Paul as he struggled for the acceptance he needed to begin his ministry. When Paul came to Jerusalem after his conversion and sought out the disciples, they all shunned him. They were afraid of his reputation and doubted his claim to faith. It took Barnabas' support to overcome the disciples' mistrust.

Paul could never have gained the early church's trust on his own. But he didn't have to. Proverbs 5:21 says, "For the ways of man are before the eyes of the Lord, and pondereth all his goings." God had it all worked out ahead of time.

So whatever it is that God has called you to do today, don't look at the obstacles standing between you and your goal — look instead at the God who called you to that task. Make your plan to take the next step in the direction He's given you. He's well aware of all the footprints you haven't even made yet — and He'll see that your feet get into them!

That We May Be One

*"That they all may be one; as thou, Father,
art in me, and I in thee, that they also may be
one in us: that the world may believe that thou
hast sent me."*

— John 17:21

God doesn't want there to be any partition between us as
believers or between Him and ourselves. That's why Jesus made
the request above a part of His High Priestly prayer.

This prayer was not prayed just for the sake of establishing
peace among ourselves, although that would be wonderful to experience. It's also a missionary verse: God wants us to be one so
that the world will believe in Jesus. If we're going to do world
evangelism, the world will have to see the unity of the Spirit among
us. This is why PTL, I believe, probably wins more souls to Jesus
than any other ministry in the world today.

When I have a United Methodist pastor, a Presbyterian pastor,
a Pentecostal pastor, Roman Catholic priests and nuns — and I've
had them all sitting on our set — the world is looking on and saying,
"My lands, these Christians really do love one another! They're getting together. And if it works for them, it's going to work for us!"

Because for so long people said, "Oh, those Christians! They
fight and fume — the Baptist fights the Methodist, the Methodists
are battling the Lutherans!" Now they're amazed to see us getting
along. And it makes them feel that there's a way out of their own
hatred, sin, and anger.

There *is* a way out. And the more you can demonstrate, right
where you are, the kind of love and oneness that Jesus prayed for,
the more others around you are going to want the Jesus you serve.
Pray and ask God if there might be something you can do to spread
harmony among the believers in Christ where you live.

Music

"Let the word of Christ dwell in you richly in all wisdom; teaching and admonishing one another in psalms and hymns and spiritual songs, singing with grace in your hearts to the Lord."

— *Colossians 3:16*

I'm glad that God's endorsement of music didn't stop with the Old Testament. I love music, and from this verse, it's clear that God sees it as an important way of getting Christ's word into us.

Here at PTL, our music program costs us a lot of money. In fact, I've been told it costs as much as the technical personnel that is needed to produce the PTL Club.

Some people think that's extravagant. During our most serious financial crisis, some people went around saying, "Dump the music! Your whole 'ship' is going down, and you've got to throw out the excess weight — the music costs too much!" But, I said, "I plan to leave the ship last, and I'll throw the music overboard just before that."

Music is praise, and I'm not going to give up the "praisers." The key to this ministry is worship and praise as well as talk. Notice the verse above again: The richness of Christ's word comes not only through teaching and admonishing, but also through singing thankfully to God.

God demonstrated the power of music and praise several times in the Old Testament by sending out the praisers and musicians ahead of the Israelite armies. On these occasions, the battle was won without a sword being raised as the praise threw the enemy into confusion.

If you've got musical gifts, don't just think of yourself as a frill or fringe on the Body of Christ. You're a part of bringing the Word of God to people.

Your Steps Are Ordered

"The steps of a good man are ordered by the Lord: and he delighteth in his way."
— *Psalm 37:23*

You know, the way the Lord works in our lives is so wonderful. He watches us and knows exactly how our paths are going to unfold. He knows if they will be straight, crooked, narrow, or wide. He is so good.

Uncle Henry and Aunt Susan Harrison truly had their steps directed by the Lord a few years back. They were flying from Charlotte to California to do the work of the Lord and they missed their flight connections in Atlanta.

So what, you say? Well, their reservations were from Atlanta to Chicago. They were to connect in Chicago with a flight that would take them on to California, but if they had made the flight the way it had been scheduled, they would have been on the DC-10 that crashed at O'Hare Airport after take-off! It was one of the worst air disasters in our history and our own Uncle Henry and Aunt Susan were booked on that flight! You know that the Lord was directing their footsteps because they weren't on board.

Being the jovial and congenial people that they are, the Harrisons didn't think anything about missing their connections in Atlanta. Instead of getting all upset and panicking because they missed their flight to Chicago, they calmly made connections with a later flight and arrived safely in California.

Isn't it wonderful how God works in our lives? Aren't we truly blessed to have a God like ours to direct the paths we take everyday? He won't lead us down the wrong way and we know that whatever direction we are taking, God has a reason and purpose for it.

Put your trust in the Lord today and let Him direct you down the right path.

Keep Working That Field

"And let us not be weary in well-doing: for in due season we shall reap, if we faint not."
— *Galatians 6:9*

If you're anything like I am, there are times when you get weary of trying to be kind or good — even of being loving — especially if those around you just don't seem to be responding. It's then that we need the reminder of this promise of God.

Today's verse has an interesting background. When it was written, most people wore long, flowing garments that stretched down to their ankles. When they went to work in the fields, they would tie their garments around their waists so as not to trip themselves. When their work was done, the laborers would unloose their garments and walk out of the field. When the Bible says, *"if we faint not,"* in the original Greek it means, "if we don't let down our garments and leave the field."

God has given you a "field" to work. It might be your home, school, ministry, or job. Conditions there might be hard for doing good. But, God says that you're there to find opportunity to do good to all men (Galatians 6:10). The beautiful part of it is that your work will bear fruit — "treasures in heaven" (Matthew 6:20); "life everlasting" (Galatians 6:8); souls saved and delivered; and the friendship and favor of your fellow men (Romans 14:18) — if you'll just stay in that field and not give up. Isn't that what we all want? Who could ask for more!

So if you're tempted to get tired, stop and take a "prayer break" to get the strength you need from God. Whatever happens, keep working for Him. Don't step out of the "field" where God's placed you. Keep looking forward to the fruitful harvest ahead!

The Freedom Of Truth

"And ye shall know the truth, and the truth shall make you free."

— *John 8:32*

Why is the truth always so difficult to tell? As Christians, we know the truth of Jesus Christ and can afford to practice the truth in our own lives. Once you begin practicing the truth, it will set you free!

Why then is the world afraid of the truth? The wicked know that the truth about their deeds will bring about their downfall. They are scared that the truth won't be accepted — they need to know the truth of our Lord so they can be set free.

When I was working at CBN with Pat Robertson, I was faced with a situation I always think of when I hear this scripture about truth. CBN was in financial trouble and it looked like it might go under. But, we had to keep up our image before the camera in those days, so the staff was instructed not to tell of the financial trouble during a crucial telethon.

I didn't understand this approach at all. I was fully committed to Christian television and I felt I needed to tell the people the truth or we could go off the air. The cold fact was, if the goal wasn't met, the station would have to close down.

Near the end of the telethon, I broke down crying in front of the cameras. I had tried to hold back my feelings, but I was over-whelmed with the situation. The Holy Spirit came upon me and led me to say, "People, it's all over. Everything's gone. Christian television will be no more, unless you help us pay our bills." Within hours, the entire telethon budget was met as God moved on people's hearts to give.

You see, the truth gave people a chance to minister to our needs. God wants you to be honest about your hurts and needs so He can minister to you. God, who knows the whole truth about you, loves you. As you live openly, you'll help others open up and also find freedom.

The Ministry Of Second-Fiddling

" . . . It is written, As I live, saith the Lord, every knee shall bow to me, and every tongue shall confess to God. So then every one of us shall give account of himself to God."
— *Romans 14:11-12*

Some people are so busy out running around in the limelight trying to be a "spiritual giant" that they don't have time to be what God wants them to be, and they end up frustrated because of it!

What they need to understand is that God made different people to fulfill different functions, and one is no more "spiritual" than another!

I often praise God from the bottom of my heart for Uncle Henry. Another man might have gotten tired over the years at having to play co-host all the time. But Henry is so secure in God's love for him that he doesn't have to wonder why God always seems to have him supporting someone else's ministry.

One day I had to tell him how much he meant to me, and how deeply I appreciated his never-failing support. There have been times when I've felt that the person in the co-host's chair beside mine had aspirations for my job. But I've never felt that about Henry. Also, when I can't think of a way to end a thought, Henry always has the right words. All I have to do is just glance at him, and he's off and running.

When I told Henry how I felt about him, he simply replied, "Jim, God just naturally tuned me to second fiddle." That sounds just like Henry, doesn't it? I told this story over the air, and a woman wrote back, "Brother Henry, you may be tuned to second fiddle, but in my book, you're a genuine Stradivarius!"

I believe that when Henry gives an account of himself on Judgment Day, the Lord is going to pronounce him a genuine Stradivarius, too! He's content in the place God put him, and instead of harboring ambitions, he's become the best at fulfilling the ministry God created him for. Today, you too can start working on becoming the best in your ministry, whatever it may be.

God's Visible Love

"And the bow shall be in the clouds; and I will look upon it, that I may remember the everlasting covenant between God and every living creature of all flesh that is upon the earth. And God said to Noah, This is the token of covenant, which I have established . . . ."
— *Genesis 9:16-17*

Cold rainy days can sometimes make us feel downright dreary. It's not always as easy to see God during dismal weather like that, either, as it is on beautiful spring mornings where every single flower seems to shout God's name. But the Lord,the author of the entire universe, puts His signature on every act of His creation, and those who are willing to search confidently through the darkness will always find God's hand leaving a token of His love.

Noah must have found it hard to see God's face through the dark storm clouds that never seemed to stop raining. But Noah knew the God he had served for so many years well enough to keep him looking out a window in the Ark for the light.

Noah's faith in God's unwavering love was rewarded at the end of the journey with a beautiful sign of God's new "everlasting" covenant with all mankind — a rainbow of colors arched high across an azure blue sky as the token of God's promise to never destroy the earth by water again.

That reminder of God's love for man still hangs in our sky today, and those who look for God, even during a storm, will always be rewarded with the sight of a rainbow at the storm's end.

Today if your world feels dark and dismal, and there seems to be no sign of God, keep watching in faith, and you'll see your rainbow!

Rebuke The Spirit Of Fear

*"For God hath not given us the spirit of fear;
but of power, and of love, and of a sound mind."*
— *2 Timothy 1:7*

God doesn't want His people to be afraid. We are told in today's scripture that God didn't give us the spirit of fear. Therefore, we know that if it didn't come from God, that if we have fear, then it came from Satan.

For instance, one of the women on the PTL staff lost her husband after he had a heart attack. She had been married to him since she was eighteen years old and had never had to provide for herself or her children.

Suddenly, she was faced with the reality of life alone. She was going to have to provide totally for herself. Satan immediately decided that this was the time to knock her out of the spiritual ball game of life.

At first, the devil would attack her during the day while she was teaching school. But, she would always come back with one of God's promises and Satan would have to flee. But, as you know, Satan is always on the job so he began to attack her at night while she slept. She would awaken with extreme fear — not of external things, but a fear within her subconscious. Satan would be telling her that she couldn't make it by herself, that she would probably get sick and not be able to work, and all the other bad things he could think of. But, God's Word put Satan to flight. She would lie in her bed in the middle of the night and quote today's scripture aloud.

Now, we know that faith comes by hearing and hearing by the Word of God. By quoting the scripture aloud, she was both hearing and saying it. Eventually, Satan learned he couldn't even get near her at night with fear, and he was defeated by the Word of God.

If you have fear in your life, use the Sword of the Lord to put Satan to flight because truly God hasn't given us the spirit of fear, but rather of "power, and of love, and of a sound mind."

Suffering For Christ

"For even hereunto were ye called: because Christ also suffered for us, leaving us an example, that ye should follow his steps."
— *1 Peter 2:21*

You know, it is so easy to say you are living the life Christ meant for you to lead, but are you willing to suffer for Him?

Peter is telling us in this scripture that we shouldn't expect our Christian walk to be a bed of roses all of the time. Many times, during our life, we will stumble and fall. We may even have to walk across a bed of "nails" every now and then in order to live our life for the glory of God.

Just as Jesus suffered on the cross for our sins, we are to follow in His steps using Jesus as our example. It will take guts and determination to continually stick up for your belief in Christ, as your Lord and Savior, but the rewards will be worth it all!

I can't tell you how many people I have known who could really give a good witness for this scripture. There was one preacher, in particular, who really gave up everything he had to enter the ministry. He was a very successful engineer and he felt the calling to become a minister. Once he had completed his studies, he became the pastor of a very small country church. The church only had about thirty or forty members at the very most. Since it was such a small church, the congregation couldn't afford to pay him a very large salary. He was blessed to receive what he did, but that amount barely covered expenses for food for his family. There was a constant struggle to make ends meet, but eventually, he was given a larger church and a bigger salary. He endured all these hardships because of his love for the Lord.

Just as Jesus carried the cross for us to Calvary, so can we carry our own cross for Him when we are faced with difficult situations. By firmly believing in Jesus, we can overcome all suffering we might pass through during our lifetime.

We're Blest!

"And all these blessing shall come on thee,
and overtake thee, if thou shalt hearken unto
the voice of the Lord thy God."
— *Deuteronomy 28:2*

TAMMY: You know, folks, we are a blessed people! Even when the housework has got us Moms down, and the kids have colds, and we've wiped one too many noses — we're still blessed with children and a home! And you, sir, even though you might be a little tired of your job and think you just can't face one more day working the same old job doing the same old thing — remember, you're blessed with a job!

A lot of those around us are not as fortunate as we are — people who are in wheelchairs, or can't walk, or see, or hear, or talk. Here I am, though, able to do all those wonderful things.

I can jump out of bed in the morning, and even though I'm tired, I can run into the bathroom and splash cold water on my face. Oh, I'm blessed!

We don't deserve it but we have houses filled with televisions, dishwashers, furniture, and we have our health and strength, our families, and friends.

We ought to be the most thankful people in all the world. In America, there's no reason for us to go around with frowns on our faces, discouraged and downhearted. Praise God, we are a blessed people!

Even in the valleys we pass through from time to time, we can say we are blessed, because God always brings us to the mountain top of victory, a stronger and happier person because the struggle has made us grow.

People, we truly are blessed. We don't deserve it but yet we are blessed. Count your blessings today!

A Mixture, Not A Compound

"And the very God of peace sanctify you wholly; and I pray God your whole spirit and soul and body be preserved blameless unto the coming of our Lord Jesus Christ."
— *1 Thessalonians 5:23*

A chemistry teacher was demonstrating the difference between a mixture and a chemical compound. He dropped a few marbles into a glass of water and stirred them around. When he stopped stirring, the marbles naturally dropped to the bottom of the glass. "That's a *mixture*," he said.

Then he took another glass of water and stirred a teaspoon of sugar into it. As he kept stirring, the sugar gradually disappeared. Pointing to the now clear glass, the teacher said, "Now, this is a *compound*."

But a lot of people think that salvation is just some kind of *mixture*. They think they asked God to save them, and then the Lord dropped in the Father, Son, and Holy Ghost like three marbles. They kind of settled to the bottom and stayed there, without changing the "flavor" of their lives too much. They don't see much hope for growing as Christians, because they don't see God being "stirred into" them.

But God's Word says that salvation is a *compound*. God stirs Himself into every part of us. After a while, if we grow in Him, He changes the way we "taste" and "disappears" into our being until we can't tell where He begins and we end. God sets us apart completely — spirit, soul, and body. And we become a compound of God and us, sharing His nature through and through.

If you haven't experienced this "compounding" of God in your life, ask God right now to "stir" Himself into you as never before. Tell Him you want Him to permeate every part of you. Tell Him to come and "be lost" in you — so you can be lost in Him!

Are You In Death Or Life?

"We know that we have passed from death unto life, because we love the brethren. He that loveth not his brother abideth in death."
— *1 John 3:14*

Many people who claim to love the Lord today have doubts about their salvation. This isn't altogether a bad thing. We should take a hard look at our lives from time to time to see if we are really representing God to the world through real faith and love or just lip service.

A good way to measure our faith is told to us in this verse. Do you love your fellow Christians? If you can answer yes, then you have passed out of the death of sin and into the life of Jesus. But, if you answered no, you need to take another look at your faith because you haven't gotten there quite yet.

The road to heaven sure would be a lot easier if you didn't have to love anybody. But, you can't make it unless you love one another. You can't say you have passed from death to life just because you give large sums of money to the church or because you serve on the board of deacons. Nor, can you say this because you faithfully attend Sunday school or because you always seem to know what is right and wrong with everyone in your fellowship. And, just because you know the Scriptures backwards and forwards doesn't let you pass from death into life. When you can honestly say that you love the brethren, then you can know that you have passed into life.

Have you done all you can to love the person who is weak in their faith and are always going up and down? Have you cared for them enough to show them the right way? Have you reached out in love to that backslider who's returned? Have you welcomed them into the fold and said, "I love you, what can I do to help?" Have you spoken well of that sister who has been gossiped about when she wasn't there? If you have, you know you have life in you. But, if you haven't, turn your whole heart over to Jesus today and He'll make you truly alive!

Trust

"But let all those that put their trust in thee rejoice: let them ever shout for joy, because thou defendest them: let them also that love thy name be joyful in thee. For thou, Lord, wilt bless the righteous; with favor wilt thou compass him as with a shield."

— *Psalm 5:11-12*

God will surround those who believe in Him. You must put your complete TRUST in the Lord in everything you do. With His guidance and defense, you can build a ministry, such as PTL, on His trust alone.

Did you know that in Hebrew the word "trust" stands for "a move toward place of refuge." By learning to lean totally on Jesus, the path to salvation is paved. But, before a person can commit their life to Jesus, they must realize their need to be saved. To live their life for God, they must know that they can't do it alone. They must seek God's help and trust Him every step of the way.

Trusting God completely doesn't come overnight. You must take it step by step. The key to learning to trust God is to try. Make your move today. You don't have to take a giant leap, just a little step toward Him will begin your journey.

I remember when it took every ounce of my faith to trust God for two hundred dollars a month. Now, we have a monthly budget of far, far more. But, when you make that first step and you see God's faithfulness, you learn to trust Him more and more with every step you take.

Begin your journey to trusting God completely today. Turn something over to Him that you have never trusted Him with before. Shout your joy out to the world and trust Him — He won't let you down.

A Fringe Benefit?

*"Yea, and all that will live godly in Christ
Jesus shall suffer persecution."*
— *2 Timothy 3:12*

Persecution is one of the less popular "fringe benefits" of serving the Lord. I doubt the promise above is one you'll ever want to claim.

But sometimes, as you live a godly life, you may have to experience some type of persecution. Maybe someone will make fun of your belief in God when they discover you're a Christian. Or, perhaps somebody will resent the cheerfulness and joy you have in the Lord, even when you're going through hard times, and they'll accuse you of being a hypocrite.

Whatever form the persecution takes, my friends, praise God with all your hearts when it happens, because that means you're on the path to victory! Persecution doesn't come because you are doing something wrong in your Christian walk — it comes because you're doing something *right!*

You see, the devil can't stand happy Believers who are trying to serve God, because they're usually responsible for influencing others to become Believers. So Satan will throw everything he can at you to distract you or take your eyes off the Lord.

If you watch the PTL Club, you know how much trouble the devil tries to stir up for us because we want to serve God. Sometimes I cry out, "God, I've tried to serve you faithfully and I've obeyed you — why all this turmoil and opposition?" Then God reminds me that persecution is bound to come *because* I'm serving Him with all my heart. Of course, God never lets anything happen to me that I can't handle with His help!

Don't get discouraged when you face persecution — rejoice! Realize that your faithfulness to God must be hurting the devil a lot more than he can ever hurt you!

Victory In Praise

"And at midnight Paul and Silas prayed, and sang praises unto God: and the prisoners heard them."

— *Acts 16:25*

Tammy and I can recall many times in our ministry when things seemed to go wrong, but through praise, we were led to victory.

Once, we were outside an Atlanta shopping center for a promotional appearance. It started to rain, and we were forced to go into the shopping center's basement. The situation seemed hopeless but we praised the Lord just the same. After the program, people came up and asked for healing prayer. Now, we later learned that God had done a great miracle by guiding us into the basement. We wouldn't have been allowed to pray for the sick in the parking lot!

In today's scripture, Paul and Silas had been unjustly thrown in jail. They could have grumbled and complained about their circumstances, but instead, they began to sing praises to the Lord, right there in their chains. Soon the jail began to shake, and the doors were opened. Their chains broke, and the jailer and his whole household got saved!

Just as God delivered Paul and Silas, He can free you from the jail cell of your problems. He can give you peace in the midst of the storm. He can give you joy despite heartache. He will loose your chains and free you totally if you'll just give praise to His holy Name.

Circumstances around you today may shout nothing but "Defeat!" But if you'll lift your heart and your voice and cry "Victory in Jesus!" God will pour down that victory from on high and make something great out of the situation. Start learning to praise God and look past the circumstances to the God who's Victor over all!

Let Someone Know You Love Them

*"A new commandment I give unto you,
That ye love one another; as I have loved you,
that ye shall also love one another."*
— *John 13:34*

It is very important to show people you care about that they are special to you. That is especially true with your wife or girlfriend. Valentine's Day is set aside to allow us time to express our feelings to that special person.

I feel like Tammy and I are still newlyweds. We are constantly joking with each other and just having fun. Of course, there are serious times, too, but she knows how much I love her from the way I talk or act.

If you have a hard time expressing your feelings, break out of your shell on Valentine's Day and let your special someone know that they are tops on your list. It doesn't matter if you have been married fifty years, a little note or even a gift on Valentine's Day will make it seem like you are still on your honeymoon. That little extra "I Love You" means so much.

You don't have to wait until Valentine's Day to show how much you care. Why not send a card for no special reason sometime? I bet you will see a grin "from ear to ear" on that special someone's face.

Jesus told us to love one another, and what better time to start expressing your love for your fellow man than today! Giving your wife or husband a big bear hug and kiss at the end of a long day, or just stopping and talking to someone who is down, are both expressions of love. You don't have to have gifts in your hand to show you love someone — all you have to do is let them know how very much you care.

Tell them how important they are to you and that they are loved.

The Right Labels

"Therefore each of you must put off falsehood and speak truthfully to his neighbor, for we are all members of one body."
— *Ephesians 4:25*

If you have ever done any filing, whether at the office, or of recipes or something else at home, you know how confusing things can get if you don't put the right identifying tag on what you file. Go looking for "apple pie" and you find "chili." There's a big difference when the labels are wrong.

As Christians, we, too, can make "labels" for things we do that don't reflect the truth. We can even be sure we're right about something wrong in our lives, if we put a pleasant label on it.

An elderly man, squinting at his newspaper, muttered, "Print just isn't what it used to be." He was positive his eyes were still good, so he blamed his struggle to read on the print!

After a lengthy pause before a mirror, a mother confessed to her teenage daughter, "I guess I'm just too proud of my beauty." The young girl answered, "No, Mom, it's not pride — you've got too much imagination."

How do your life's labels read. Does your label for worldliness read "broadmindedness?" Does your label for gossiping read "stating facts?" How about the one for sin — does it read "maladjustment?"

If the label on your whole life's file reads "Christian," you need to make sure that the contents are accurate. Make sure today that the way you live and your conversations are honest and true. Walk with God in such a way that when people in the world look into what you are, they don't read "Christian" on the label — and find a "hypocrite" in the file!

Run From Lust

"Flee also youthful lusts: but follow righteousness, faith, charity, peace...."
— 2 Timothy 2:22

This isn't a popular message in America today. In fact, kids are being told more and more every day to do just the opposite. "Go ahead, experiment with sex. We've got the pill now, you can do your own thing! Try it, you'll like it!"

Hold it! The Bible says to run from lust! I've heard of Christian young people who've gotten themselves into some compromising situation and actually prayed, "God, forgive us for what we're about to do," or "Lord, if you don't want us to do this, stop us!" God doesn't say to play with sin like that — He says, "Run from it!"

There was an eagle who woke up one winter morning with a fierce appetite, so he flew off to search for food. Over an icy river, he spotted the dead body of a deer floating downstream. He swooped down onto the body, dug his claws into it, and started to eat the cold flesh. Suddenly he heard a roar up ahead — a waterfall! The eagle took one more bite, and then tried to fly off to safety just before the deer plunged down the falls. But when he flapped his wings, nothing happened — his claws had frozen into the carcass! Screaming and flapping his great wings, the eagle went down to his doom.

That's the way it is with sexual appetite. It seems so right to satisfy that hunger. While you're doing that, you think you've got control of the situation. But in reality, it has control of you! When you want to let go, you can't — you're stuck in lust, and it can destroy you.

Don't play around with lust! You follow after God instead of your appetites — and you won't go over the edge! That's a promise from God!

Something You Can Hold On To

"Now faith is the substance of things hoped for, the evidence of things not seen."
— *Hebrews 11:1*

Some people think faith is a pie-in-the-sky wish upon a star that they hope against hope will come true. That's not what God's Word teaches, though. The Bible says that faith is "a groundwork, something to subsist on, a reality."

The Greek word is used in the sense of "a title deed." If you've got a title deed to something, it belongs to you, right? So faith, in the now, is the title deed to something that's yours.

It's also the "evidence," the "proof," of something that's yours, though you don't see it. It's kind of like a guarantee in writing of something that you've bought by mail. So according to the Word of God, faith for something is just as sure as having the thing itself! Hallelujah!

We all have a measure of faith according to the Word of God. Yet, some people seem to accomplish much more with their "measure" than others. "Why is this?" you may ask.

The problem may be that you are doing more "hoping" than believing. I have prayed for people who were sick, and then asked them, "Are you healed?" They have said, "I hope so."

I know when they walk away that they are not healed because they are "hoping" instead of looking for the "evidence" of their healing.

When God gives you a desire to pray for a need or a healing, don't hesitate and wonder whether you have enough faith to make it happen. Stand firmly on the Word of God and begin to do what is necessary to bring it about, and it will happen. Give faith a try today! It will be well rewarded, and you'll probably find it increasing, too!

Sight To The Blind

" . . . eyes have they, but they see not; they
have ears, but they hear not . . . . "
— *Psalm 135:16,17*

There are some people who are not blind, but just don't see the beauty in things around them. I really love the sights at Heritage Village. I love the flower gardens, the red brick walks, the large, sheltering trees and green lawns. The mansion and the spire of PTL's studio inspires me often as I drive along past the fountain in the Avenue of Flags.

I've tried to make everything about Heritage Village harmonious and lovely. I tell you, I'd hate to walk around those grounds with a man and say, "Isn't that a beautiful sight?" and have him answer, "I don't know, I'm not much for looking at scenery." That would probably ruin my day!

At PTL, we try hard to make our music as beautiful as possible. Next to the ministry of the Word of God, music is the most important part of the PTL Club. It would downright depress me to hear the PTL Singers and Orchestra wind up a glorious number and have one of my guests say, "I didn't hear anything great — I'm tone deaf." I'd think, "My, how I pity him, he's missing out on so much in life."

Imagine if someone like that would start arguing with me and say, "Jim, you're wrong to get so excited about such sounds and sights. There's nothing to them." I couldn't be angry with him. He couldn't help it. But I'd sure be sorry for him.

Some people just seem to be blind to the beauty of Jesus Christ. They say, "Well, being a Christian is great for you; I just don't see anything in it." Doesn't your heart go out to them? Pray today that the eyes and ears of those who are deaf or blind to Jesus Christ will be opened to see what a beautiful Savior He is!

Are There "Goliaths" In Your Life?

"And David girded his sword upon his armor, and he assayed to go; for he had not proved it. And David said unto Saul, I cannot go with these; for I have not proved them. And David put them off him."

— *1 Samuel 17:39*

You know, many times in a ministry, and not just here at PTL but any ministry, people are asked to do something and don't rely on their God-given abilities to accomplish the task. Instead, they try to use armor belonging to someone else to fight their battle. But, we need to be like David. He used what he had and that was his faith in God.

This scripture really talks to me. Here we see King Saul outfitting David in his (Saul's) armor so he can go out and fight Goliath. But, David was very wise. He told Saul that he couldn't wear his armor. David gave the armor back to Saul and went out to fight the powerful Goliath with only five simple stones, he had taken out of a brook, and his shepherd's sling.

Now, does this tell you something as a child of God? God will never call you to do anything that you aren't already equipped to do. David went into this battle using his faith in God that had been tried when he was a shepherd boy guarding his father's sheep and a bear tried to take off with a lamb. David knew his faith in God was better than any armor he could wear.

When you come against the "Goliaths" in your life, remember what David said, "The battle is the Lord's!" If you remember this, God will deliver your enemy into your hands just as he delivered the Israelites from Goliath and the Philistines.

God's Eternal Love

"For God so loved the world, that He gave His only begotten Son, that whosoever believeth in Him should not perish, but have everlasting life."

— *John 3:16*

All of us have probably looked up into the sky as youngsters, and marveled at the countless number of stars. Some of us may even have attempted to count them, but there were always too many.

Scientists say there are billions of suns and solar systems in the universe. Yet, the Bible says that for just one planet, Jesus came to earth and died. The Son of God, who was "from everlasting to everlasting" (Psalm 90:2), gave His life to give us everlasting life! That's mind-boggling!

Why did He do it? Astronomers can see through their telescopes whole galaxies being born and dying every year. Once Adam sinned, didn't God have a right to give up on little planet Earth, too? Yes, in His holiness and justice He did. But in His mercy, even back there in the sin-stained garden of Eden, He gave the promise that He would send His Son because of His great love for us.

How can a heart as small as yours and mine know that kind of love? When I think about how much pride and selfishness we humans have, it makes me weep to think that God somehow found us in this vast universe and saved us!

What a far-sighted love God must have! He looked, in His love, down ages of human history glutted with greed, lust, murder, and ambition and saw eternal life amid all that death. Yes, it was to a world like this that He *gave* His only Son!

Jesus is God's gift to you today. Whatever your hurts, faults, fears, or doubts, He has searched the whole universe and all of time for you — and loved you. Oh, believe it today! Right now, receive your portion of that love that will last forever!

Our Lord And Our God

"Jesus said unto them, Verily, verily, I say unto you, Before Abraham was, I am. Then took they up stones to cast at him: but Jesus hid himself, and went out of the temple, going through the midst of them, and so passed by."
— *John 8:58-59*

In today's verse, Jesus clearly states His claim to deity. He gives Himself the same name of God that was revealed to Moses: "I AM" or Jehovah," as it has been translated. To the Jews, this was blasphemy — no wonder they tried to stone Him!

While we wouldn't stone a man who claimed to be God today, we might well put him into an insane asylum, or assume he was a dangerous person, because he was a liar and leading others into deception.

One English author pointed out that we don't have much choice when it comes to Jesus — either He was a liar (in which case we wouldn't claim that He was a good man); He was a lunatic (how then could we respect Him as a teacher); or He was who He said He was — God in the flesh and Lord of all. There aren't any other options. No one can sit on the fence when faced with the claims of Jesus — and that is just the way He wanted it.

It has got to be all or nothing with Jesus. It could be that you have read thus far in this book and said, "Yes, that statement is true, and that teaching is true," but you haven't made up your mind about Jesus.

The decision is yours to make. Right now, decide where you stand with Jesus.

Obeying God

"But this thing commanded I them, saying Obey my voice, and I will be your God, and ye shall be my people: and walk ye in all the ways that I have commanded you, that it may be well unto you."

— *Jeremiah 7:23*

Have you ever wondered why some people have exciting things happen in their lives and others don't?

I'll tell you why — obedience. The Lord said, "Some will obey Me and some will not." Why can Jim Bakker build buildings and go on television and believe God for a million dollars a week? You might think, "I can do better than he."

Well, that's true. I bet there are millions of people that are more suited for this than Jim Bakker. But, why did God pick Jim Bakker, a frail vessel? Because I was a willing vessel, I am willing to obey.

The old nature in us is always saying, "I want my way." And God can't use us as long as we are striving for our own way. But, as soon as we start seeking God's way — then great things start happening!

I don't know what your prayer needs are today, but God does. I believe with all my heart that if you take down the walls of "self" and start seeking the will of the Father . . . right in the midst of your need . . . He will answer your prayer.

If you have a financial need — sow some seed. Apply God's principle of giving. "Give and it shall be given unto you," the Bible says.

Do you need to be healed? Then pray for others to be healed. That's what the Bible says!

Seek to obey God in a new and more powerful way today. Then sit back and watch God work in your life!

We Can Win

"And the angel of the Lord appeared unto him, and said unto him, The Lord is with thee, thou mighty man of valor."

— *Judges 6:12*

TAMMY: We may say Jesus is our Victor, but when we look at our fears we don't believe it. I don't care how many sermons you hear on how Jesus is everything we need, when you look at your fears you won't think you have had a victory in years. Satan wants us to doubt ourselves so we can't think of carrying out God's will.

With God, we will continue to have victory. He transforms ordinary people into soul-winning Christians. Gideon was a good example of a man who was fearful and blamed God for all his fears.

Just like the rest of Israel, he was scared of the oppressing Midianites. The angel of the Lord appeared to Gideon and called him a "man of valor," while he was hiding from the Midianites. Can you imagine that! Here he was hiding in fear from his enemy and he is called a "man of valor." God saw Gideon's potential, just like he sees our potential. Even if we are afraid, God sees the victory we can have.

I was reminded of how I used to feel when I read the story of Gideon. He asked the angel how in the world a poor child could save Israel and I remember telling God I didn't think I could have victory over my fears because I came from a poor family in northern Minnesota. I didn't have any great abilities and I didn't think I could ever be a winner.

God told me the same thing He told Gideon — that He was with me and I could win the victory. Just as Gideon won his victory over the Midianites, so could I win my victory over fears today. Even though we are weak, God is strong. He sees our potential and guarantees us victory when we put our trust in Him!

Run To The Roar

"Fear not . . . . "

— Genesis 15:1

Throughout the Bible, God tells us not to fear. Fear will do more than cripple you emotionally, it can cause terrible sickness. The mounting fear and anxiety in our nation has been termed a "crisis in confidence."

There is a lack of trust in our political leaders, in our government, in our schools, in our businesses, and in ourselves. People are concerned about oil shortages, food shortages, and so many other things. Many are even afraid to go out shopping . . . afraid to go to stores. Others are afraid to go to church or auditoriums and if they do go, they sit in the back so they can get out quickly. Many doctors are saying that fear causes 90-95 percent of our sicknesses.

Fear is sin. It is a direct disobedience to God's order to "Fear not!" But, it can be defeated just like any other sin. My wife, Tammy Faye, used to be frightened at the thought of flying in an airplane. No amount of logic could change her mind. She knew that statistically, air travel was one of the safest ways to travel. Yet, she was still afraid. This was a difficult situation for us, because our ministry often requires a great deal of long distance travel . . . travel by plane.

Today, Tammy has conquered her fear. She just gets on the plane, curls up in her seat and goes to sleep. She isn't the least bit afraid of flying anymore.

What was the key to Tammy's victory over fear? With God's help, she faced her fear. We call it "running to the roar" because it is illustrated by the story of the old, toothless lion in the jungle. His job is to confront a prey with a loud roar in hopes of causing the animal to turn and run into the clutches of the awaiting young lions. Safety is only possible by running toward the roar — toward the safety of Jesus!

God Answers Prayer

"Now the Lord had said unto Abram, Get thee out of thy country, and from thy kindred, and from thy father's house, unto a land that I will show thee: And the Lord appeared unto Abram, and said, Unto thy seed will I give this land . . . . "

— Genesis 12:1, 7

Most people don't really understand or realize what a man of real faith Abraham was. Abraham was seventy-five years old when God told him to leave his father's house and land and go to a country that He would show him.

Now, at this time, there weren't any super highways or jets, not even a Hardee's or McDonald's along the way. In fact, Abraham didn't even know the route he was to take. He was to take one day at a time and go in the direction God told him to go.

Abraham didn't question God, but started out obediently with his wife, Sara, and nephew, Lot, and all of their earthly possessions.

Sara had never been able to give Abraham a son, but after they arrived in Canaan, God spoke to Abraham again and told him that the land would be given to his seed, or descendants.

Now, Abraham probably thought this was strange since he didn't have a son. Nevertheless, he did not doubt God. One thing about the Bible that fascinates me is that even though Abraham and Sara didn't see the fulfillment of the heir of promise, Isaac, for twenty-five years, he never doubted that God would not be true to what He promised. And God was true to His Word. Isaac was born when Sara was ninety years old and Abraham one hundred.

How many times have you asked God for something and felt in your heart that God said "yes," and yet, because it did not happen immediately you doubted God? God doesn't work according to man's timetable. Sometimes, He closes a door temporarily because the time isn't right and we need a lesson in learning to walk by faith.

Remember, God never forgets a promise He has made even though sometimes we may feel He has. Let us determine in our hearts to be like Abraham and wait patiently for the fulfillment of God's promises in our lives.

A Form But No Power

"Having a form of godliness, but denying the power thereof: from such turn away."
— *2 Timothy 3:5*

Some of PTL's worst critics are the kind of people Paul is talking about in this verse. These critics never talk about sin or the blood of Jesus. They don't believe in the Virgin Birth or the Resurrection. They don't believe in miracles. Yet, they'll attack us as "out-of-date" and "frauds," without doing anything to meet the real needs of the people.

The largest television ministries in the world are run by people who believe in the power of God. The critics can't do what we're doing. It takes a miracle a day to keep PTL alive — and you can't do something that takes a miracle if you don't believe in miracles. A religion without power isn't important to people. Oh, some will go to church on Sunday morning so they can ease their conscience. If you call them at the office about a pledge or donation, they might give you a check because they can write it off on their taxes, but you have to come collect it.

But, it's the people who love a living Jesus and His resurrected power who are producing Christian television. You can hardly go to any city in America without turning on your television set and finding Christian programs that are reaching out to this generation. Now, God is bringing the miracle of salvation to France — and that's not a godly place. In Australia, less than 10 percent of the people go to church. In Japan, less than 1 percent profess Christ. But, we don't think that makes those places hopeless. The power of God is transforming nations right now.

Don't listen to the critics who want to dampen the message of a powerful God. Turn away from them — and turn to the God who can make a real difference in this world — and in your life.

The Faithfulness Of Christ

"Let us hold fast the profession of our faith without wavering; (for He is faithful that promised.)"

— *Hebrews 10:23*

God's blessings, in our lives, are controlled by our faithfulness to Him. Sometimes our faithfulness wavers when God asks us to do something for Him that demands a sacrifice on our parts. We might complain or even rationalize away God's voice speaking to our hearts, turning back to what we'd rather do, instead of facing God's call.

What would have happened if Jesus had done that? Our sins would never have been forgiven at Calvary if He had turned away from the agonizing mission God placed before Him.

But Jesus obeyed the Lord because of His love for mankind and His faithfulness to God to fulfill the promise He had been sent to deliver.

The Psalmist wrote in 89:1, "I will sing of the mercies of the Lord forever, with my mouth will I make known thy faithfulness to all generations."

Are we shouting about God's faithfulness with our mouths or are we saying things that will only discourage others? As Christians, we should shout our thanks from the highest mountain so all can hear us, not from the basements where we can't be heard.

We can't allow ourselves to fall into a rut with our faithfulness. We must learn to be faithful, as He was, with even the job we least want to do.

When we are faithful to God's calling, He is faithful to pour out His blessings on us. God richly rewards us when we are obedient to Him. Today, concentrate on accomplishing the job God asks you to do — and rely on His faithfulness to bring it to pass.

Encouragement

" . . . but David encouraged himself in the Lord his God."

— 1 Samuel 30:6

A little bit of encouragement can be like a cup of water handed to a marathon runner as he runs by. It can be just enough to strengthen you as you run the race of life.

In sports, encouragement is a very important factor. Many writers refer to it as the "home field advantage." They recognize that the support of local fans — the encouragement they give the players — has a positive effect on the team. This effect could very well spell victory in the final score.

The other day, I received a tremendous amount of encouragement when I read a letter from a young man who had been contemplating suicide. He wrote: "I was contemplating taking my life I had attempted suicide before. I saw PTL with a friend and I experienced the presence of the Lord. I called PTL and asked for your prayers. My life is completely changed and I am living for the Lord."

That letter encouraged me so much. When I hear from people who have been blessed by PTL, it gives me the strength to run my race and defeat Satan.

We all need encouragement to run life's race, to keep our eyes on the goal, to keep going forward. Sometimes it seems that there is no one to encourage us. But remember, there is always one — and that is God! By His Spirit, He is here to comfort, strengthen, and encourage, just as He was for David, when his own men talked of stoning him after a defeat.

If you're in need of encouragement today, if you're downcast and just feel like you can't go on, look to Jesus right now. Remember the love He has for you and the precious promises that are yours in Him. If someone you know needs an encouraging word, be sure and give them that lift that will help them get across the finish line, too!

Help The Weak

"We then that are strong ought to bear the infirmities of the weak, and not to please ourselves."

— *Romans 15:1*

Every now and then, God gives us a snow here in Charlotte, and we get all excited. The Northerners who live in Charlotte have just got to bear with the Southerners — they just don't know how to handle the snow.

When I was growing up in Muskegon, Michigan, I can remember looking out my window and seeing the snow falling at night. The snow banks would be piled high and there we were safe and sound inside our warm house.

I don't think there is anything cozier than a big, heavy snow and I would love to be out in it when I was little. But, in Charlotte, you stay inside if you know what's good for you. When it comes to driving in the snow, most Southerners are crazy! And they are the first to admit it. They just don't know how to drive on it, and you will find them in the ditches, on the shoulders, and running into everybody. My dad just goes driving along because he's used to driving on snow. Up where Tammy comes from in Minnesota, they live on the snow. They just pack it down on the streets and go on with their usual day. There's no other way. At forty below zero, it isn't going anywhere!

It seems like in every church, ministry, or group of Christians, there are young or weak ones who are just like those Southerners trying to drive in the snow. The Christian life isn't familiar to them, or they never learn to negotiate it, and they're always making mistakes and getting in the way. They're sincere, but just not able to function very well.

Those of us, who are stronger or more experienced, have to bear with them and help to support and guide them. If they get stranded along the way, pick them up and get them back on their feet. If you "run into" someone like that today, don't get mad at them, help them — and you'll be stronger for helping.

Be Ready!

"Be ye therefore ready also: for the Son of Man cometh at an hour when ye think not."
— *Luke 12:40*

A lot of people believe that Jesus is coming again soon, and I'm one of them. Almost all the "signs of the times" that Jesus gave are present in this very day and hour. And I believe PTL is directly involved in the fulfillment of the prophecies about the last days, as we're helping extend the outreach of the Gospel around the world.

But as sure as I am that Jesus is coming very soon, I'm also sure that His coming is still going to be a surprise. In the scripture, Jesus was talking to His disciples, and He was telling them that, with all these signs, He wasn't going to come back when they thought He was!

I think that's just as true today. Jesus is going to come back at a single moment in time when nobody expects Him! How He is going to arrange that, I can't imagine. Perhaps some great natural calamity will take place that will take everyone's mind off His coming. Perhaps there will be a time of persecution or discouragement which will distract the people of God for a moment. But in that instant, Jesus will return.

There have been groups of people who have thought they knew the exact time of Jesus' return. They've gone up on top of mountains to wait for Him. But they've always come down discouraged. Can you imagine what would have happened if He had come while they were down and sorrowful because He hadn't come at the moment they thought was right?

Jesus said, "Look up," but He also said, "Be ready!" We ought to always be doing something that will glorify Him, so that if He comes, we will be ready to meet Him. If you're not ready to meet Jesus today, get ready. Try to please God with your life today, so that if He comes, you can be glad He finds you faithful to His will.

Get In Touch With God

"In those days was Hezekiah sick unto death. And the prophet Isaiah the son of Amoz came to him, and said unto him, Thus saith the Lord, Set thine house in order; for thou shalt die, and not live."

— *2 Kings 20:1*

Hezekiah is remembered as one of the best kings who ever ruled Israel. But, we know from scripture that even Hezekiah had his times of sickness and problems. But, what was the secret of Hezekiah's success? He knew how to pray and get in touch with God!

In today's scripture, we see that Hezekiah is sick and Isaiah, the prophet, was sent to him with a word of wisdom from God. He told Hezekiah to "set his house in order" because he was going to die.

Now, what did Hezekiah do? Did he say, "Oh, woe is me," and give up? No! You know what he did? He turned his face toward the wall and began to cry out to God.

Hezekiah reminded God of his faithfulness to Him in the past and how he had always tried to please Him. God heard Hezekiah's prayer and, I think, He remembered Hezekiah's faithfulness. Anyway, we know from scripture that before Isaiah could leave the courtyard of Hezekiah's house, God spoke to him (Isaiah) and told him to go back inside and give Hezekiah another message. He told Isaiah to tell Hezekiah that He had heard his prayer and that he would live another fifteen years.

Hezekiah prayed to God to spare him because of his faithfulness and God listened to his prayer. You, too, can remind God of your faithfulness to Him in your times of need. God does listen to your prayers and wants you to be in touch with Him!

Rebuking Or Reproving

"Let the righteous smite me; it shall be a kindness: and let him reprove me; it shall be an excellent oil, which shall not break my head . . . . "

— *Psalm 141:5*

Nobody likes to be "told off." Everybody wants to be praised and agreed with. I know I do, yet flattery can be dangerous! You can get a swelled head, and besides bursting easily, heads that size don't fit well in tight spots! The Bible even goes as far as to say that a rebuke given at the right time, from the right lips, is actually good for us!

If we stray away from God, words of correction from a friend in the Lord are a great blessing to have, though we may not see it that way at the time! While the rebuke may sting our pride at first, it might cause us to get back into fellowship with the Lord again, after we let the truth of the words sink into our hearts.

Of course some Christians abuse this verse mightily. They seem to believe that God gave them the "ministry of rebuking!" They go about "reproving" their brothers right and left, all for the sake of their brothers' souls, of course! Now I don't hold with that kind of rebuking — that's just plain out and out criticism.

But when you see a pitfall a beloved friend is about to step into, it is a kindness to point it out to him, in a gentle way, and your friend is more than likely to thank you for it at a later date.

Today, if the Lord happens to point out a fellow Believer to you who's about to walk into trouble, tell him gently. Also, be willing to receive a loving rebuke from a friend in the Lord, just in case the Lord may have chosen to speak to you in that manner. If you're open to this possibility, your blessing may be great.

Be An Encourager

". . . But to the counsellors of peace is joy."
— Proverbs 12:20

Hurrying out of a store, a young man accidentally bumped into an elderly lady. After apologizing, he was greeted with the words, "Why, thank you for that pat on the back! I've been needing a little encouragement."

Good-natured people are like a vase of fresh flowers — you love being in the same room with them. Think of the people you enjoy being with. They probably say nice things and have a good sense of humor. Their sense of inner peace and joy always seems to give them the right words of advice or soothing concern — as well as perfect timing when they laugh or smile.

It's great to know someone like that. It's even better to be one! And you know, you don't have to be born that way. Growing up in a happy family helps, it's true, but an inner peace and joy is something every man, woman, and child can receive and develop. The way to get it is to seek God: "Ask and you will receive; seek and you will find; knock and the door will be opened" (Matthew 7:7). Jesus said that, and He will give you that peace and joy if you ask Him for it.

Then, start giving away good feelings, like love, concern, and encouragement, to someone else. Before you know it, you'll start getting the same response from others. You'll find yourself changing fast, and your life will have a brighter side to it.

Right now, sit down and write out the feelings you have that you would like to exchange for better ones — and then put across from them the good ones you want. Then just start giving a little kindness here and love there, and God will return to you a hundredfold what you give in love to others. It's the truth — you'll get back what you give away. Decide today which side of the page you want your life to be like.

Jesus' Transforming Love

"Jesus said unto him, Thou shalt love the Lord thy God with all thy heart, and with all thy soul, and with all thy mind. This is the first and great commandment. And the second is like unto it, Thou shalt love thy neighbor as thyself."
— *Matthew 22:37-39*

Rejection is one of the most severely painful experiences you'll ever live through. Opening yourself up to the possibility of being hurt in this way takes a willingness to be vulnerable that only love can develop. And, opening yourself up, knowing most people will reject you takes the kind of love that originates only from God.

His love for us is so powerful, that it can take rejection time and again without faltering. If you sometimes feel you've let the Lord down one time too many — that your rejection of Him is greater than His love for you, you're wrong. There was once another person who probably felt that same way, for a time, too.

After Jesus had been arrested, He happened to look into the eyes of a man who had been one of His closest companions over the past three years — the same man who had just denied their friendship to curious bystanders.

As Peter looked back, the memory of the three times he'd denied his loyalty to this misunderstood man stung his conscience. But love hardly noticed. When Jesus went to the cross a few days later, He went for Peter, too. And one day, much later, Peter, transformed by the love of a man he'd rejected, stood before a crowd, sharing the news of a Savior who would grant eternal life to those who would have it.

If Jesus' love could take the rejection of a close friend, just at a time He needed His friends most, and transform that man into a mighty preacher of the Word, His love can transform you also. Let God's love transform you the way it did Peter. It doesn't matter if you've rejected Jesus before — Love's hardly noticed. Accept that love today.

Use It, Don't Lose It!

*"Verily, verily, I say unto you, The servant is
not greater than his lord . . . . "*
— *John 13:16*

I have a slogan for all of us today. Here it is: "Use it, don't lose it!"
Maybe you've never heard this one before, but very simply, it
means this: Use what you have, and you'll get more; if you don't,
you'll lose what you already have.

The first step, of course, in being used of God is to put to work
the talents God has given you. If you don't use what you have for
God, soon you'll have nothing. Looking at that pile of dishes or that
repair job facing you, you may remark, "Jim, that's fine for you,
with your big ministry and all. But me? I don't have any talents."

Wait a minute! Did you know that cooking, cleaning, and listening are all talents in God's kingdom? A lot of us today, though, shun
work like that — it bothers with our pride. Most people would laugh
in my face if I asked them to clean up after someone they didn't
know. But there is a real need for people who are willing to swallow
their pride and serve others.

Jesus knew the value of service long before the modern era, as
today's verse points out. He put in a lot of years of carpentry repair
work before He started ministering. Maybe you've never sat down
and considered the talents God has given you. You need to recon-
sider those talents today. The Lord is going to bless anything you do
for others in His name. Whatever you do, do it for Jesus. Think
about that today, and begin to use those talents for His glory.

Remember — it's better to use them than to let your talents be
lost!

Jesus' Compassion

*"... Go to the village ahead of you, and at
once you will find a donkey tied there, with her
colt by her. Untie them and bring them to me."*
— *Matthew 21:2*

TAMMY: I'm a real animal lover. You've probably heard Jim share
on the show about all the little animal friends I somehow manage to
collect, even though we have to give many of them away.

I think all those precious fuzzy critters are just another way
God says "I love you" to His children, because they sure enrich my
life.

It touches my heart to know that Jesus cares about animals,
too. That's why this verse of Scripture means so much to me. Have
you ever noticed, in reading over this verse, that Jesus had so much
compassion, He wouldn't even allow a little baby colt to be
separated from its mother?

Just think — Jesus had so much love in Him that even His common day-to-day instructions to His disciples while He was here on
Earth automatically took in the feelings of a baby animal — that's a
whole lot of love!

If Jesus would show that much kindness and tender mercy to
one of His animals, then imagine the gentle way He deals with you,
His most treasured creation!

When I really stop to consider how much Jesus must love me, it
makes me love Him all the more.

Oh, I know I don't always "feel" His love for me — especially
when He's showing me some area of my life that needs to be
worked on! But deep down inside I have the assurance that Jesus
can't do *anything* that's not in love. He can't even take a mother
from her colt!

Today, rest assured that no matter what the Lord is doing in
your life, He's doing it with great tenderness and love.

Buffeting

"And lest I should be exalted above measure through the abundance of the revelations, there was given to me a thorn in the flesh, the messenger of Satan to buffet me, lest I should be exalted above measure."

— *2 Corinthians 12:7*

Early in the weeks of basic training, the army teaches the new recruit how to shine his boots. In soldier slang, the polished look is called a "spitshine," and must be bright enough that the sergeant can see his reflection on the toe of the shoe.

After marching through miles of mud or sand, the boots get dirty. It only takes a short time to clean off the soil, but putting the shine on again takes much longer. First there is another coat of wax and then countless strokes with a shoe brush until the shine is buffed and shiny. A half effort on the soldier's part will result in a loud lecture from the sergeant and more buffing.

Just as polishing boots teaches a soldier discipline, so are believers buffeted by the trials of life. These trials help smooth rough areas of our character which if not dealt with through discipline, our witness to reflect the life of Christ will be dulled and hidden. In the buffeting that God allows Satan to pour on us, we learn two important virtues — patience and humbleness.

A daily Christian walk with God is an exciting life of blessing and trials. They are more precious than gold, which only becomes precious when molded and polished.

Buffeting is not a pleasant experience because the problems and hardships it causes hurts. But, the result is growth in character. One day, Jesus will come again to see just how closely we have followed His commandments and have endured the buffeting.

Accept your trials so you can reflect and illuminate the love and life of Jesus.

Assurance

"If any man will do his will, he shall know of the doctrine, whether it be of God, or whether I speak of myself."

— John 7:17

My wife, Tammy, has stood by my side for so many years and especially through these last two years — the most dreadful, exciting, beautiful, wonderful years of our lives. We are survivors, but only because we have known, without any doubt, that we were in God's will.

Other voices have attempted to influence us and cause us to doubt, but we have not wavered because of the inner peace we had knowing we were definitely in God's will.

When you know the will of God for your life, you can be steadfast and unmovable. No one will be able to change your mind. You will know without a doubt that the vision God has given you is His will — never deviate from it. Don't go to the right or to the left, but keep your eyes on the vision and constantly work toward your goal. Ignore the voices that will try to influence you.

Surrender your will to God. Surrender is not giving up — surrendering is saying, "God, I know it was you — You told me to do it. All hell is against me, and God, if You want to take this — it's yours. I surrender it."

You may have your vision called crazy, but every time man has attempted to do something new — he has been called crazy. The man who invented the sulfur match created a match that changed the world. But he was murdered because they thought he was crazy. He had invented a stick that would light a fire! Every person living today is affected by this man's vision even though he died because of it.

When one is in God's will, nothing done for Him is wasted. You may not always see the proof or the results, but if it were done in God's will, victory will be yours. God is sovereign and you'll never understand Him — just obey Him.

The Death Of Death

"And God shall wipe away all tears from their eyes; and there shall be no more death, neither sorrow, nor crying, neither shall there be any more pain: for the former things are passed away."

— *Revelation 21:4*

There's never been a funeral in heaven. Angels have sat in a grave — Jesus' tomb, one at the head and one at the feet, when the disciples found it empty. But they were only visitors there.

There's nothing about angels that worms can feed on, and no grave can shut in their free spirits. Death can't hold them for a minute.

So it is for all those who have been set free in Jesus Christ, who've passed through the grave and are now with Him. They cannot die. Ages and ages may roll on, eternity will spin on forever. But there will be no greying of hairs or wrinkling from age. There'll be no more infirmity of limbs, no more aches and pains. All of that will have passed away, along with the old order of things that God is soon going to bring to an end.

Do you long to see again that loved one who suffered so much for Jesus' sake during his life? Oh, praise God! Jesus Himself has tenderly wiped every tear from his eyes.

Was there a friend who died suddenly from a painful illness? I tell you, he's better off than we are — he's with Jesus and he'll never feel pain again!

Do you sometimes feel as if your cup is full with suffering and sorrow? Jesus understands. He knew the sorrow and the agony of death for the whole world. How wonderful it will be someday when He takes you in His arms and caresses all your pain away forever!

The Unity Of The Bible

". . . And the Scripture cannot be broken."
— *John 10:35*

I read recently, in the newspaper, one of the major denominations is about to have a drawn-out battle in its leadership conference about the Word of God. There's a large body of pastors and church leaders who do not believe that all of Scripture is the Word of God; they believe that it *contains* the Word of God, along with a lot of human errors.

It's a tragedy to see this. They are on dangerous ground. To put yourself above God's Word is to court trouble and confusion. When you begin to pick and choose what you're going to accept and reject in Scripture, you soon have lost your basis for belief. If you don't like what Paul says about women, you simply cut it out. If one of the Ten Commandments isn't "relevant," you do away with it.

Some of these "scholars" want to cut all the miracles out of the Bible. Some of them, bowing to women's lib, want to revise all the descriptions of God as "He" out of Bible translations. Others say Moses didn't write the Book of Genesis, Peter didn't write II Peter, and Paul didn't write some of his own epistles! Where will they end? They'll have no sure guidelines for life at all.

If you claim Jesus as your Lord, you've got to take seriously what He Himself thought about Scripture. In today's verse, Jesus insisted that the Bible can't be broken. Every time He quoted Scripture, He used it as the total final authority.

In my experience, it has never been the Bible that was wrong, it has been Jim Bakker that has been confused! And that was a healthy and safe attitude to take when approaching the Word of Truth.

Tithe To Your Church

"Bring all the tithes to the storehouse so that there will be enough food in my temple. If you do, I will open up the windows of heaven for you and pour out a blessing so great you won't have room enough to take it in."

— *Malachi 3:10*

How many times have you sat back in church and quietly moaned at the words in the church bulletin. "Sermon topic — Tithes and Offerings."

Believe it or not, it is not any more fun for your pastor to preach on that subject than it is for you to hear it. But, he has to do it. First of all, because God says we must tithe, and he has to relay the Word of God to his "flock."

Plus, more often than not, the church finances are in trouble. Sure, not all churches are always on the brink of bankruptcy, but a lot of them are.

A good friend of mine, Cliff Dudley, was once a pastor. He lived in poverty while his parishioners rode around in Cadillacs and wore three hundred dollar suits. The rich wives made pointed comments at his wife when, after months of wearing the same dress, she bought a new one. He almost lost his salvation over it.

We have an obligation to God to give ten percent of our income to our church. That portion of our pay isn't even ours, it's Gods. And to keep it is to rob God.

God wants to bless us through our tithes. He promised that He will open the floodgates of blessings in your life so great you won't be able to contain it. If you tithe, you know it is true.

In verse 11, God challenges us to put this truth to the test, "Try it! Let me prove it to you, your crops will be large for I will guard them ... These are the promises of the Lord of Host."

The Pearl Of Great Price

" . . . The kingdom of heaven is like unto a
merchant man, seeking goodly pearls: Who,
when he had found one pearl of great price,
went and sold all that he had, and bought it."
— Matthew 13:45-46

A while back, a Hindu published an article in an Indian magazine, suggesting that India adopt Christianity as its national religion. His reason? Because, he said, "It's the cheapest religion in the world."

"I know what I'm saying," he wrote. "Here in India, we give all for our religions, and often make ourselves poor in doing so. But I have been to America, and I have seen millions of professing Christians in that land who spend more for gasoline than they do for God, more for personal pleasure than they do for the advancement of their faith."

What a sad criticism from a so-called heathen! Yet, it's more true than we want to admit, isn't it? If every Christian tithed and gave to God some of his time, energy, and love, do you know what would happen? There'd be no welfare system in the country. The insurance companies would shut down. The hospitals and nursing homes would have to sell their beds. Instead, we pamper ourselves and give God crumbs from the table. Then we wonder why our country's blessings are dripping away like water down the drain.

A lot of Christians think this verse means that Jesus came down and gave His all for us, because we were the pearl of great price. That's not it, friend. It is *Jesus,* who's the Pearl of great price, and anyone who truly sees His worth will go out and give everything he's got for a chance to receive Him. Yes, salvation is free, but anyone who knows what it's worth will spend his whole life for it, even if he doesn't have to do so.

Don't Push God Away

"Looking diligently lest any man fail of the grace of God; lest any root of bitterness springing up trouble you, and thereby be defiled;"
— *Hebrews 12:15*

When we experience a great disappointment or live through the loss of a loved one, we sometimes feel like taking our hurt and loneliness out on God, turning on Him for allowing misery into our lives, instead of turning towards His loving arms for help and comfort.

We seem to forget that our brief stay on earth isn't supposed to be Heaven, yet — that we will see and experience tragedy as a natural part of our lives, until we pass through those pearly gates.

We need to realize that in the midst of any hurt, Jesus is there, and He wants to carry us through our sorrow, making us stronger, more sensitive Christians as a result.

When we angrily push God away from us, we push away our source of comfort and healing.

God never feels joy in seeing us hurt, nor does He deal with us unfairly. God is not to blame for the hard times in our lives. But if we allow ourselves to grow bitter towards God, spurning the hope in His love, we lose our faith and our joy. Bitterness only results in a miserable life of resentment, and we do ourselves no favor by allowing a bitter root to remain and grow in our lives.

Today, take joy in knowing that in the darkest valleys of your life, God is beside you, ready to shower you with love and compassion.

If you have a hurt in your life, reach out to God, and He'll lift it from you, healing your heart at the same time, because God never wants to see you suffer.

Signs And Substance

"But he answered and said unto them, An evil and adulterous generation seeketh after a sign . . . ."

— *Matthew 12:39*

When we walk by faith daily, we have no need for signs. God's Word is full of the evidence of His goodness, but some people still need to be reassured that what they are doing is truly God's will.

People who are constantly putting out "fleeces" justify what they are doing by saying they are following Gideon's example. But, they should also remember that Gideon was living under the law and we are living in the day of grace.

During Gideon's day, Israel had forsaken God and, as a result, was constantly being raided and terrorized by the Midianites. Also remember, Gideon was hiding from the Midianites when the angel appeared to him.

Gideon wanted to be sure that God was really calling him, so He put out a fleece. His faith was strengthened when God answered him by wetting it with dew as Gideon had requested.

We don't need to "fleece" God today. In fact, Jesus is warning us against "fleecing" in this scripture. Jesus tells us that "sign-seekers" are evil and adulterous. When the scribes and Pharisees asked Jesus for a visible sign, He rebuked them.

Why should He change His mind today? He hasn't! The Word is still the same and His promises are still in effect. Many miracles have been happening lately that have opened people's eyes so they can see the shortness of time left. But, you must be careful not to seek after these signs. They will only confuse you and Satan will try to trick you into following them.

If you need an answer from God, seek it in faith. Listen to the guiding voice within you instead of relying on external signs and wonders.

Don't Give God Junk

"And if ye offer the blind for sacrifice, is it not evil? And if ye offer the lame and sick, is it not evil? Offer it now unto thy governor; will he be pleased with thee, or accept thy person? saith the Lord of hosts."

— *Malachi 1:8*

These words of God are from one of the angriest passages in the Bible. God was mad at the priests of Israel. They were telling people that somehow God wanted junk!

They got the idea that God would accept sick offerings. They told the people to bring lame animals and sacrifices that nobody could eat because the flesh was rotten. "Give God what nobody else wants," they said to themselves.

Sadly, things haven't changed much since then. Some of my critics complain because PTL always tries to do things first-rate for God and His people. But the critics seem to feel we should use second-hand equipment and hand-me-downs to be spiritual. They say I shouldn't pay my staff but a mere pittance, because if you work in a ministry, you should sacrifice for God.

Well, I'll tell you, God was angry with that way of thinking then, and He hasn't changed. Did you know that the Tabernacle alone, which was nothing but a big tent, was worth, according to Bible scholars, more than thirty million dollars? And God designed every inch of it! He demanded the best. That's why everything we've put into PTL has been the best. Let the critics cry "Waste!" We're going to obey God.

Give God your best today. Offer Him something that costs you. He wants to be praised from the rising of the sun to its going down. Give Him your best in everything — and then you'll have a right to expect Him to give you His best. He will, too, because God always goes first-rate!

Let God Heal You

"He sent His word, and healed them . . . . "
— Psalm 107:20

TAMMY: I had a guest on the PTL Club once who said, "If people who are sick would take the Word of God as often as they take aspirin, they would be healed." I believe that is true!

Most of us are so "programmed" by the commercials we see on television, that the first thing we do when we get a headache is to reach for a bottle of aspirin. Or if we get a stomach ache, we reach for the medicine cabinet.

I'm not saying that these things are not good, and that they aren't useful. What I am saying is that's not the best solution for the believer.

God sent His only Son, Jesus, to die a terrible death for us. Before He went to the cross, the Bible says He was beaten. Through His death we are saved, and "by whose stripes (the wounds of the whippings) ye were healed" I Peter 2:24.

He has already paid the price for our healing. He wants us whole . . . He wants us to accept His gift of healing.

All He asks is that you have faith in Him. How do you get faith? "Faith comes by hearing, and hearing by the Word of God."

The answer is in the Bible. We have to get in the habit of reaching for the Word instead of for a bottle of pills. When you put your faith in action through the Word, God's healing power can take over your life.

So, instead of taking a pill "three times a day and at bedtime," try taking the Bible that often. A few doses of "Rise and be healed," "By whose stripes ye were healed," and "He sent His Word and healed them," and you'll begin to see what God can do.

Who Changes?

"For I am the Lord, I change not; therefore ye sons of Jacob are not consumed."
— *Malachi 3:6*

One morning a preacher woke up and heard from God. The Lord said to him, "Bob, you and I are incompatible — and I don't change!" That didn't leave much doubt as to who would have to change if there was any changing to be done!

God doesn't need to do any changing; He's absolutely perfect as He is. He has never been any less perfect than He is now, and can't ever possibly get any better. Scripture clearly tells us that.

But we need a lot of changing. We like to think we can't stand improvement, but life has a way of proving to us that we don't have it all together.

Have you ever been able to say that you've done anything without a single flaw whatsoever? I can't say that I have. If I can come close with any consistency, I'm happy. I'm pleased that the PTL Club has gotten high marks in the television industry for the quality of our production, color, audio, and other technical aspects. But at PTL, we're always trying to do better.

If God is perfect, and He doesn't change, I wonder what He thinks when He looks down at His very imperfect children? One thing I know: Even though we may make mistakes, or somehow stray away from God into sin, His love for us never wavers and His mercy is always reaching out to us, giving us another chance.

Isn't it comforting to know that God's not moody like we humans are — that His compassion towards us doesn't depend on how good we've been, but flows naturally from Him — just because He's God! Today rest in that knowledge that no matter what, God's love is always there for you, and it will never change or weaken.

The Animal School

"Now there are diversities of gifts, but the same Spirit."
— *1 Corinthians 12:4*

A group of animals decided to better themselves by starting a school. They set up courses in swimming, running, climbing, and flying.

The duck was a great swimmer, but he was worried about his weakness in other areas. So he decided to take climbing, running, and flying, though he was not good in any of them. He worked so hard flopping over logs and waddling around and trying to loop his nose through low clouds that he almost forgot how to swim!

The rabbit could run swiftly, but he spent so much time trying to master swimming that he lost most of his speed. The squirrel dropped from an "A" in climbing to a "C" because his instructor spent hours trying to teach him to fly and swim. An eagle had to stay after school because he got bored with trying to learn to climb and just flew up to a treetop.

This little story is a laughable illustration of what all too often happens painfully in the Body of Christ. God's given each of us a gift. And our gifts differ. But some of us are trying to do so many things that we foul up in the thing for which we're most qualified. And the whole Body suffers.

In Romans 12, Paul says to use the gifts we have. Don't get upset because someone else does something better than you. If God made you a duck saint, you're a duck. So swim with all you've got! Don't get all bothered because you waddle when you run. Running isn't your thing. You just concentrate on swimming. If you're an eagle saint, stop trying to get squirrel saints to fly like you do, or rabbit saints to build nests like yours. Let them do their things, using their own gifts. That's what'll make the Body work as it should.

You know, the Holy Spirit is pretty versatile. He can swim or fly or run quite well — in a willing vessel. You help Him school you well in your things — and He'll take care of the lessons others need to learn!

Work That Satisfies

"Wherefore do ye spend money for that which is not bread? and your labor for that which satisfieth not?..."

— *Isaiah 55:2*

Experts in business management are now confirming what experience has shown for a long time: If an employee doesn't like his job or place of employment, he's better off finding another place to work than staying where he is with an unhappy attitude. If he stays, he may hold down his job, but he won't be really productive. And chances are, his feelings will spill over into grumbling and complaining that may affect others around him.

So Isaiah's question is a very good one: Why are you working for or in something unsatisfying? You'll never be happy that way, so why bother?

This has implications for the whole of life. Day after day, you read the newspaper or watch television and hear about people who "have it all," but aren't happy with it. Many rich and famous people express their dissatisfaction with life — but they don't do anything about it. They don't think of turning to God. They need to consider Isaiah's question.

The devil will never give you any real satisfaction in life. He can give excitement, pleasure, riches, and knowledge of sorts, but never satisfaction. With him, you're always looking at life as if through the wrong end of a pair of binoculars: The satisfaction you expect to get always eludes you.

You'll never be dissatisfied if you give your every waking moment to serving the Lord. The only people who can never be happy doing God's work are hypocrites, who don't really have Jesus in their hearts, but are just going through the motions. And if you're a born-again Christian, and you're not satisfied with what you're doing, either it's the wrong thing or you should be doing more of it. If you're not content with your life, ask God to show you why, right now. Get it straightened out with Him — He can satisfy your every need and question.

Being Considerate

"He that blesseth his friend with a loud voice, rising early in the morning, it shall be counted a curse to him."

— Proverbs 27:14

I'm sure you've heard someone say, "Don't bother me in the morning until I've had my cup of coffee!" You may have even said it yourself! Many people just can't get "fired up" in the mornings. Only after they have their cup of coffee or wait until mid-morning are they alert and ready to face the rest of the day.

But there are others who come bounding out of bed ready to "eat nails!" They charge through breakfast, sing in the bathroom, and almost dash out the door without opening it.

Science has discovered that there are indeed "day people" and "night people." Day people do their most productive work in the morning hours and after that slowly run down. By evening, they're ready to settle down with some hot chocolate and fade into dreamland. But, night people — in the morning, they are just like a slow fuse burning. The fuse keeps on sputtering slowly all day until evening. Then the "bomb" goes off! They want to go out on the town, stay up talking till all hours, or watch the late movie. They're the kind who always bring "homework" home from the office, too.

I like to think that the difference between these two types is a "comma." When the alarm clock goes off, the day person shouts, "Good, Lord — it's morning!" The night person grumbles, "Good Lord — it's morning!"

Solomon certainly was a wise man to recognize that difference. Take a tip from him. Try to take stock for a moment of the kinds of people with whom you live and work, and the way God made them. Learn to be sensitive to their needs, and considerate of their habits and "quirks." Be quiet around the night person in the morning. Don't badger a day person at night. Don't let your greeting become a "curse" to anyone today.

The Growing Season

"To every thing there is a season, and a time to every purpose under the heaven: . . . a time to plant, and a time to pluck up that which is planted."

— *Ecclesiastes 3:1-2*

One of the hardest things for us to do, as Christians, is to wait on God's appointed timing. If we could have our way, we'd plant a seed one morning, and come back the next day to find a whole crop ready to harvest! But God didn't create things to work out quite that way. Instead, He has much He wants to teach us during the seemingly endless growing season between planting and harvesting!

Kenneth Copeland talks about how as a little boy he planted some watermelon seeds by his driveway. He remembers going out every day to check on the seeds' progress, impatiently waiting as the vine finally began to come out of the ground, and buds began to appear. But he wanted it to grow faster.

One day, as a treat, his dad went out to the store, bought a huge watermelon, and hid it under the vine. When little Ken went out to check his plant the next day, and discovered a big watermelon suddenly lying there, he says he screamed at the top of his lungs in excitement!

Brother Copeland says he has learned, though, that while God will sometimes surprise us by performing a miracle to help us, the way his earthly father surprised him with a huge watermelon, as a rule the Lord won't produce our "watermelons" for us with a "stroke of divine power." He expects us to go through the process of doing our own gardening, even though the patience it takes to wait through the slow growing stage comes only after a struggle with our impatient natures.

Today, accept the divinely appointed times of planting and harvesting, and accept also the waiting stage between. The patience you'll grow during that time will be a sweet fruit indeed.

Thy Will Be Done

"Thy kingdom come, thy will be done in earth as it is in Heaven."
— *Matthew 6:10*

Sometimes we repeat prayers like "The Lord's Prayer" almost mechanically — we've said them so many times before, that the meaning of the words don't really sink into our hearts anymore.

The Lord hears every word we utter, however, and He's more than likely to remind us that if we're going to pray about His will being done here on earth, the best place for Him to start working on that "prayer request" is probably with us!

The fact that we may be at the top of God's list of "Things To Do" might bring us up short for a minute, but you know, if we honestly do want to see God's Kingdom here on earth begin looking more like the one He rules in Heaven, the biggest obstacles to be overcome are really our own selves, if we'll admit it!

Of course, change isn't always fun, or comfortable. In fact growing more like Jesus can even hurt sometimes — any kind of growth is always a little painful. Especially when it involves giving up our own will to follow God's will instead. There is something in our natures that causes us to want to be in control of our lives.

We may have other changes to face, also, like giving up some habits that aren't pleasing to God, or getting rid of a bad temper.

But whatever God asks us to do to help make this earth more like His kingdom in Heaven, He'll also give us the grace to help us do it! If you've been praying the "Lord's Prayer" lately, don't be surprised if God answers by pointing out a few things in your life that need some work. The result, though, will be more Heaven on earth!

Repentance

" . . . But now God commandeth all men everywhere to repent."

— Acts 17:30

As Chuck Colson would tell you, perhaps one of the most shocking things about American prisons today is the large number of inmates who are there for the second, third, or fourth time. I doubt if a single man in prison hasn't been sorry he ended up behind bars. But it's obvious from those repeated stays in jails that being sorry for getting caught is not enough to keep criminals from committing crimes again!

While you may never have been in prison, I'm sure there have been times when you were sorry for having been found out for doing something wrong. If there's one thing that characterizes this kind of feeling, it's feeling sorry for yourself. It feels bad to be caught, and perhaps humiliated and punished, doesn't it?

But when God talks about repentance, He's not talking about just feeling sorry for having been found out for sin. He's talking about such a change of heart and mind that a person turns his will away from that sin, hates it, and feels sorrier for the grief he's caused God than the grief he may feel for himself.

We are told to repent. To change our heart and mind concerning sin. If a mind changes its "shape," it's going to think differently. Rather than dwelling on sin, it's going to dwell on good things. It's not going to dwell on the wrong it did, it's going to concentrate on the right things there are to do.

This is what Jesus commanded all men to do — to make a 180 degree turn around in their actions and their thinking. Can you think of any part of your life or thinking that isn't "shaped" God's way or turned in His direction? Ask God right now to change your heart and your actions.

The One Thing Needed

"Jesus answered and said unto him, Verily, verily, I say unto thee, Except a man be born again, he cannot see the kingdom of God."
— John 3:3

The Lord spoke to me more than a year ago that it was time for us to talk much less about being Charismatic and talk more about the Body of Christ, with all its true believers.

Don't get me wrong — I'm not knocking the Baptism in the Holy Spirit. Tammy and I are Spirit-filled, and so is most of the PTL staff. But the Bible doesn't say, "Ye *must* be filled with the Holy Ghost." Now, God urges us to seek that — but "Ye must be born again."

If you're born again, you're my brother and my sister. There are a lot of good things that God gives that He wants us to have. But I'll tell you what, if someone doesn't even believe in the Baptism in the Holy Spirit, but they love Jesus Christ as Savior, they are still my friend, whether anyone likes it or not — my friend, and my brother in Christ.

You see, Christianity is no private club open only to people holding some special doctrine. I don't think the thief on the cross was baptized in the Holy Ghost. I don't think he had time! He wasn't baptized in water, either, unless his own sweat counts for that. Yet, Jesus said the thief would be with Him in Paradise that day.

I believe that if you're alive and well, you ought to be baptized in water in obedience to Scripture. But the most important thing is to be born again — and then to follow the Lord Jesus in whatever He tells you to do.

Don't shut anyone out of the kingdom of God because their doctrine is a little different from yours. If they have Jesus in their heart, if they've been born again, embrace them as brothers and sisters. Love them a little — in spite of all your faults, the Lord loved you more than a little!

Childlike Trust

"Therefore take no thought, saying, "What shall we eat? or, What shall we drink? or, Wherewithal shall we be clothed? (For after all these things do the Gentiles seek:) for your heavenly Father knoweth that ye have need of all these things."

— Matthew 6:31-32

Children really know how to trust. They never worry if there'll be food or clothing or shelter for them. It's their very nature to trust their parents' love and care. It's growing up, with its disappointments and broken promises that teaches them distrust.

There's not a lot of trust in the Mafia. A thug taught his baby son a lesson about trusting one day. The little one was taking his first steps. "Come on to Papa," said his Dad, and the baby toddled across the room. His father caught him in his arms before he fell, set him upright, and then moved a few steps away. Again, the son stumbled toward his father, but this time, the man kept moving backwards until the baby fell on his face. His father picked him up, dried his tears, and said, "You see, son? Don't trust anybody — not even me!"

It seems strange to me that as untrustworthy as people are, most of us still find it easier to trust men than we do to trust God, especially with the "little things" in life. We can trust God to keep the moon and sun up in the sky — but not to keep food on our table! We stew and fret about whether God's going to come through and meet the bills — we need some re-education concerning God's promises!

If there's one thing that God claims in the Bible, it's that He's absolutely trustworthy. What is it going to take for us to start believing Him? Every now and then, He just has to take the control of things out of my hands so I have to trust Him. Friend, He's never failed me, and you know some of what I've been through. If you're born-again, act like it. Learn to trust like a child again — and let God be Dad.

The Secret To Success

" . . . for my heart rejoiced in all my labor:
and this was my portion of all my labor."
— *Ecclesiastes 2:10*

A little wooden box setting on my desk in my office has attracted a lot of attention. Written across the top of it are the words *The Secret to Success*. Nearly everyone who comes in opens the box to find out the answer. Most people groan when they do! For inside is written just one word — WORK!

Most people are expecting some bit of philosophy, I guess, or a key to riches instead of the simple word "work." But personally, I believe there are three ways to success — work, work, and more work!

Our PTL Orchestra and Singers do a really super job. I hear as many compliments about this great group of young people as anything at PTL. But their beautiful sound didn't come just because they're beautiful people — which they are. Each one of them has special talents. But first, they had to get together. They worked and rehearsed and rehearsed and worked. Somebody had to write the music; someone else had to write the words. Then somebody had to write the arrangements. Only then could they all get together and put their talents to work. Only then did harmony and beauty come forth — because they worked at it together.

A saying I grew up hearing often was "anything worth having is worth working for." That's a principle that's worked all my life. You know, Jesus is worth working for. Sure, salvation is a free gift — but Jesus is the Pearl of Great Price, and He's worth every ounce of energy and bit of time or money the whole human race could ever spend.

Give everything you've got to working for Jesus Christ for your whole lifetime. That's what real success is. Start working today like there's no tomorrow — you'll be a stunning success forever.

He's Coming Soon!

"He which testifieth these things saith, Surely I come quickly. Amen. Even so, come, Lord Jesus.

— *Revelation 22:20*

If you don't think Jesus is coming back soon, just look around you! All the ingredients are here: Wars, rumors of wars, earthquakes, vast increases in knowledge, signs and wonders in the heavens, false teachers with "miracles" trying to fool God's people if possible. You say all those things have happened before? Well, there's one prophecy which has never come close to being fulfilled before this age — the Gospel message reaching to the ends of the earth! That goal is now within reach — and I'm proud to say that PTL is a part of it!

Dino and Debbie Kartsonakis were telling me not long ago about some friends who were recently driving through the desert. They don't usually pick up hitchhikers, but they picked up a young man on this occasion. This young man kept saying to them, "Jesus is coming soon." And they said, "We believe that — we're Christians." He said, "No, you don't understand what I'm saying — He's coming *very* soon!" After he'd said this for about the fifth time, the wife sitting in the front seat looked around to the back seat — and he had disappeared! Well, these weren't people prone to seeing things, and they decided to report it to the local authorities. The sheriff said, "You're the seventh or eighth couple in the last few days to tell us the same story."

Wasn't that strange? Could it have been an angel? I don't know. But I do know that we've got the assurance of the Word of God that Jesus is coming soon. In the turmoil of the world today — that may be touching your life right now — Jesus is laying the foundation for His coming. So child of God, rejoice greatly! Don't look down. Look up! Victory in Him is sure!

Cultivating With God

"In the morning sow thy seed, and in the evening withhold not thine hand: . . . "
— *Ecclesiastes 11:6*

Farming is an occupation that requires a lot of work. A farmer knows his crops won't grow by themselves. He's got to work if he's going to get results. He's got to get on his tractor and plow the fields. After he plants his crops, he also has to tend and harvest them.

Nature, God's creation, gives the important ingredients of sunshine and rain and the miracle of the tiny seed that grows into a plant. But nature alone won't produce a crop. Just so, life and breath are given to a person at birth, along with great possibilities for learning and growth. But it's whatever efforts are put into cultivating a productive life that will determine the kind of person — and the kind of fruit he bears.

Yes, it takes more than your own efforts to be the person you know you should be. That's where God and His love become an added ingredient in your life. But, you've got to work with Him. God provides, yet you must do your part. He gave His only Son, Jesus, to die for your sins, but you have to accept forgiveness and salvation.

Suppose a farmer couldn't decide what crop to plant until the growing season almost ended. It would be too late then to expect a good harvest. The longer you delay in dedicating your life fully to Christ, the more futile your best efforts at productive living will be.

As you cultivate a daily relationship with God through prayer, studying and reading His Word, He has promised to supply every need of your life. That will require working hand in hand with His tending and planning today and every day. God and you make up the essential ingredients for the best person you can be. Work with Him, and you can't fail to be "the cream of the crop."

Plain And Simple

"Seeing then that we have such hope, we use great plainness of speech."
— *2 Corinthians 3:12*

Believe it or not, my English was far better when I was a teenager than it is today. I learned, as I was preaching in country churches and back in the hills, that there were certain words in my vocabulary that nobody could understand. So when I began ministering over television, I took those words out and to speak very simple English. I had to in order to reach everybody.

I'm not telling English students to throw their grammar books away. But people can be turned off by great big words they don't understand. What good is preaching or sharing if no one knows what you mean?

Experts in the languages spoken in Old Testament times have come up with some interesting insights on how Jesus Himself spoke. He gave His messages in Aramaic, and scholars say that much of what He said, like the Sermon on the Mount, was probably said in something like rhyme. In fact, His way of speaking was a lot like the folk songs and sayings of His time. Jesus was from Galilee, which was considered "the sticks" of Palestine. His style was probably a lot like a country preacher's today!

No wonder the Scribes and Pharisees couldn't stand Jesus. Here was a man saying the most profound things ever spoken — so plainly and simply that anyone could understand Him! God made sure that the New Testament was written in the most common business language in the Roman world.

God was so interested in saving people that He made it as easy as He could for them to understand the Gospel message. When you share Jesus, do you make the Gospel message as simple as you can? Make it easy to meet Jesus. Many people have met Him just because at the end of every PTL Club telecast, I say, "God loves you, He really does!"

Works Laid Out

"For we are his workmanship, created in Christ Jesus unto good works, which God hath before ordained that we should walk in them."
— *Ephesians 2:10*

Two preachers were driving down the road to a meeting one day. As the miles passed, they talked about the wonders of God's saving grace apart from the Law.

Then up ahead, they saw a car parked on the shoulder of the highway. The driver was walking around it, obviously muttering to himself. The preachers slowed down a bit and saw that the car had two flat tires. The driver, seeing them, waved his arms and pointed to the tires.

The two preachers looked at each other. "Should we help him brother?" asked the preacher at the wheel.

"My friend, I am disappointed in you," the other answered, "Are you trying to be saved by works?"

"Of course not," said the other.

And then the reverends went on down the road, leaving the driver and his crippled car stranded there.

There are too many Christians like those preachers in the little story. They think that when they got saved, God gave them a free ride to heaven, with nothing to do but enjoy the trip. But today's verse says that God didn't just save you — He saved you for a purpose. And that purpose is to do good works.

No, good works do not get you to heaven. They are just what you're supposed to be doing along the way. God has made so sure of that, He's got a whole bunch of them prepared in advance for you to do, according to this verse. How do you know which ones to do? If they're in front of you, do them, and fulfill God's plans for you today!

Rapid Communication

"And it shall come to pass, that before they call, I will answer; and while they are yet speaking, I will hear."

— *Isaiah 65:24*

Have you ever called up someone on the telephone and gotten an answer even before the phone rang? Isn't that a strange experience? Sometimes the phone does ring on the other end of the line, but maybe it didn't register on your end. So, it was a shock to you when they answered.

When Isaiah wrote these words, communication was very slow compared to today. Sending a message any distance in those days often involved considerable time and travel. But somehow, I don't think Isaiah would have been too surprised if he could have caught a glimpse of today's telephones and other means of communication. After all, by the Spirit of God, he had seen something even faster!

The verse above is absolutely amazing to me. Can it really be that whenever I lift up my voice to pray to God, He's already got an answer on the way? That's what He says here.

There are times when I'm tempted to think that for some reason, God just doesn't pay attention to my prayers. Did you ever feel like that? Someone once said, "God answers every prayer He gets. Sometimes His answer is 'No!'" I think we may on occasion miss God's answers to our prayers because they aren't the ones we thought He'd send!

It's great to know, isn't it, that there's no time lag in getting through to God! At any time, day or night, He knows your prayer is coming. He knows just how to respond. He cares so much, He's acting out there ahead of your need. What confidence you can have in coming to Him with every hurt, every request, every need, knowing that there's no one you can get through to faster than God.

Make It Happen

"For every one who has will be given more, and he will have abundance...."
— *Matthew 25:29*

God gave me a philosophy I call "Make It Happen," that has guided my ministry. It means that if God tells me to do something, I get out and do it — because I'm created in the image of God, and He's a Do-er.

When I was just starting in television, Tammy and I made barely enough to get by. But we used what little we had to buy and sell and invest as best we could. Before long, we had more than others making a lot more money. Jesus' parable of the talents tells us that God wants us to be action people. Those who invest their talent and money in God will get more back. God doesn't want us to sit around and take the safe route. You say, "Well, I might lose." That's true — but you might win, too! You need enough faith in the God who holds your heart to realize that He can take care of you and guide your decisions.

I used to have young people on my staff who'd say that they'd like to buy a home but couldn't because they were too expensive. I'd reply, "That's right, you'll never have one if you keep confessing and believing that. If you really want a house, you'll go out and start looking for one." Those kids began to believe what I was preaching, and one after another, they began moving into brand new houses.

Why? They weren't making any more money. It happened because they got their faith into action and began dreaming and meditating on it. Some made arrangements to plant shrubs, paint the house, and do other things to reduce the cost of the home. But by faith and action, they made it happen.

Have you got a need or God-given desire in your heart today? You can make it happen, too, if you'll start putting your faith into action right now.

Starting Without Jesus

"And when they had fulfilled the days, as they returned, the child Jesus tarried behind in Jerusalem; and Joseph and His mother knew not of it."

— *Luke 2:43*

It seems somehow preposterous that Joseph and Mary could have packed up and headed for home without realizing their son wasn't with them.

How, we've probably asked indignantly, could they lose Jesus? Actually, when you go back and study the customs of their day, you find that it's really not so unreasonable for that mix-up to have happened.

In those days, people traveled together in groups. When they were ready to leave a place, they'd start out in two stages. First, the women and children would leave, while the men remained behind to finish packing the tents. Later that day the men would set out, catching up with the women by evening, when they would make camp for the night.

Jesus, at twelve years old, was in that in-between stage — neither a "man" of thirteen, nor still a child. It is more than likely that in the hustle and bustle of packing up and setting out, Mary assumed Jesus was with his father and the other men. Joseph probably believed Jesus to be with Mary and her group. It wasn't until they met in the evening and got settled that they had a chance to discover Jesus had traveled in neither group.

This story makes me think about the times we, enthusiastically, start off on some new project "for God," assuming He's right there with us. But while God never leaves us, He does sometimes withdraw His blessing from certain tasks we take up when they're really for ourselves, not for Him.

Before you start off on any new venture today, first check to make sure the Lord's with you, or you may have to do some backtracking, like Mary and Joseph did!

Satan Never Changes

"Be sober, be vigilant; because your adversary the devil, as a roaring lion, walketh about, seeking whom he may devour."

— *1 Peter 5:8*

Of one thing we can be certain, in a world that's ever changing; everything's under the control of a God who is immutable. But while God never changes, unfortunately, a certain "fallen angel" I know hasn't done much changing in the past few eons, either — he just likes to make you think he has.

Satan is the master deceiver. If he can cause you to believe that he's merely some abstract principle floating around, or a misjudged misfit, or, better yet, a creature that exists only in the fertile imagination of ignorant fanatics, then he's well pleased.

But, don't let him fool you! Satan is the same dirty destroyer today that he was centuries ago, because he is incapable of changing his nature. He reminds me of this scorpion I heard about in a story once. This scorpion needed to cross a river. It approached a turtle to ask for a ride. The turtle, aware of the scorpion's reputation, was wary.

"If I agree to take you across the river, we'll get to the middle and you'll reach under my shell and sting me," the turtle objected. "I know you." But, the scorpion reasoned, "See here, if I stung you in the middle of the river we would both drown. Now why would I do anything to hurt myself? Please take me across. I'm not such a bad fellow when you get to know me." Reassured the turtle agreed, and the scorpion crawled onto his back. Halfway across the river, though, the scorpion reached under the turtle's shell, and stung him. "But we'll both die!" exclaimed the turtle beginning to sink. "I know," replied the scorpion, "I guess I just can't change my nature."

Satan is just like that scorpion! He may seem to be a reasonable fellow at times, but I guarantee you that under that pleasant exterior lies the nature of a scorpion that must sting!

Do You Hate?

"Thou shall love thy neighbor as thy self."
— Mark 12:31b

TAMMY: Have you ever known anyone that is consumed by hate? It's a sad, sad sight to see.

A bunch of us gals were eating lunch at a hamburger stand the other day, and one of them was talking about one of her relatives. The woman had gotten mad at her sister twenty-five years ago and hadn't spoken to her since!

Now, both of these ladies are up in years, yet neither one will make a step toward the other. A seed of bitterness has grown over the years, and I guess if they don't do something soon, they will die still hating each other over something as silly as how to direct a wedding!

Hate is like a cancer. Once you let it start growing in you, it will continue to grow and reach into other areas in your life.

The sad thing is, God can't live where hate is. God is love. If we have God in our hearts, we can't hate. We don't have that right.

Over the years, Jim and I have had many people do hateful things to us, to try to take over or destroy our ministry. And I've been tempted to hate, in fact, at times I have hated for a while. But God always brings this truth back to me. I have to forgive — or He won't forgive me!

Search your heart today. Is there anyone you hate? Your boss or former boyfriend . . . an ex-best friend that spreads gossip about you . . . Whoever they are, whatever they did, forgive them today. Release the hate!

Believe me, you'll be happier. Love will cover a multitude of sins — it really will people!

Look For The Good

"For thou, O God, hast proved us: thou hast tried us, as silver is tried. Thou broughtest us into the net; . . . Thou hast caused men to ride over our heads; we went through fire and water: but thou broughtest us out into a wealthy place."
— *Psalm 66:10-12*

As a child it was never fun to get a tetanus shot, eat liver, or take medicine, but my mother always told me, "It's good for you." Now that I'm a parent, I realize the value of shots and spinach and medicine. Over the years, I've learned that even if something isn't pleasant, it doesn't mean it's bad.

Being an adult, life certainly isn't without its uncomfortable requirements. There may be many a problem you'd like to exchange for a bite of liver or a spoonful of castor oil, like having a root canal, broken car transmission, or house payment. But in studying your situation, there is something valuable in every problem. You may want to ask, "Why is this happening to me?" If you look back on your life, see if you can attribute some of the knowledge you now have to the rough experiences you have been through. In every experience that cost you something, you got the benefit of learning from it. It's likely that your hardest times are the most priceless.

Looking for the good in everything that happens to you is a sure way to discover something good. Cursing a problem never solves it. Struggling with a problem often only makes it worse. Ignoring a problem allows it to grow out of proportion. Oftentimes, God uses our circumstances to tell us something or to guide us. When you're confronted with confusion, fear, or any emotion that is unpleasant, ask God what it is He's trying to tell you. Instead of allowing yourself to become resentful in your circumstances, first go to God in prayer and ask His help.

The next time you are faced with something you don't understand, instead of looking down and getting out of sorts, look up and get some light on the subject. There is something good in everything God allows to happen in your life.

Not Of This World

"I pray not that thou shouldest take them out of the world, but that thou shouldest keep them from evil. They are not of the world, even as I am not of the world."

— *John 17:15-16*

You only have to look around you to know that we are living in the last days. The pattern is set for the coming of the Lord. I believe the stage is ready.

It isn't always easy for the Christian today to know what to do because of the things we encounter daily. But, remember, the disciples were facing difficult times when Jesus prayed this verse. Just as Jesus prayed for the disciples to be kept from evil because they were not of this world, so can we pray and rise above the problems and evil we come in contact with daily.

Most of our lakes and rivers are polluted today, yet a boat floating on a lake can be in the dirty water, and still not be a part of it. It may be bobbing along with the filth and debris, but that boat is still serving its purpose by ferrying people across the water so they don't get drenched with the dirty liquid. Only if the boat were full of the water would it be considered a part of the lake.

The same is true with the Christian who gets too involved with the things in the world that will pollute him. If he is not careful, he will take in too much and sink right out of sight! Or if he tries to take himself out of the world completely, he will no longer be serving his purpose here on earth.

Today, don't ask Jesus to remove you from the lake of life — just ask Him to help you keep the dirty water out of your hull as you serve the purpose Jesus created you for!

His Masterpiece

"Faithful is He that calleth you, who will also do it."

— *1 Thessalonians 5:24*

God didn't call you to save yourself. He called you to trust Him, love Him, and obey Him — and to let Him do the saving.

This is a hard truth for some of us to grasp. Here in this country, we much admire the "self-made man." We have great respect for people who with great will-power pull themselves up from lowly beginnings and achieve success. It's part of the American Dream. While there's much to be admired in that kind of accomplishment, it's not what salvation is all about.

It's quite a blow to your pride to admit that you can't make it to God on your own, isn't it? You can be anything in this world, if you're determined enough. But nothing you can do will ever get you a step closer to heaven. Only Jesus the Creator can make a new creation out of you.

Spiritually, every man is like a rock, and God is like a sculptor. The Lord can see in that lifeless stone the marvelous shape of what you'll someday be. And it's not long after you meet God, that He starts chipping away what isn't Christ-like from your life. Sometimes the blows of His "chisel" drive deep into old habits and cherished secret sins, and it hurts. It would be so much easier on us if we could do the cutting ourselves, wouldn't it?

If only we could see the finished product God has in mind. We would rather be self-made, but we could never make what God can make out of our lives. Today, let God have complete control of your life.

A Place Of Agreement

"Again I say unto you, That if two of you shall agree on earth as touching any thing that they shall ask, it shall be done for them of my Father which is in heaven. For where two or three are gathered together in my name, there am I in the midst of them."

— *Matthew 18:19-20*

PTL is a place of agreement. If a visitor to PTL doesn't believe this when they walk in the door, they will feel the power of the Holy Spirit during their stay. People have their lives touched and changed when they pray together at PTL, at home, or at church. Prayer helps heal scars.

Everyone has problems. Whatever your needs may be, whatever is foremost in your heart — I want you to believe in God to heal what is bothering you. Prayer is the beginning of miracles performed by the power of God.

While God is not a legalist, who demands we always say certain words when we pray, or maintain a certain position, sometimes we do need to get down on our knees, with our face before the Lord. When we kneel humbly before God, we're acknowledging His Lordship over our lives — we're saying we recognize our place as God's servant.

I believe that when we humble ourselves, admit that God is God, and worship, then we will hear from the Lord. Joining with other believers when we pray like this enables us to send up powerful prayers to Heaven.

Christians, praying together, can win many battles. As children of God, we can intercede for one another in prayer and expect answers. Those who are fighting us are fighting God and they have a fight on their hands they can't win. We must stand together and pray, remembering that He is with us always.

A Time For Action

"When the righteous are in authority, the people rejoice: but when the wicked beareth rule, the people mourn."

— *Proverbs 29:2*

You can feel the spirit of the Anti-Christ in our nation today. The Supreme Court has made it illegal to pray in the public schools and has even made it hard to celebrate Christmas. They don't want you to sing Christmas carols in school, and many cities have started moves to make it illegal to even decorate the streets at Christmas. They are trying to take Christ totally out of public life.

Yet, do you see any happiness and joy being brought to America because of these moves? Of course not! God isn't going to bless a nation that turns its back on Him. It's time we started standing up for the Christian way of life and not let public officials intimidate our views.

We need to stand up against abortion, gay rights, and "revolving door" justice that upholds the guilty rather than the innocent. Christians need to start doing their homework on the public officials who represent their area. Find out how your congressman and senators are voting. Ask how your mayor stands on certain issues and make sure your school board is upholding the Christian views in the schools.

We need to start putting men and women of God in high places. Let's stop battling one another and start loving each other and hearing the voice of God. America was founded by men who revered the Word of God, not by those who hear the devil.

There is still hope. If we stand together, we can turn things around. Pray to God right now to minister to this land and let it be a place where we have the freedom to preach His Word everywhere.

Small Enough To Fill A Heart

"But will God indeed dwell on the earth? behold, the heaven, and heaven of heavens, cannot contain thee, how much less this house that I have builded?"

— *1 Kings 8:27*

I've heard many people call God "the man upstairs." It is kind of easy to imagine a nice old man, with long white hair, sitting on a cloud, isn't it? I think most people want as much of God as they can manage in their lives. That's why they like this idea. But the Bible says that there's much more to God than that.

Some things you might imagine as God aren't God. John 1:18 says, "No man hath seen God at any time." No one can comprehend all of God at once. He is infinite, without limit, in power, knowledge, love, justice, mercy, and goodness. As one of Tammy's favorite songs puts it, "My God is bigger than any mountain that I can or cannot see!" And yet, by His Holy Spirit, He can live in my heart! I don't claim to understand that, but I know it!

A famous skeptic once came upon a farmer while strolling in the country. He asked the farmer where he was going. "To church, sir," was the reply. "And what are you going to do there?" the skeptic inquired. "To worship God," the farmer replied. "This God of yours — is He big or little?" questioned the skeptic. "Why, He is both, sir," the farmer answered emphatically. "How can He be both?" the skeptic persisted. The farmer answered, "He is so great, sir, that the heaven of heavens cannot contain Him; and so little that He can dwell in my heart." The skeptic later remarked that this farmer's simple words had gripped his mind more than all of the scholars who had opposed his views.

If you'll only meditate today on the greatness — and smallness of God, you'll experience Him in a new way — in the world around you, and in the tiniest corner of your heart.

True Beauty

"Whose adorning, let it not be that outward adorning . . . But let it be the hidden man of the heart . . . a meek and quiet spirit, which is in the sight of God of great price."

— 1 Peter 3:3-4

My mom and dad enjoy sitting in the studio audience to watch the PTL Club and greet the visiting Partners. One day, Mom came dressed up like she was ready for Christmas, all decked out in red and white — and wearing slacks!

That may not seem shocking to you, but it was just unheard of when I was a kid. The ladies of our church just didn't do that. And heaven help them if they wore any make up or jewelry! Well, now the ladies wear slacks to church. My mom's gotten modern. She even wears earrings!

To tell you the truth, I'm glad we're not hung up on that anymore. I even like to think that a little paint job helps keep the house looking fresh, if you know what I mean! When we were hung up on all those things, we almost forgot the souls of people. We were so interested in how they looked on the outside, that a lot of times, we failed to see that people hurt. We failed to recognize some of the most beautiful, tender hearts among us because our eyes were on externals. We even drove some of those people out of church.

I'm glad to see the church loving people today. I'm glad the Spirit of God is giving believers eyes to see past color and race and dress — past all the prejudice to recognize a meek and quiet spirit. That's always been the most important thing to God.

It's all right to do your best to look nice. But, don't forget to dress up your inner person, too. When you put on Jesus, you're the "best dressed" in any crowd. Wear Jesus well today — and be sure and compliment others who are showing His beauty in their lives, too.

Believe In Your Answer

"If any of you lack wisdom, let him ask of God, that giveth to all men liberally, and upbraideth not; and it shall be given him. But let him ask in faith, nothing wavering. For he that wavereth is like a wave of the sea driven with the wind and tossed."

— *James 1:5-6*

Has anyone ever told you about a problem they've been wrestling with? They've tried solution after solution and wonder why God hasn't helped them yet. But many times God's already given His answer — He's just waiting for them to use it!

A famous professor of mathematics once assigned his college class a very difficult problem for homework, telling them that he expected a correct answer by next morning. Well, the students went back to their rooms and struggled far into the night. The next morning, the professor looked out over the classroom and asked, "Who has the correct solution to the problem?" One young man raised his hand quickly. "Write it on the board," the professor said. The young man did so, and the professor said, "That is not the correct answer. Who has another?" Several other students volunteered answers, all of which the instructor rejected.

Then the first young man who had stood up raised his hand once more. "Sir," he said, "I am aware of your greatness as a mathematician. But with respect, sir, you are mistaken. I worked that problem out carefully and spent hours rechecking my steps. My answer was the correct one." "Yes, you are right," the professor replied, to the shocked gasps of his class. "You see, in today's world, people will challenge your answer, even if it's correct. It is not enough to have the right answer — you must believe in your answer and stand up for it."

If you have asked God for an answer to a problem in your life, you can rest assured that He will give you the wisdom you need. Then, believe that you have indeed heard from God, and start acting on that answer. Try it today.

Render Unto Caesar

*"And Jesus answering said unto them,
Render to Caesar the things that are Caesar's,
and to God the things that are God's. And they
marveled at him."*

— Mark 12:17

It's no wonder they marvelled at Jesus for this answer! Who could imagine a better one? Some Pharisees had come trying to trick Jesus by asking Him whether He thought it was lawful to pay taxes to Caesar or not. Now, Israel was a captive nation at that time, under the control of Rome, and the Jews didn't like that one bit. These men wanted to trap Jesus into saying something that would get Him into trouble with the Romans or with the Jews, who resented the taxes.

Jesus had them bring a coin. There is more irony in this story than first glance will show you. For on one side of this coin, historians say, was a picture of the Roman emperor. On the other side was a picture of the Roman god, Zeus. So Jesus showed them, first the side of the coin with Caesar's picture — and then the one with the Roman god! He was saying, "Well, it's Rome's money all the way. If you're going to use it at all, give Caesar all that he asks. But don't be self righteous about it, if you don't have any real convictions.

It's not much easier to give to "Uncle Sam" today than it was to give to Caesar. Recently, our government spent one hundred thousand dollars trying to figure out why hermit crabs choose to live in one sea shell over another. Over three billion dollars was spent by the government just to print forms and reports that it created! Uncle Sam needs our prayers!

As Jesus said, we need to pay our taxes. And I think that rather than complain about taxation and government spending, prayer would accomplish a great deal in bringing things in line with God's will. So, give to "Caesar" today — and pray for him as you do!

A Broken Promise

"... Though all men shall be offended because of thee, yet will I never be offended ... Though I should die with thee, yet will I not deny thee...."

— *Matthew 26:33, 35*

Just a minute, you say, what's that passage doing there as the Word of God for today? Isn't that Peter talking, just before Jesus was arrested and sent to Calvary? Didn't Peter deny Jesus three times that same night? Yes, that's Peter, and he did deny Jesus.

But remember, Peter was just like you and me. He was a man and became confused by the events that occurred so rapidly in the hours preceding and during the arrest of Jesus.

How many times have you gone to the altar during an invitation at church or some meeting and promised God that you would never commit a certain sin again? How many times have you, on some spiritual high, vowed never to get upset with financial or physical circumstances again? Probably as many times as I have — and that's all too many. I don't think there is one of us who hasn't, like Peter, failed God or denied Him at some time or other.

Take a good look at Peter after the denial. He preached to some of the same people on the day of Pentecost that he had denied even knowing Christ to on the night of Jesus' arrest.

What made the difference? He had gone through the "upper room" experience and had been filled with a new holy boldness. Never again was he the cowardly Peter, but instead, he became the spokesman for the early church because he was established in the Word.

God wants to make His Word established in you. Trust His Word totally today — and become a spokesman for God.

It Is Finished

"Then Jesus said, "Father forgive them; for they know not what they do."
— Luke 23:34

Take a few minutes today to let your imagination drift back in time . . .

The sweaty smell of an angry mob drifted through the busy streets. An unruly crowd swarmed at the base of a government building. Before them stood the target of their venom . . . a man who called himself the Son of God.

Because there were no crimes He had committed, they shouted at Pilate that He was found "perverting the nation." (v.2) "Crucify him . . . crucify him," yelled the mob. And Pilate gave the sentence. Meanwhile, the soldiers fashioned a crown of sharp thorns, and they forced it onto His head with such force that blood trickled down his cheeks from the wounds.

They stuck a reed in His hand to mock the sceptor of this "king," and bowed before Him as they made fun of Him. Then they began to spit on Him, and hit Him violently on the head. Wounded, they led our Lord away to nail Him to a tree.

Stripping Him of his clothes, the soldiers began to drive huge rough nails through His hands and His feet. Naked and wounded, Christ stood before the jeering crowd bleeding and dying.

When He was thirsty, they offered Him vinegar. Over His head they nailed a sign, "Jesus — The King Of The Jews."

The earth knew a terrible thing was happening to Jesus, the Son of God, and the sun refused to shine as darkness covered the earth in the middle of the day (Matt. 27:46).

Only a few of his loved ones stayed at the foot of the cross. I'm sure it was a sight many couldn't have stood. Yet, his mother, Mary, sat weeping at his feet until a disciple took her home.

I'm sure His followers thought their world had come to an end. Their Master died . . . painfully . . . slowly . . . he gasped, "It is finished."

The Earth Shook

"And the graves were opened; and many of the bodies of the saints which (were dead) arose, and came out of the graves after his resurrection and went into the holy city, and appeared unto many."

— *Matthew 27:52, 53*

The earth reacted violently to the death of Jesus. The veil of the temple was torn from the top to the bottom, (v. 51). The ground shook in a terrible earthquake.

The holy city of Jerusalem trembled as dead people walked the streets. Note that the Word said it wasn't all of the dead . . . but many saints. Hm-m-m-m.

Why all of the uproar? Man didn't seem to be upset that this Jesus was killed. But the earth . . . the earth could hardly stand the shock of the murder of the Son of God.

As the earth shook, the Bible tells us that some "centurions" were with Jesus after he died when the earthquakes began. And they feared greatly. "Truly this is the Son of God," they acknowledged (v.54).

Nevertheless, some refused to believe. The day after He died the chief priests came to Pilate remembering that Jesus said on the third day He would rise again. They told Pilate that if they didn't guard the tomb, the disciples would steal the body, and they'd go around saying Christ had risen. (v. 63-64)

Taking every possible precaution, they sealed the huge stone that filled the entrance to the tomb, and placed a guard at the grave.

They were sure this would finally stop all the talk about this Jesus Christ being the Son of God . . . the King of the Jews.

How wrong they were!

He Is Risen

"And he saith unto them, Be not affrighted:
Ye seek Jesus of Nazareth, which was crucified:
he is risen; he is not here: behold the place where
they laid him."

— *Mark 16:6*

How quickly we forget what the Lord tells us! Jesus had told everyone that He would rise three days after He was buried, but with the shock of His terrible death . . . either no one remembered . . . or no one believed.

Early that morning, Mary Magdalene and Mary, the mother of James, made their way to the grave. They had brought sweet spices and planned to anoint Jesus' dead body with them.

The sun was just coming up as they slowly walked up the hill. Then it occured to them, "Who will roll away that stone?"

As they got within sight of the tomb, they were surprised to see someone else had rolled it away. When they entered, they saw a young man clothed in a white garment. And they were amazed!

I don't think that we could even dream of the joy that must have leaped into those ladies' hearts as this angelic being told them that Jesus wasn't there. As they looked on the empty bier, surely they wondered, scared to even think it, "Could He have really risen?"

Yes! He arose! Later that day, Jesus appeared to Mary Magdalene, and when she told the others about it, they wept.

Jesus has spoken to all of us through His Word that He is coming back for us soon . . . yet, how many of us forget that we know that and continue on in life like we have forever to prepare for the rapture.

Our Lord meant what He said to His followers then, and if they had believed Him, they would have saved themselves a lot of grief.

The same is true today . . .

What Kind Of Love?

"But a certain Samaritan, as he journeyed, came where he was; and when he saw him, he had compassion on him."

— *Luke 10:33*

What a message there is in the familiar story of the Good Samaritan. Jesus is trying to tell us that the love He wants us to show others is more than just doing service in the church ... it's more than just going through acts of religious piety ... it's more than just going and taking communion, though that is important ... and, it's more than just going to a church and singing some hymns and directing a service.

The "religious" people in Jesus' story walked on by the wounded man. But Jesus is saying, "I want you to do what the Good Samaritan did. I want you to go and minister to the needs of people. I want you to minister to the sick. I want you to minister to the hurt. If they have sores, I want you to pour in the wine and the oil — I want you to give the kind of ministry that's going to heal them in the area of need.

That Samaritan undertook to help the suffering man in every way possible. I'm sure the Samaritan was a busy man — he could not stay but one night at the inn before he continued on his journey. But even after he left, he made sure the wounded man received attention. He took responsibility for seeing that the man was restored to health. Jesus wants us to have that kind of complete involvement. He wants love in action now.

Folks, look around you. There are people hurting. You can touch the lives and minister to the needs of some of them. You can get on your face before God and pray for them. Let your heart be open to minister to the need or hurt that's there. Be like the Samaritan and put the oil and wine where the wound is. Really love someone today — and see that love fulfilled.

In One Accord

"And when the day of Pentecost was fully come, they were all with one accord in one place."

— *Acts 2:1*

When the Spirit of God came to that little band of followers in the Upper Room, the revival began that we're experiencing right now. Such great things happened! Tongues of fire came down, the disciples spoke in languages they hadn't learned, and 3,000 souls were converted that very day!

I tell you, there's power in being of one mind. But do you know, they could have gotten bogged down in all kinds of discord and gossip that day, if they had let it happen. Think of the humdinger group of people in that Upper Room. They could have looked at Mary Magdalene and said, "What is she doing here? I heard she used to be a harlot. What makes her think the Holy Ghost is going to fall on her."

Oh, they had a lot to talk about. There was Peter. Someone might have whispered, "Why is he here? He's the one who betrayed Christ! And the nerve of that one showing up!"

But no, they weren't gossiping. They weren't tearing one another apart. They were there with one accord. And when they waited in one accord, the Holy Spirit came upon them and filled them with His power, and they went out from there and turned the world upside down!

If there's anything that's going to change the world, it's the unity of the Holy Spirit. Look at what these people began to do: "And by the hands of the apostles were many signs and wonders wrought among the people; and they were all with one accord in Solomon's porch" (Acts 5:12).

God can use us with the same power today, if we'll just get in one accord. What does what one or the other of us used to be matter when there are souls out there needing salvation? Let's forget our differences and join in the work that has to be done. God never said, "whosoever's just right," He said, "whosoever will!" To be willing to serve is to be right enough for God.

The Liberated Woman

"And the rib which the Lord God had taken from man, made he a woman, and brought her to the man. And Adam said, This is now bone of my bones, and flesh of my flesh: she shall be called Woman, because she was taken out of Man."
— *Genesis 2:22-23*

The most liberated women I know are Christians! I know that may sound like a ridiculous statement to those who believe that true women's liberation will come only with the ERA amendment, but I challenge them to take a closer look at what the Bible says about women.

Tammy delights in reminding me that the Hebrew word used to describe man's creation in the Bible is something like "blopped," while the Hebrew word that describes the creation of woman is closer to "artistically created." Eve and her female descendents can hardly be referred to as second-rate citizens!

Also, Eve was fashioned neither from Adam's feet, symbolizing an inferior position compared to his as a servant or slave, nor from his head, symbolizing a function superior to his.

Instead, God chose to form Eve from Adam's side — a significant decision when we realize God was showing us that he designed woman as man's equal — as his companion and helpmate.

Eve shared not only Adam's body, soul, and spirit, but also his commission to fill the earth and subdue it, working alongside of her husband.

To anyone who declares that God has unfairly placed the female sex in an inferior position to man's, I reply, read Genesis!

Eyes and Light

"The light of the body is the eye: if therefore thine eye be single, thy whole body shall be full of light."

— *Matthew 6:22*

How many times have your eyes given your true feelings away? Even though you may be hiding your emotions inside, your eyes will always tell the truth.

The way you look at someone can tell them how you feel. A noted Christian child phychologist has been discovering the great need for eye contact with children so they will know they are loved. One of the first sights a new baby sees is his parents eyes. The baby is searching for a familiar face. Children can feel, through the loving way their parents look at them, a love that mere words can't possibly express. The reassurance your loving look can give children is amazing.

This is one reason blind children have such a hard time adjusting in the world. They can't see the love in their parents' eyes. A parent needs to minister love to a blind child intensively in many other ways to make up for the lack of the love in their eyes.

Your eyes are the "windows to your soul." Children have got to have the right things in front of their eyes so they won't be guided down the wrong path in life. With all the advertising, movies, television, and other sights in the world, children see an illusion through their eyes that is very tempting. What they see will influence their lives. That's why it is so important that young people, especially, know the true look of Christian love. They are going to see so many other "looks" in everyday life and they need to be able to "see" the difference.

Christian adults also need to be able to look into each others eyes and see Christian love. They need their eyes filled with good things. What will your "windows" see today? Will they tell others about Christian love? Open your eyes and shout your joy to all!

The Unseemly Parts

"And those members of the body, which we think to be less honorable, upon these we bestow more abundant honor . . . ."
— *1 Corinthians 12:23*

There are going to be a lot of surprises on Judgment Day. One preacher calls it "The Great Embarrassment." I think we're going to realize that we've taken credit for a lot of good things in our lives and ministries for which God and other faithful servants of His are responsible.

A preacher was once holding a street service in one of the busiest business sections of a great city. As he raised his voice this particular day, he found that he was drawing a vast crowd. His words echoed from the tall buildings around him with an authority he'd never before felt in his ministry. People of all ages were hanging on his every word. He saw tears trickling down many cheeks.

Even as he spoke, he began to congratulate himself. "Hey, you're really in the power of the Holy Spirit today. You've got it, brother. My, how God's using you!" But just then, he heard that familiar, still, small voice: "Wait a minute, son. Direct your eyes over to the right. There, under that lamppost — do you see that old man, with his hands lifted, his eyes closed and his lips moving? It's not you who's responsible for this great move of My Spirit. It's that little man, who's interceding for you with all his heart. He's the one." The preacher quieted his proud spirit and went on preaching the Gospel, mightily, but with a new humility.

I know how that preacher felt. Heaven only knows how much the prayers of our friends have meant to the ministry of PTL. Pray for ministers of the Gospel everywhere. We only stand as we're propped up by the prayers of other people. It may be that the brightest crowns will adorn the heads of those who've won the greatest battles through prayer alone.

Totally Forgiven

"If we confess our sins, He is faithful and just to forgive us our sins, and to cleanse us from all unrighteousness."

— 1 John 1:9

Have you ever questioned your Christianity? I mean, downright wondered whether Christ could really forgive you of all your past sins? I used to wonder myself how the Lord could wash away my sins until I heard this little illustration.

A small boy had recently become the proud brother of a baby sister. One day as his mother sat holding the precious bundle, the boy came up and took a wide-eyed look and said, "Mommy, the baby's got a new tooth! Can I touch it?" "Certainly," replied his mother, "but first, go wash your hands."

The little boy's face fell: "Both of them?" His mother held back a grin and said, "Well, just wash one — but I want to watch you!"

Now, of course you can't just wash one hand, because when you wash one, the other will get cleansed, too. Well, the Lord doesn't do a halfway job of cleansing sin, either — He cleanses completely, according to our verse for today.

The Bible tells us even more: Once God has cleaned a heart, He fills it with something rather than just leaving it empty. Yes, He takes the sin from our lives and replaces it with His love. And, if we give ourselves to loving Him and others, there's no room for sin to creep back into our lives.

Don't let the devil try to trick you into thinking you're not completely forgiven. If you've given your heart to Jesus, God's Word says that He doesn't even remember your past sins any more. God will be just as ready to forgive you of anything you do wrong today, if you sincerely confess it to Him and resolve to turn from it. So trust God's Word right now and walk in His love, knowing that your sins are totally forgiven.

Tithing Trucks?

"Bring ye all the tithes into the storehouse, that there may be meat in mine house, and prove me now therewith, saith the Lord of hosts, if I will not open you the windows of heaven, and pour you out a blessing, that there shall not be room enough to receive it."

— *Malachi 3:10*

In Old Testament days, people who loved God would tithe ten percent of their substance unto the Lord. It would be the finest of their flocks and produce. And God honored that.

Mr. and Mrs. James O. Adcox of Baytown, Texas, have a modern-day version of that tradition of worship. From their fleet of trucks, they chose the finest, and gave it to the Lord.

During an illness, Mr. Adcox was ordered by his doctor to stay off his feet. And during that time, he and his wife, Neva, started watching the PTL Club and soon rededicated their lives to the Lord.

One morning, they heard me talking with Floyd Wilson, our man in charge of volunteers, about our needs at Heritage USA. The first thing on the list was a dump truck. Immediately, Neva thought of the truck they were going to sell to help pay a large tax bill. They knew, from a realistic financial viewpoint, that they couldn't afford it but they just called and gave that truck to PTL in spite of it!

We sent someone down to pick up the truck. And God sent down a blessing for the Adcox's. The tax people called and informed them that they owed less than they thought. The money to pay that soon began to come in by miraculous means. Praise God!

We've tried to make PTL a giving ministry. And we've never seen God fail to pour out His promised blessing. This Word for today is so sure that God says, "Go ahead! Try Me!" Lay aside something today to give to the work of God. Try Him, and I guarantee you'll find Him true!

Contentment

*". . . For I have learned, in whatsoever state I
am, therewith to be content."*
— *Philippians 4:11*

Contentment is something that a Christian can have in any circumstance, if he knows he's in the center of God's will.

I'll never forget the night of our first Heritage School graduation. The students and teachers were decked out in their caps and gowns. I even had a cap and gown on! We had planned to televise the ceremony in the Amphitheater at Heritage USA, and the seats were packed with relatives and other friends. We were going to follow the festivities with the PTL Singers and the Heritage of Sacred Song musical spectacular and a fireworks show. But God had other plans.

A big thunderstorm came up, and our remote truck took a direct hit of lightning in a power surge and was wiped out. We were able to record only a little bit with a small camera. We wiped off the seats and the platform, and out came the students and faculty and sat down there in the rain. To my amazement, hardly any spectators left. I prayed for each student individually and we didn't get around to the fireworks until 2 a.m.

I believe it was more than fitting that they received their diplomas in the rain. They had weathered, with the PTL ministry, the storms of the past years, and they'd learned that the skies aren't always going to be clear over their lives and ministries. They cried and laughed and praised the Lord, right there in the rain. That's why they will be able to go out and win the world for Christ. It takes that kind of spirit, that can come through and smile in the rain.

You can only learn real contentment in adversity. Unless the storms come, you won't know that God and you can weather them. The storms teach you what you're made of in God. Remember that, in whatever kind of weather today brings you.

Let The Tares Be

". . . The servants said unto him, Wilt thou then that we go and gather them up? But he said, Nay; lest while ye gather up the tares, ye root up also the wheat with them."
— *Matthew 13:28-29*

Tares were a weed that looked a lot like wheat while it was growing up. It took a sharp eye to tell the two apart until both were nearly grown.

In this passage, Jesus was telling a parable about the kingdom of God. He likened it to a field of wheat, in which tares were discovered by some laborers. They told their boss about it. The boss recognized that an enemy must have sown the tares. But he told his workers not to pull them up, because they might pull up some wheat along with them. He advised them to wait until they were full grown, then gather the tares and burn them up, and put the wheat into the barn.

You know, in every church or Christian ministry, you'll find "tares." Our enemy Satan puts them there, and at first glance, they look like Christians and seem to be growing like Christians. It often takes a while to spot them. And when you do, it's not hard to get angry at the bad influence they usually have had and want to rise up and "root them out."

But Jesus is saying here not to disrupt the whole fellowship trying to get rid of these "tares." He says you've got to take care — because you might uproot too much of the "wheat" in the process. You've got to let God take care of the "tares" and deal with them in His own good time.

Remember when you find a "tare" in your church or field of ministry; don't go around creating a furor and getting all self-righteous and turning other people's eyes away from Jesus! Just hold your peace and entrust the situation to God. Minister to that person if you can. You'll never know but that the Lord may want to turn that "tare" into "wheat!"

We're Winners!

"For the devil is come down unto you, having great wrath, because he knoweth that he hath but a short time."

— *Revelation 12:12*

God's people never have to be liars or cheats, because we're winners. It's the losers of this world that have to play fast and loose with the rules. I don't want to be on a losing team, do you? The Bible says that the devil's team is a loser. That's why he's stealing and killing, telling lies, deceiving whoever he can — he knows it'll soon be "curtains" for him and all his wicked angels.

He's like a gangster, who's holed up in some abandoned warehouse, surrounded by well-armed policemen. He's trapped in there, but he's still shooting at anyone who sticks his head up. "Come on in and get me!" he shouts, "But if you do, I'll take a lot of you with me before I go!" That's what the devil's like. But let me tell you: We don't have to bow and scrape to him! I've read the back of the Bible, and do you know what? *We win!* If you're serving the God who made you and me and the whole universe, you're going to rule and reign with Him some day. And you can tell the devil to back off and get out of your way!

Jesus didn't come to this world to hurt you or take from you. He came to give you life, and "that more abundantly" (John 10:10). I call that a winning strategy: Giving rather than taking, building up instead of tearing down, telling the truth rather than lying.

So if you belong to Jesus, don't listen to that lying voice that puts you down. Don't let Satan cheat you out of the joy and peace that belong to you. "Resist the devil, and he will flee from you" (James 4:7). He's got to, because he's a loser. Be what you are for God today — a winner.

God Loves Backsliders

"Turn, O backsliding children, saith the Lord; for I am married unto you . . . . "
— *Jeremiah 3:14*

God loves the backslider. I don't know how many people I've met who think they have committed a sin that might be unpardonable and are suffering horrible anguish because of it. It's not hard to backslide or fall into some area of sin as a Christian. We're weak in the flesh, and the devil is constantly waging war against us, trying to tear down our Christian testimony with his devices.

No, it's not hard to backslide. But it seems to be hard to regain again that privileged place with God. I said "seems," because it isn't really hard. The devil tries to make it seem hard by playing on the guilt. He makes backsliders feel like they're trash, like they're not fit to come into God's presence ever again, like they've sinned, too much, and can never be forgiven.

But, I want to tell you today that God loves backsliders. Look at the verse above — He says He's married to the backslider. And for God, that's a serious commitment. He's not fickle like we are, He doesn't just pitch out, like trash, His people who might have a black mark against them. Instead, He cries, "Turn, O backsliding children!" In Jeremiah 3:22 He says, "Return, ye backsliding children, and I will heal your backslidings!" And He wants us to answer, "Behold, we come unto Thee; for thou art the Lord our God" (Jeremiah 3:22b).

You may be saying right now, "Oh, Jim, I wish I could believe that — but you don't know what I've done." No, but God knows, and He says to your heart today, "Yes, you've backslidden, but I'm there with you. I'm married to you. I love you. I will not leave or forsake you. I'm your God. I died for you. Will you return to Me and let Me heal you today? Will you let Me cleanse you right now and make you whole! Come to Me, and I will receive you, this moment!"

Who We Really Are

"But ye are a chosen generation, a royal priesthood, an holy nation, a peculiar people that you should show forth the praises of Him who hath called you . . . . "

— *1 Peter 2:9*

It can be downright discouraging to be a Christian when people of the world put you down for what you believe. "Christians? Oh, they're weak, gullible people who need a 'crutch' to get through life," some say. Or: "Nice people, but they're out of touch with the times." Others accuse Christians of being narrow minded or fanatical. Afraid of such putdowns, many believers are silent about their love of Jesus Christ.

I believe we shouldn't feel ashamed. We shouldn't feel like second class citizens. In fact, it's time we found out who we really are! This scripture gives us a pretty good idea. Read it again. That hardly sounds like a bunch of castoffs to me. Don't be fooled by that word "peculiar." It doesn't mean weird or odd. It means "a called out or separate people."

So who are we? We're a generation chosen and called out by God Himself — and it's time we started acting like it! I'm convinced that the world will never totally accept us, but if we keep winning souls to Jesus, at least we'll be the majority! As for those who have nothing better to do than belittle Christians, realize that they're just spokesmen for the devil, who's mad about the short time he has left.

Don't let the devil harass you through these people. Resist his voice. Remember, the voice that tells you you're no good and can't be an effective witness for Jesus comes from Satan. The voice that lifts you up is God's. Once you get those voices straightened out, you'll be a successful Christian.

Today, be proud of your belief in Jesus. You don't ever need to feel inferior — you've been "called out" to spread the Gospel, an honor even the greatest angels don't have!

Be A Good Witness

"And this Gospel of the kingdom shall be preached in all the world for a witness unto all nations . . . "

— *Matthew 24:14*

The greatest witness for Christ that the world can see is for Christians to unite and love one another. This is what we are trying to do daily at PTL.

Through our PTL Satellite Network, the Gospel is broadcast twenty-four hours a day. Some nations are receiving the Good News of Christ for the very first time. By sharing our common love of Jesus we are serving as good Christian witnesses.

It is those nations that haven't heard what Christ can do for their lives that I am so concerned about. Few people understand the need to spread the Gospel into foreign lands. On my visits to India and other poverty stricken areas, I have seen firsthand the inhuman conditions in which these people must live on a day-to-day basis. My heart aches for these countries and I know the people need to have Christ brought into their lives.

Reaching out into foreign lands is a must! PTL's missions outreach program is helping feed, clothe, and educate many of the children in those underprivileged nations, but PTL can't do it alone.

National hosts for foreign productions of the PTL Club have helped many lonely souls in those nations come to Christ. By showing our common love for Christ and sharing the Gospel, many have seen what a uniting force the love of Jesus can be.

Let's begin praying for all the souls throughout the world that don't know Jesus as their Savior. We, as Christians, must unite and go out into the world and proclaim what Christ has done in our lives so others can be brought closer. By doing this, we will be witnessing unto all nations!

Noah's Single-Mindedness

" ... Which sometime were disobedient, when once the long-suffering of God waited in the days of Noah, while the ark was a preparing, wherein few, that is, eight souls were saved by water."

— *1 Peter 3:20*

God's way of doing things is so different from man's that often the world will make fun of you for obeying the voice of the Lord. To those who don't know the Lord, Christians don't make much sense, and they're more than likely to dismiss us as "fanatics."

I wouldn't be a bit surprised if Noah was known as a "religious nut" in his days. I'm sure his neighbors must have made fun of him when he explained that the Lord had told him to build a big boat. Some may even have been a little irritated when he relayed God's message that the earth would be destroyed by water unless the people repented.

It must have been hard for Noah to work on year after year, listening to his friends and relatives mocking him. It must have been frustrating to try and warn people who were unwilling to listen about what would happen unless they turned to God and gave up their wicked ways. But Noah knew he had heard from God, and in spite of his neighbor's scorn, he continued to work faithfully on the huge project the Lord had given him to accomplish.

Noah had the kind of single-mindedness of purpose we've got to have in our lives today. PTL would never have become the great soul-winning ministry it is today unless I had held on determinedly to what God told me, in spite of those who branded me a fanatic and made fun of me. So it is in your walk with the Lord — hang on for dear life to what He's shown you, even during the hard times when people may laugh at you. The Lord will reward your faithfulness with the fulfillment of your vision!

Uphold Your Leaders

"Remember them which have the rule over you, who have spoken unto you the word of God: whose faith follow, considering the end of their conversation."

— Hebrews 13:7

No one is immune from problems in this world — especially not the shepherds of God's flock. They're the ones who so often have to "stick their neck out" for God.

Many times I've had to do that. But I've found out that every time I stick my neck out, it's not really my neck I'm sticking out — it's God's neck I'm sticking out! And God's neck doesn't break, beloved!

A black preacher was on the radio one morning, preaching his heart out. He said, "Sure, preachers are going to have problems. The reason preachers have problems is so they can go through those experiences and have the fiery darts of the enemy come at them. That way they can flex their faith in God and people in their congregations can see that they have the victory. As your pastor goes through a hard time, all you want to do is vote him out! But, instead of throwing him out, you need to get down on your knees and pray for that man. Seek the face of God and get revival back in your church. If we had more praying and less criticism in the pews, we'd have more revival in America!"

I say, "Amen, brother!" to that. God never changes anything through bad feelings. It's prayer that changes things. Your pastor and other ministers of the Gospel need your prayers, not your criticism. Will you resolve today to put the same energy you may have used criticizing your spiritual leaders — into praying for them? You'll see revival in your fellowship if you do!

The Gambler

"My sons, be not now negligent: for the Lord hath chosen you to stand before Him, to serve Him, and that ye should minister unto Him . . . ."

— *2 Chronicles 29:11*

I'm sure we have all met the kind of person I want to tell you about today. I call him "the gambler." But, he isn't a gambler in the sense that he goes to nightclubs and places bets. To me, his gambling is far more serious. He gambles with his salvation and that of his family.

This man may go to church every now and then or he may tell his family that it doesn't matter if you don't attend all those Bible studies, prayer meetings, and worship services. He believes he already knows all he needs to know about God and doesn't see any sense in wasting his time attending all these church activities. He is betting, with his soul and the souls of his wife and children, that they will still be saved even though they don't seek after Jesus as their Lord and Savior.

He's laying odds that he can ignore Jesus' teachings on sowing and reaping. He thinks his luck will hold out while he fails to give as God prospers him — and that God will continue to bless him financially. He looks at all the lost souls around him with a "poker face" and tries to "bluff" his way into heaven.

This "gambler" thinks he has really found the way to "beat the house." But, he doesn't realize that he is betting against God. He is ready to "lay his cards on the table" and the devil will "call his bluff."

If you have ever known people who liked to "play the odds" like this, please let them know what the score is. Let them know they must stop playing this game and lay everything they have on the altar of God. His hand is always open to you and ready to give. His "odds" are always in your favor.

The Body Will Take Care Of Itself

"I have been young, and now am old; yet have I not seen the righteous forsaken, nor his seed begging bread."

— *Psalm 37:25*

Christian, God's promised to take care of His people, even in times of famine and shortages. That's something to remember when the headlines scream out "Double Digit Inflation!" and "Food Prices Skyrocket!" Recession need not be a cause for crippling fear in the Body of Christ.

It's important right now to be a part of the family of God. My mother and father went through more than a recession. They went through the Great Depression, and you may have, too.

But do you know something? When people were standing in breadlines, starving and hungry, do you know not a member of that little group of people on the outskirts of town called the "Holy Rollers," a "bunch of fanatics" — not one of them starved, not one of them went hungry, not one of them jumped out a window! Why not? Because they had a strength outside themselves. Their hope wasn't in money. Their hope wasn't in their homes. Their hope wasn't in the things around them. They had their hope in Jesus Christ, and God sustained them in the midst of that depression!

How did it happen? It was like the New Testament Church. If one family had a chicken, they shared chicken dinner. One of them had a bean patch, they shared the beans. They shared together. I asked God what would be the solution to coming world crises, and He answered me, clear as a bell, "My Church, My Body, will take care of itself."

A lot of people today don't think much of the family of God. But I'll tell you, one day you'll be glad you got deeper into the people of God. Make up your mind today to take care of the business of God and His people. You do that, and He'll take care of you!

Stand Firm

". . . So the sun stood still in the midst of heaven, and hasted not to go down about a whole day. And there was no day like that before it or after it, that the Lord hearkened unto the voice of a man: for the lord fought for Israel."
— Joshua 10:13-14

We don't have to live discouraged, defeated lives — Christians were meant to live an exciting life full of victory, because in every battle we go through, God is right in there with us! He is able to arrange for whatever it will take to snatch His children from defeat at the hands of the enemy!

We serve a God who is even able to stop the sun in its orbit, and keep it from going down for a whole day, because of the prayer of a single man. When we ask God for help, we can rest assured we're going to get it! All we have to do is to stand firmly on God's word, and wait for Him to act on our faith.

I remember when we were struggling to get the Heritage Hall Auditorium built in time for the Labor Day celebration and I would hold on to God's promises, but sometimes discouragement would creep in.

One evening God spoke to me, reminding me of His perfect track record so far. This encouraged me and so I said, "OK, God, I trust You — I'll stick my neck out and hang on to your promises." I don't think God was too impressed, because then He reminded me that it wasn't my neck I was sticking out, it really was His! Anytime I stand on His Word, it's His reputation that's at stake, not mine!

Just as the Lord went as far as to stop the sun in order to help the Israelites win their battle, He will do whatever is necessary to help you win your battle. Today, stand firm on God's promises, remembering it's His reputation at stake, and God will honor your faith by fighting for you!

United By Faith

"And if one prevail against him, two shall withstand him; and a threefold cord is not quickly broken."

— *Ecclesiastes 4:12*

God has set forth a challenge to every Christian in the world — to join forces and spread His Word. PTL has taken this challenge and is doing something about it.

By joining forces with ministries in the United States and around the world, PTL is helping to reach the lost and lonely. All gifts of money and manpower to mission outreaches are causing God's kingdom to spring up everywhere. God is truly training His army for battle.

We have learned that most ministries are working for the same goal and our battle is not with each other, but with the devil. In Christ, we already have that battle won.

Working together, in mutual love and cooperation, for God's kingdom is such a good feeling. By uniting our efforts with other ministries, we are bringing millions of Christians together for the very first time.

This uniting effort is very important. The Church of today is faced with an identity crisis. Even though more people than ever are being born again, into a personal relationship with Jesus Christ, there is turmoil within the Church. God wants His church to be one family and we are coming closer to that than ever.

When Christ comes again, all judgment will start in the Church. I want all fellow brethren in Christ to join together under the direction and unifying love of the Holy Spirit. If we are all as one, then the Church can show the world the love of God in Christ. Jesus is speaking to his church every day. Let us seek God's truth in his Word and in love. We know we have all passed from darkness into light because we love one another and Christ loves us all.

Payday Wages Of Satan

"For the wages of sin is death; but the gift of God is eternal life through Jesus Christ our Lord."

— Romans 6:23

You know, the devil will never offer you something for nothing. He makes you work for everything he gives you — and the "wages" he pays only add up to one thing: death.

When people look around the world today and see the desperate shape it is in, they tend to wonder why it is like that if God is a good God. They ask, "How can God be good if He allows sickness and murder, war and children starving?" When Adam and Eve did their first chore for the devil in the Garden of Eden, Satan started paying "wages" for work done for him. The very day Adam sinned, God promised that he and Eve would face death, hard labor, and pain. But God wasn't going to put all this on them — the devil was. This was their pay for working for him.

Instead of blaming God for the situation in the world today, we need to thank Him for being just and kind. But, most of all, thank Him that, unlike the devil who makes us earn death, He gives us life as a free gift because of Jesus Christ.

I don't care how much effort we exerted, we couldn't earn eternal life as humans. But, Jesus paid the price for our chores at Calvary and through His perfect life. Salvation comes to us free of charge, but it cost God dearly — the life of the precious Son He loved.

Don't blame God for the "wages" Satan has dumped on the world. Thank Him instead for His great mercy and love. He gives the precious gift of salvation freely to whomever will call upon Him in faith. There's more goodness there than an eternity of work could ever earn.

The Value Of A Good Wife

"Who can find a virtuous woman? For her price is far above rubies."

— *Proverbs 31:10*

How well I know this scripture to be true! My Tammy Faye is the greatest asset to me and to my ministry at PTL. Not one day goes by that I don't thank the Lord for her.

I met her at Bible college, and fell head over heels in love. When I asked her to marry me, I had nothing at all to offer her. I was a busboy at a restaurant, and didn't even have the money to buy her a ring. She had to lend me the down payment!

But, she always believed in me. In spite of the fact that we had to quit school to get married, she always believed God was going to use me — even when I didn't believe it myself.

All through our marriage, she has always been the source of constant encouragement that I need so badly. When it looked like we were going to have to sell Heritage USA, she is the one that always ministered to me that, if it were God's will, nothing could stop Heritage USA from being a reality.

In all honesty, she put her own feelings behind to say that to me. She knew once we started a building project, she'd see less of me and I'd be preoccupied with the project.

Why did she encourage me then? Because she loved me. And she was willing to prefer my needs over her own feelings. That's real love.

Tammy Faye is as much a part of PTL as I am. Without her strength, her love, and her help, I doubt PTL would be what it is today.

You husbands, if you're like me, telling your wife how you feel isn't always the easiest thing to do. Somehow, we think they know how we feel. But they need to hear it . . . often!

Tell her how you feel. And thank the Lord with me this day for a "virtuous woman."

Break Down Those Doors!

". . . And on this rock I will build my church, and the gates of Hell shall not prevail against it."

— *Matthew 16:18*

I think it's time born-again Christians stopped thinking of themselves defensively and started thinking more offensively in dealing with the devil. Too often, we see ourselves as his helpless victims, kind of like a walled-up city under siege. The devil and his demons are pounding at the door with a battering ram, and it's all we can do to hold the fort. But the Bible says that we're the ones who ought to be on the offensive. It's the devil who's on the run, and we should be the ones beating down his door!

Take a look at that verse above. It says that the gates of hell will not prevail against God's church! Hallelujah! When are we going to get this message straight in our minds? The devil may try to bar the door, but if we'll just head toward it in the power and authority of God, it will have to give way! Why? Because the devil is a defeated foe — my Bible says it, and I believe it! If I didn't, there wouldn't be a PTL.

You may say, "Well then, why is the devil still giving me so much trouble? The Bible says sin can't stand in the presence of God." I'll tell you, sin is not standing in the presence of God, it's collapsing before Him! Have you ever seen a slow-motion film of a building falling after being hit by a wrecker's ball? The greatest turmoil and noise comes at the moment of total collapse! And that's the state of the devil's kingdom right now!

I assure you today that the devil's strongholds in your life will not stand against you, if you will plant your feet firmly on the foundation of Jesus Christ and move forward! If you have been held back in your walk with God lately, I urge you to take a "giant step" — and you'll see the devil give way!

Love Is Action

"If a man say, I love God, and hateth his brother, he is a liar; for he that loveth not his brother whom he hath seen, how can he love God whom he hath not seen?"

— *1 John 4:20*

If you want to love God, love your fellow man. Love that Catholic, that Protestant, that pastor in another denomination or that neighbor. Love one another and demonstrate the love of God. Serving God is more than lip service. Love's actions speak louder than words in any relationship.

I think of Mark Buntain, the great missionary to India, and all the thousands of little children he has helped to feed. He loves to help people in any way he can.

Author Doug Wead talks about one of Buntain's workers who contracted leprosy. The missionary kept the man from committing suicide, and personally took him to the leper's colony hundreds of miles away. Buntain hugged him at the gate and promised him Jesus would never fail him. The man wasn't a Christian at the time.

This busy man of God wrote the leper every day, constantly expressing his unconditional love, and telling him about Jesus. One day, the leper finally accepted the Lord. One month later the Lord healed him of his leprosy, and he returned joyously to the man who'd kept promising him that Jesus would never fail — a promise he firmly believed now!

God honors you when you reach out to touch others. Jesus said, "Verily I say unto you, Inasmuch as ye have done it unto one of the least of My brethren, ye have done it unto Me" (Matthew 25:40. Living the Christian life is a lot more than just you and the Lord, incorporated. It's you and everyone you meet whether your teacher, the woman at the grocery counter, the policeman, or your co-worker at the office. It's even your landlord and the tax collector!

If you want to prove your love for God today in the way that would please Him most — treat everybody you meet just as well as you would treat Jesus!

The Wickedness of the Heart

"The heart is deceitful above all things, and desperately wicked: who can know it?"
— *Jeremiah 17:9*

Satan loves to flatter people by saying that man is basically good; he just needs a little encouragement and steering in the right direction. Give man half a chance, and he'll do right. Some of the devil's spokesmen go so far as saying that what makes men bad is law enforcement and morality! If we could only do away with those, they say, crime would cease.

I'll tell you, God knows better than that, and His Word doesn't pull any punches. He says man's heart is desperately wicked — and the evidence is on His side!

Several years ago, the police force of Montreal, Canada, went on strike. According to eyewitnesses, that was a fearful day. Normally law-abiding citizens went absolutely wild. They smashed over a thousand windows in the business district, and then went on a spree of theft and violence, looting stores, dashing out with television sets, whole racks of clothes, and anything else they could get their hands on.

Investigations after the forces of law and order took control again revealed that most of these people were not criminal types or needy people. They were folks that others described as, "nice, neighborly people." Some of them were shocked themselves at their own behavior. But when there was no reason for "respectability," the masks came off, and their real colors showed.

The Bible tells us that the presence of God's people and the Holy Spirit in the world are what are restraining this sort of behavior from being an everyday occurrence. But a day will come when God is going to take His Holy Spirit and His people out of the world. Work and pray that God will save many souls while there's still time!

Don't Grumble!

"Do all things without murmurings and disputings:"
— *Philippians 2:14*

That's a tough one! *All things,* Lord? That's what the Word says. That doesn't leave out much, does it?

God doesn't like grumbling. The children of Israel murmured against Him in the wilderness, and He allowed a disease to torment them that killed thousands. So this is a commandment that we'd better take seriously!

What makes it so difficult is that complaining seems to come so naturally with just living in an imperfect world. Things never go quite the way you want or expect them to, and you just want to say something about it.

Your roast gets overdone because the preacher's Sunday sermon is too long. How do you stay "spiritual" about that? You buy a jungle gym for your children, and the first thing you know, there's a scream, and little Johnny has fallen down and broken a leg. Your boss takes you off a vital assignment at work and puts you on a job that you can't stand. How do you do it without disputing or grumbling? It seems like almost too much to ask.

Well, it *is* too much to ask, in a way. Everything about godly living is impossible without God in our hearts to give us the power to do it. But God wouldn't have given us this commandment if He didn't want us to keep it. Tammy sings a little song that gives a clue — it goes like this: "If life hands you a lemon, then start making lemonade! Praise God for the situation, and thank Him for the day He made!" That's a good start.

If you find yourself in a frustrating situation, try this: First, just hold your tongue a minute. Don't let that grumble get out of your mouth. Then just say silently to God, "Lord, you know I'll complain like crazy if you don't help me. Right now, just take control of my tongue and quiet my Spirit. You knew this situation was going to happen. I praise you that you are in it with me. Turn it into good for your glory, Lord. Amen." You'll be amazed at how the Lord works it all out!

Not One "I"

"After this manner therefore pray ye: Our Father which art in heaven, Hallowed be thy name."

— *Matthew 6:9*

It's remarkable that the words "I," "me," and "my" never once occur in the Lord's Prayer! In a way, Jesus meant this to be our prayer more than His. The disciples asked Jesus how they should pray, and His answer was, pray like this. Perhaps there's some importance to those "I" and "we" words not being there!

How many times have you prayed this prayer and translated it "*my* Father" in your mind? Instead of "give *us* this day our daily bread," thought only "give *me* this day *my* daily bread?" Made a mental "switch" from "forgive *us* our debts" to "forgive *me my* debts?" How many times do we remember to ask God to give others the same blessing we're asking for?

Here is a little poem by Charles Thompson that might help you to include the needs of others in your prayer:

You cannot pray the Lord's Prayer,
And even once say, "I."
You cannot pray the Lord's Prayer,
And even once say, "My."
Nor can you say the Lord's Prayer,
And not pray for another;
For when you ask for daily bread,
You must include your brother.
For others are included
In each and every plea:
From the beginning to the end of it,
It does not once say, "Me."

Oh, Jesus, help each of us to pray for good to come to all people, not just ourselves and those we love. Help us to have the needs of others close to our hearts. For your sake, Amen.

Battling

" ... who shall prepare himself to the battle?"

— *1 Corinthians 14:8*

Monuments to our American heritage have been constructed on battlefields across the land. They remind us of battles that marked key victories or turning points in the wars of our nation's history.

When you read the Bible, you realize that Christians go through battles. Oh, boy! Do we go through battles! The children of Israel faced constant conflicts along the journey to the Promised Land. Many times they were outnumbered and still defeated their enemies. Neighboring nations, after scoffing, began to fear them and their God.

Someone once said that the fiercest battles rage within a man's soul. Each of us face struggles within when deciding right from wrong. Temptation, fear, and depression war against the soul, and conquering self-will seems an endless fight.

The battle of Gettysburg, the turning point of the Civil War, signified the intense division of our country. Soon after the war, our nation was reunited. The tragic loss of lives was costly, but the renewed unity caused our country to grow.

Some of the most tragic times in my life have been turning points. A near-fatal accident involving a child and a car I was driving as a teenager brought about my total dedication to God's service. As a result, there's a worldwide outreach for Christ through the PTL Television Network.

God will help you fight your battles as you surrender your life to Him. Singer Andrae Crouch has written, "If I'd never had a problem, I'd never know that God could solve them." Your victories in the battles of self-will and temptation will shine out in landmarks of peace, love, and joy in your walk with God. People will be able to read your growth in the life you live. You'll be glad to say with the apostle, Paul, "I have fought the good fight, I have kept the faith" (2 Timothy 4:7).

Learning To Give

"Give, and it shall be given unto you; good measure, pressed down, and shaken together, and running over, shall men give into your bosom. For with the same measure that ye mete withal it shall be measured to you again."
— *Luke 6:38*

TAMMY: When I was little I always valued everything that I had because I came from a family of eight children. With eight children around, you don't have much of anything. I used to be a very selfish person because of this and I never knew the joy of giving.

Early in our ministry, Jim began preaching on the joy of giving and what God would do if we gave to Him. Right after that, God spoke to us, "You are preaching that message and now I want you to live it."

We never thought God would ask us to live the giving part of our preaching. But, we began to give to God and God gave back to us. We really learned a lesson when we began to give to God.

The first twenty-five dollars God asked us to give will always be in my mind. We were in church and there was a special need. God had spoken to Jim to put in twenty-five dollars and I gasped when he told me what God had spoken to him. That was all the money we had! It was our grocery money, but I felt good inside because we were giving it to Jesus. Before the service was over someone had asked us out to eat and he gave us twenty dollars after dinner. And, that night in church we were given two more twenty dollar bills. The Lord had returned sixty dollars to us for our twenty-five!

Now, I give to God because I love to give so much. We serve a God who is faithful and who is abundantly able to give above what we could even ask or think of.

Mercy Is For The Needy

*"And the publican, standing afar off, would
not lift up so much as his eyes unto heaven, but
smote upon his breast, saying God be merciful
to me a sinner."*

— *Luke 18:13*

A person who thinks he's "got it all together" will probably
never make it to heaven, because he will never ask God for mercy —
he doesn't think he needs it!

In this story of the Pharisee and the publican, what a mistake
the proud Pharisee made! He tried to tell God how wonderful he
was and how much he had done for God. He had a whole list made
out to recite to God. He didn't know that, as one man put it, "the only requirement for membership in the true Church of Jesus Christ is
that the applicant be unworthy." This Pharisee had no compassion
for the need of the heavy-hearted man beside him.

The publican, on the other hand, knew he had done wrong. He
knew he had cheated people. He knew he had no good thing in his
life with which to "bribe" God. He was a sinner with nothing to
recommend him. He could only cry to God in his anguish, "God, be
merciful to me, a sinner!"

God isn't interested in hearing about all the things you've done
for Him or how good you are — His heart belongs to those who
recognize they are nothing apart from Jesus and tell Him so.

Have you seen today how much you really need God? I don't
care if you've been saved sixty years or sixty minutes, you still need
Him. You know, God doesn't "need" anything you can do for Him.
But He does want an humble heart, empty of pride, that He can fill
with His mercy for others, too. Humble yourself right now, and let
God know how much you need Him and love Him.

Use Tongue For Good

"And that every tongue should confess that Jesus Christ is Lord, to the glory of God the Father."

— *Philippians 3:11*

You read in the Word of God the evil the tongue can do. I guess all of us at one time or another have trouble keeping that "little member" of the body (as James refers to it) in line.

However, there is one thing that little member is supposed to do and that is confess Jesus as Lord. The best way to win an unbeliever to Christ is by talking to them, sharing the good things of the Lord.

If you want to feel the presence of the Lord, start using your tongue to praise the Lord. He inhabits the praises of his people. That honors Him.

When we honor Jesus Christ, we honor the Father. God created us to fellowship with Him, to talk to Him, and to praise Him. And it is only when we are doing what God created us to do that we are totally happy and complete.

There is great power in the tongue. In Genesis 1 we read that God *spoke* the world into existence. The Bible says that through confession we are saved.

If we, as children of God, could ever come to the place in our lives where we spent more time talking about God and to God than we spend talking on the phone about our neighbors and making fun of other people, how much more pleased God would be with us!

Evaluate what you say today. It will take some effort, but concentrate on spending more time confessing Jesus and praising God. You'll be happier for it.

Don't Limit God

"He that is faithful in that which is least is faithful also in much."

— *Luke 16:10*

God's blessings in your life are governed by your faithfulness to Him.

The world is still shocked by that terrible catastrophe in Guyana with the People's Temple and Jim Jones. About two years ago, hundreds of people committed suicide because they were misled by someone who claimed to be a prophet of God.

I believe that terrible event took place because God gave a man a gift and he took it and misused it to his own destruction. In the process, he dragged hundreds of others into the same terrible fate.

Many times I have heard fellow staff members at PTL complain that they don't have the new house they want or the new car they want. Some are wanting a promotion or a different job and they just don't understand why God hasn't given it to them.

So, I ask them, "Are you keeping the house God gave you clean and in good order? Are you keeping that old car in the best repair you possible can? Are you doing the best job you possibly can in the job God has you in now?"

Often they walk away from me shaking their heads. It's a hard lesson to learn, but if we, as Christians and as children of God, could ever learn that our own blessings are governed by how we handle the blessings He has already given us, we can then see God's floodgates of blessings open wide in our lives.

Whatever your need is today, try not to concentrate on it, but on the blessings God has already given you. Make do with what you have and do the very best you can, and do it joyfully as unto God.

You'll see that this principle is true. God wants you to have your heart's desire. Just release it to Him today.

Baptized In The Spirit

"For he that speaketh in an unknown tongue speaketh not unto men, but unto God: for no man understandeth him; howbeit in the Spirit he speaketh mysteries."

— 1 Corinthians 14:2

Some children of God who are seeking the Baptism of the Holy Spirit believe you have to follow a formula, like saying the "right" words; praying in a properly "spiritual" place, such as at an altar; or asking in the right position, in order to receive it. There are plenty of "helpful" church people around, too, who egg on this belief.

When I was a teenager seeking the Baptism, some people would tell me to kneel down, others advised me to stand up; some said hold back, others told me to turn loose; some said to sing, others to praise God, and raise my hands at the same time. I tried all of their suggested "tried and true" methods. I tell you though, God will never let Himself be confined to formulas!

It wasn't until I finally gave up my struggling that God baptized me in His Spirit in a basement that had once been a wine cellar. God doesn't want you to go through a certain ritual in a sacred place — He just wants you to ask Him and let Him do it. We don't serve a predictable God who always does the same thing in the same way.

When my Affiliate Director, Walter Richardson, asked for the Baptism in the Spirit, God answered his prayer somewhere between North Carolina and Illinois — 35,000 feet above the ground!

Walter was flying to Chicago when the Lord baptized him, and he kept running to the restroom so he could try his new language! I wonder what the flight attendants thought, especially the ones who could hear him!

If you've asked God for the Baptism in the Holy Spirit before, and nothing has happened, don't keep struggling — the Lord has the perfect place and time for you picked out!

Give It All To God

"I beseech you therefore, brethren ... that you present your bodies a living sacrifice...."
— *Romans 12:1*

Suppose a surgeon decides not to operate on anyone for several years. No matter how skilled a surgeon he may be, he is of no use to his profession if he refuses to use his abilities.

Sometimes God doesn't use people with great ability because they don't give Him a chance. For instance, a talented musician who'd rather be in the spotlight than sing sacred music. God is looking, in every life, for availability and useability. He'll use people willing and able to serve Him.

How are you using your abilities to serve God? If you're using your talents and abilities to help and bless others, you are serving God. At PTL, cameramen use their ability to shoot programs that share the Gospel. In the local church, people who can teach or sing minister to others. In daily life, all Christians can serve God by being open to His leading to share the Good News with people they meet. Every believer can do something for the kingdom of God.

We've all met people with low opinions of themselves and their abilities. They think they're useless. Many times they excuse themselves from serving God, saying they're not good enough. But who could be "good enough" for a perfect God? He doesn't ask that, just willingness to do whatever He asks of us, be that thing great or small, as well as we can.

Just as you are, you're useful to God. He wants you to present yourself. Yes, you! Be available now. God can do something wonderful with whatever you can do — right now! Don't hold back on Him. I guarantee that He will do something in your life that will amaze you — if you'll hand it over to Him.

The Price Was Paid

"For He hath made him to be sin for us, who knew no sin; that we might be made the righteousness of God in Him."
— *2 Corinthians 5:21*

Years ago, when I worked at CBN, I was doing a radio shift, a children's show, and hosting the 700 Club. Needless to say, I was working night and day to keep all of those programs going. One day, unbeknown to me, the radio station manager had asked several announcers to take a Saturday night shift.

Finally, he came to me and I told him, "I'm sorry, but I've promised to take Tammy out. We haven't been out together in months."

"Well," said the station manager, "you still have to do it."

I shook my head and told him I couldn't do it and left it at that. That Saturday night, as Tammy and I drove home from dinner, I clicked on the radio and our station was silent.

Right or wrong, I got blamed for the entire situation. The next day, Pat Robertson called me into his office. Explaining that I had broken the chain of command and discipline was in order. He told me I'd have to pay a one hundred dollar fine or resign.

Tearfully, Tammy and I left the station. We didn't say so, but we didn't have the money. A few days later, Pat called me back to his office. We both knew God still had work for me to do at CBN. Pat reached in his pocket and pulled out two fifty dollar bills. He paid my fine and I went back to work.

God has told us in His Word that "All have sinned and come short of the Glory of the Lord" and "The wages of sin is death."

But our fine has been paid by the blood of Jesus Christ on Calvary. Praise God, He has paid the price for us!

Always Awake

"... He that keepeth thee will not slumber.
Behold, He that keepeth Israel shall neither
slumber nor sleep."

— *Psalm 121:3-4*

Have you ever heard that expression, "Satan never sleeps?" He seems always to be on his job, tempting, lying, stealing, and destroying. And it can make you feel so helpless, because there's no way you can be alert enough at all times to keep up with his mischief. All too often, he can catch you napping.

There's somebody else who never sleeps, either, and that's our God. He's got a lot more on the ball than Old Slewfoot!

Who was more awake when Joseph's brothers sold him into slavery? God was!

Who was caught napping when Moses and the children of Israel were backed up against the Red Sea? Not God!

Who knew the time of day when little David went out to meet the giant with a sling and five smooth stones? God did!

Who had His eyes wide open when the prophets of Baal accepted Elijah's challenge to a duel of fire on the mountain? Not Baal!

Who had a head start on the day Mary and Joseph set out for Egypt with the baby Jesus, escaping the murderous clutches of Herod? Our God did!

Always remember that God's been "awake" a lot longer than the enemy of your soul. God was around when Satan was brought into being, and He'll be awake long after Satan's tossed forever into the lake of fire. God's been awake forever, and He'll be awake forever, too. Do you think He can take care of you today? You can let your soul rest easy, because your God will be awake today — and always on the job!

How To Handle Praise

"Let another man praise thee, and not thine own mouth; a stranger, and not thine own lips."
— *Proverbs 27:2*

Most people have a problem accepting praise. Haven't you seen someone squirming all over the sofa when someone else is telling them how well they have done something? You have probably been in the same situation yourself. The conversation may have been something like this:

"Miss Jones, you sang so beautifully tonight, and I was so blessed!"

"Oh, it was nothing. The Holy Spirit did it all."

Then, they blush and look ashamed that they have been praised and try to disappear into the woodwork.

I just don't think we should handle praise like that. You need to consider these reasons why we should accept praise from others. First, what "Miss Jones" (or whoever) did wasn't as simple as she made it sound or "nothing" as she said. It blessed someone. It moved someone's heart so much that they wanted to thank the person God used. Instead of saying it was "nothing," say thank you to whoever praises you because God has chosen to use people to win others to Christ.

Second, the Holy Spirit didn't "do it all." I'll tell you one thing, if someone hadn't been standing up there the Holy Spirit wouldn't have sung that song. God doesn't want to take all the joy out of serving Him. Not only has He given us the responsibility of serving Him, but also of having the joy that comes from being a part of what He is doing. We should share in the joy He gives us just as He enjoys doing His work through us.

I don't mean you should go all over praising yourself for every good deed you do — that would be boasting. God isn't honored by boasting, but he is honored by praise. *Do* let others praise you — don't deny them the joy of saying something nice about you. You don't have to hide from praise. Enjoy it and thank God for it, and in return, give it back to Him.

Your Sins Are Forgiven

"Verily, verily, I say unto you, He that heareth my word, and believeth on him that sent me, hath everlasting life, and shall not come into condemnation; but is passed from death unto life."

— *John 5:24*

Christians should have no fear of death. Jesus has already died on the cross to save us from being judged for our sins. Every Christian will pass from death into eternal life.

All Satan can do is try and bring fear into our lives about death and illness, but Christ has freed us from our worries. He has taken our bondage to death away, so that we can walk in eternal life in the present, and not worry about Satan's threats.

Christ paid the penalty for our sins, and because of his death, Christians are permanently separated from their sins. Our sins have been "blotted out" and God has promised He won't remember any of them.

By walking in His path, Christians are attempting to lead the life God planned. No human is without error, but should you slip off the righteous path and have fear that you will be judged, remember what the Lord said. If you hear His word and believe in Him, you will have life everlasting.

Jesus suffered for our sins at Calvary so we wouldn't have to come into judgment as sinners. All who hear the voice of Jesus need not worry, for they will have eternal life.

By walking in the path of Jesus, you have already stated your choice. You want to glorify God and serve Him for the rest of your life!

Whom Shall I Be Afraid?

"The Lord is my light and my salvation; whom shall I fear? The Lord is the strength of my life; of whom shall I be afraid?"
— *Psalm 27:1*

TAMMY: Whenever Satan wants to break our trust in God, he will use any opportunity he possibly can to create fear within us.

I always had very happy memories and experiences from school. I just loved going to school. To me, it was one of the greatest excitements in my life to start the process of learning, and I could hardly wait to get dressed and be on my way to school. But, one day when I was in the second grade, this all changed. My teacher accused me of plugging the drains with paper towels and I didn't do it! I tried to tell her that someone else must have done it, but I still took the blame.

From that moment on, I was the target for anything that happened wrong in the classroom. Every jar of paint that was broken, anything that was missing, or if a water cooler clogged or a light bulb blew — I knew I would be blamed. I was constantly afraid and I couldn't prove that I hadn't done it. For me, that has always been my greatest fear — that I am going to be accused of doing something that I can't prove I didn't do.

Have you ever thought how some children always seem to pick up the torment and fear in every situation while others don't let things bother them?

I believe much of the fear children have is developed by the attitude the family develops. If the family portrays a constant confident attitude and pays little attention to the crises as they occur, I think the children will learn to respond in the same way.

I wrote my book, *Run To the Roar,* because I felt it would relate to many people, and my hopes have been confirmed many times over.

Remember, God is always with you.

Suffering For Jesus

"For unto you it is given in behalf of Christ, not only to believe on Him, but also to suffer for His sake."

— *Philippians 1:29*

Once you enter the kingdom of God, you become part of a battle. Some people are shocked when they learn this. Rather than "babes in Christ," we ought to call new believers "recruits." Satan never bothered them much before they knew Jesus. Now, he's flailing away at them overtime, and they're almost too amazed to fight. Let me tell you: You'll never know the peace of God until you pick up the sword and start swinging. And there can't be a victory without a battle.

Oral Roberts told me not long ago, "Jim, I was asking God 'why?' Why do I have to bear the attack of the press? Why do I have to take all of this? Why do I have to fight for everything I'm doing? Why all this pain and all these scars? God spoke to me and said, 'Do you want to stand before Me one day and present a body that has been scarred for Me — or do you want to stand before Me with a body that hasn't gone through anything for Me?' There was no question. I said, 'God, I will stand before you with the scars.' "

You may feel, right now, that you've been scarred working for God. You may have known the harsh blows of the enemy. You may feel like you've been hurt. But in any battle, there will be scars.

But praise God, when we see Jesus, it will be worth it all. Perhaps, as well as the wounds in His hands and feet, He carries with Him forever the scars of the stripes He bore. When our scars are revealed before Him, He'll say, "You too? Well done — I know so well what you've been through. The gift of your suffering is most precious of all to Me." Thank you, Jesus, for the right to fight for you — and for my scars.

Wash Your Mustache!

"Thou hast put gladness in my heart...."
— *Psalm 4:7*

There is a story about a man with a real thick mustache who sat down for his evening meal. Among all the other dishes, his wife set before him a plate of Limburger cheese.

Since he really loved cheese, he gobbled it down in a hurry, then sat back to read his newspaper. Meanwhile, his wife went into the kitchen to wash the dishes.

A few minutes later, he bellowed at his wife, "What's the matter in here? It stinks ... didn't you clean the living room today?" Grumbling under his breath, he stomped into the bedroom.

He wasn't in there long before he yelled at his wife again. "It smells terrible in the bedroom, too." With that, he announced that he was going to take a walk to get away from the house's odors.

A half hour passed, and he slammed the door, "I don't know what is the matter. The whole town stinks."

Finally, his wife whispered in his ear, "Darling, did you wash your mustache after you ate that Limburger cheese?"

I think a lot of us need to wash our mustaches. If you are always unhappy with your boss ... no matter what jobs you've had over the years ... chances are the problem is you, not your boss.

If you have problems with your pastor, no matter what church you go to ... the problem is not your pastor, it's you.

Of course, learning when to wash your mustache isn't easy. But, it's a good indication that anytime you are feeling negative, to check out your own attitudes.

Experience the joy and gladness the Lord wants to put in your heart. Don't let it get blotted out by the problems of this world!

"Gray" Areas

*"All things are lawful for me — but all things
are not expedient; all things are lawful for me,
but all things edify not."*

— *1 Corinthians 10:23*

A lot of times, we as Christians try to put everything either in a "black" column (sin), or a "white" column (good). But there are some "gray" areas in the Body of Christ.

For example, I have a friend who has a terrible weight problem. His doctors have warned him, that if he doesn't lose some weight, he is setting himself up for what could be a fatal heart attack. For this man, it is a sin to eat a piece of strawberry cheesecake.

On the other hand, there is a girl on my staff who has always weighed less than one hundred pounds. She is constantly sick, and in dire need of putting on some weight . . . or so her doctor says. For her, to turn down the cheesecake would be a sin.

In both cases, it is not the strawberry cheesecake that is at fault.

Paul's wisdom was put to the test by the Corinthians when they asked him whether or not it was a sin for them to attend the feasts where their neighbors would sacrifice food to idols.

Part of the church thought it was okay. After all, the idols were just big stones. Paul agreed, but warned that new believers, their faith being weaker, should not take part.

Questions like that have turned up all through the ages. So, how do you decide in these "gray" areas?

First, check it out in the Word. If the Bible clearly says it's wrong — then it's wrong. There is no "gray" in that.

Second, check your Spirit. If you feel guilty about it, then it is wrong for you. Pray about it and let God lead you.

Third, ask the Elders. Do like the Corinthians did, and ask someone whose discernment you trust and respect. Chances are, you aren't the first person to raise that question.

With this check list, you should be able to determine what is right for you and what is wrong in any situation.

In *All* Things Give Thanks

"In everything give thanks: for this is the will
of God in Christ Jesus concerning you."
— *1 Thessalonians 5:18*

TAMMY: I remember when Jim was hosting the 700 Club one night, while we were still at CBN. His guest for the show was Merlin Carothers, the author of several books on praise. Merlin explained how praising God in everything was the fastest way out of a valley, or any other situation for that matter.

Well, after that show, Jim began praising God for all things, even the aggravating ones, knowing God had a good reason for allowing them to happen. It wasn't long, though, before God put Jim to the test!

Jim and I were on our way to Atlanta for a telethon. Our car began to give us some trouble and Jim found a garage that specialized in front-end work. The manager said, "You have bad shocks. We'll have to replace them." Jim told the man to go ahead and do the repair work. I began praising the Lord for this delay and moments later the manager was back again. Now I had been praising God all this time and the manager told us, "Sir, I'm sorry, but your ball joints need replacing."

For the next several hours, the manager kept coming back with part after part that needed replacing. Jim and I kept praising the Lord and praying for the men in the garage.

About two hundred dollars and several hours later, we finally got on the road and it began to rain. Jim started to complain and his secretary asked, "Why don't you praise the Lord for the rain, Jim?" We all began to obediently thank the Lord for the rain and in about ten minutes it stopped!

The next day, I received a phone call from a lady who told me her husband worked at the garage we had stopped at and she wanted us to pray for him. I told her we had already been praying for him and before the night was over she called back to say he had come to Christ.

If you find yourself in a difficult situation, begin to praise the Lord and just see what God will do for you!

Greater Is He

"Ye are of God, little children, and have overcome them: because greater is He that is in you, than he that is in the world."

— *1 John 4:4*

Hallelujah! Everytime I think about this verse, I get excited! And you should too, because it means that there is no more powerful force in the world you live in than Jesus Christ in you today! That's something to shout about when you stop to think about it!

I don't spend a lot of time with people who are always talking about how strong the devil is, or how much havoc he's causing in the world today. I wish they would get as excited about what the Lord is doing as they are about what Satan is doing!

After all, what has Satan done lately in any Christian's life that God hasn't been able to turn around for good? What tragedy or aggravating circumstance can the devil dream up for us that God hasn't already prepared our way out of the second we need it? Where on this planet can he stir up trouble that God won't see and control as He pleases? Satan is on a leash, and God holds him at bay as he chooses.

When we concentrate on Satan, and the dark things of his world, we do an injustice to God who has given us the power to rise above the devil's world if we want to.

God has touched lives with love and hope. He's spread joy and healing, traded peace for strife, and given eternal life in the place of death.

Thus, with Jesus in our hearts, we're going to be overcomers! Only God does great things in this world, and if we will give our whole heart to doing His will, we'll be a part of that greatness. Greater is He — much, much greater! Hallelujah!

The Still, Small Voice

". . . But the Lord was not in the wind: and after the wind an earthquake; but the Lord was not in the earthquake: and after the earthquake a fire; but the Lord was not in the fire: and after the fire a still small voice."

— *1 Kings 19:11-12*

After his great victory over the prophets of Baal, Elijah, like a lot of us who've known high points, had a letdown. The king of Israel's wicked wife, Jezebel, threatened Elijah's life, and God's man of power for the hour ran like a scared rabbit. He sat under a tree in the wilderness and prayed for God to take his life.

The Word of the Lord came to him there, telling him to go up to a mountain. And there the Lord passed by, and before Him came a wind, and an earthquake, and fire. Before the prophets of Baal, God had spoken dramatically, with consuming fire. But here, as Elijah shuddered upon the mountain, God was not in the earthquake, wind, and fire. He came in a way Elijah didn't expect — in a still, small voice that asked him a simple question: "Elijah, what are you doing here?" And that got Elijah's attention and made him ready to obey God.

Elijah had seen the spectacular. He'd known the power of God. But he hadn't known God's quietness and gentleness. A man with a bold nature like Elijah must have felt like an awful failure, ashamed of his fear, alone and defeated. But God met him there, in his weakness. God didn't meet him in a glorious way. God didn't use the "big guns" this time. They would have depressed a downhearted man even more. God used a small voice, as still as Elijah's sad spirit, to meet the prophet's need.

You may feel today as if the glory of God has departed from your life. You may have asked God for a sign and gotten none. But I tell you, listen more closely today. God may not send an earthquake, wind, or fire. But His voice will reach you, in quiet love that will bring you peace.

Being All Things To All

". . . I am made all things to all men, that I might by all means save some."
— 1 Corinthians 9:22

One of the biggest pop music hits of the last decade was a song entitled, "I Did It My Way." What a pride-filled concept of life! But it carries over to some Christians, too. "I'm going to share Jesus *my* way." "I'm going to live the Christian life my way." Well, I'll tell you something: God will be pleased to let you do it your way, once you want — more than anything else — to do it His way! Doing it His way means burying your pride and being sensitive to the needs of others.

Back in the early days of Christian TV, I worked with a dear sister named Emma McSmith, who at age eighty was quite a Bible teacher. She always wanted to preach from a pulpit, but I tried to get her into a kitchen set because I knew that some men just can't stand women preaching! I said, "Sister Emma, if I put you in a kitchen with some pots and pans, and you talk over the counter, people will really relate to that a lot more."

She agreed to go along with that. We built a set, just a wall, really, with pots and pans, a window, and a counter. One day, the set fell while Emma was preaching. She grabbed it and held it up with her hand. She never missed a lick of her message! A friend of hers, who watched the show, saw Emma's hand raised during the whole show and thought she was really having a blessed time!

God is looking for people who are even willing to be fools for Him. Winning souls is that important to God, and it ought to be that important to us. Jesus gave up His "dignity" and died on the cross to save souls. Are you willing to give up your way and accept *His* way so souls might be saved today?

Sure Direction

"Trust in the Lord with all thine heart; and lean not unto thine own understanding. In all thy ways acknowledge Him, and He shall direct thy paths."

— *Proverbs 3:5-6*

Recently I read about a young man in Pennsylvania who was interested in the oil business. He was determined to some day find oil and strike it rich. He had a Canadian friend, also seeking oil, to whom he wrote, "I want to come up there and find my fortune in oil." The friend wrote back suggesting he stay in Pennsylvania until he'd studied more about oil.

Well, the young man studied a bit, but soon became restless. Impetuously he sold his farm for $833 and moved to Canada to join his friend searching for oil.

Shortly after he left the farm, the new owners were out checking the pastures. Out from under an old board came this awful, gooey-looking black mess into the cattle water. You guessed it! That young man had high-tailed it to Canada, and one of the biggest "gushers" in America was found on his old farm. A billion dollars worth of oil has been pumped from that $833 piece of property alone!

If that young man had listened to his friend and studied a little longer, he might have known how to see oil when it was squirting out right under his own nose. But how much like so many of us, who won't accept the all-knowing advice of God and just dash off on our own steam. I'm tempted to do that from time to time. I think, "I've been in television so long, I know what I'm doing." Then God has to stop me short with His beautiful and simple wisdom.

You know, you can't fail to get pointed in the right direction today if you'll put your whole trust in God and refer everything in your life to Him. Keep in touch with Him — and you won't miss any of the good things he has for you.

Creativity

*"And He that sat upon the throne said,
Behold, I make all things new . . . . "*
— *Revelation 21:5*

God hasn't saved us to try to do something new with the same old life. He's given us a new life and new things to do with it. If you get the idea that your life has to be a set pattern, and you can only do things one way, you'll never live your new life creatively.

Christians spend too much time trying to create things that are as good as the world's, when with Christ we can create things that are far better. When you realize that you are God's creature, His unique creation, then you can invent and develop new ways of doing things. Instead of being influenced by the commercial world, you can enter the new world of God's imagination.

Basically, everything that PTL has done in Christian television, we were told couldn't be done. We couldn't buy two hours of television time a day. Nobody would sell it to us. Now we're in almost every major city in the USA. The impossibility became a possibility, and then a reality.

One of the things we teach our Heritage School students is that nothing is impossible — it can be done! If things go wrong, you just pick yourself up and keep going. You don't stop, even if the world seems to be falling apart around you.

You may have something you want to do or to make that's really new and unusual. Perhaps you have in mind a new way to do an old job more easily.

If you have put that idea on the shelf, I know a God who can mend broken dreams and broken projects. Today, take that idea off the shelf, and watch God do something exciting in your life!

Setting Your Mind

"Set your affection on things above, not on things on the earth. For ye are dead, and your life is hid with Christ in God."

— *Colossians 3:2-3*

Two men were walking side by side down a busy city street. Suddenly, one of them stopped and leaned over, cupping his ear. "I hear a cricket chirping," he said to his companion.

The other man frowned, listened intently, and then shrugged his shoulders. "I don't hear it," he said. "But tell me, with all these cars roaring by and footsteps and voices, how in the world can you hear a cricket?"

Well, the man who'd heard the cricket was raised in the country, and his ear was tuned to a cricket's chirp.

Down the street, the other man came to an abrupt halt and scanned the ground around him. He'd heard a coin hit the sidewalk! His ear was tuned for a different kind of sound!

If you have Jesus in your heart, God wants to give you a whole new attitude from the one you had before you met Him. Then, your ears might have been eager to take in gossip or foul talk. Your brain might have directed your feet and hands to go and do things they shouldn't have. Your mind might have been set on thoughts that weren't pure.

But you see, when you accepted Jesus, you became a part of the death He died for you on the cross, and a new person was born. As you and God deal with the problems and trials in your life, that new self begins to grow into a spiritually healthy adult! With God's help and your willingness to press on, you can overcome the old, dead flesh.

So today, God wants you to set your thoughts on heavenly things. Tune your mind to His love and goodness. Scoffers have said, "Don't be too heavenly minded, you'll be no earthly good." That's not true. The most heavenly-minded people have been the most earthly good. If you'll start putting the things of God foremost in your thinking right now, it won't be long before you will be bringing a little bit of heaven to earth!

Give Up The Rut

" ... Leave your country, your people and your father's household and go to the land I will show you."

— *Genesis 12:1*

In the days when roads weren't paved, it wasn't uncommon to find yourself stuck in a mudhole on your way to the market or to visit somebody. But people didn't stay in that mudhole any longer than necessary. They found someone with a good mule team or tractor to pull them out.

It's not hard to get trapped in an emotional "mudhole" or rut these days. You may have been traveling along with everything going your way when suddenly you discover you're knee deep in an unexpected problem. Well, that problem may seem bigger than you are, but it can never be too big for God. Abram, in today's verse, was in a rut in the ancient city of Ur. God told him to get moving — He had a better land for him.

If you have a dream or ambition in life, you need to get out of whatever rut you're in and move. To get out, you need something strong and sturdy to hitch your life to and pull you out. Faith in God is the winning hitching team!

Some people seem to prefer mudholes. They fall into them, and instead of going for help they stick up a "Home Sour Home" sign. They make camp at their mudhole. But, when you have a dream to follow, don't give it up because you're in a rut. Give up the rut! Whether your problem is financial, marital, physical, or emotional, don't settle into it. If you've put down any stakes at your mudhole, pull them up and go for help. Hitch up to the faith in God. He can get you out of that rut and back on the road to your dream.

You can change your outlook by looking past where you are now. Don't give up on your dream or yourself. Whatever that secret dream of yours is, join it to God with prayer and effort right now — and move on!

God Is Love

"... God is love...."

— *1 John 4:16*

This is one of the most amazing statements in the whole Bible. Notice that it doesn't say, "God *was* love," or "God *will be* love." It doesn't say, "God is *in* love, either." All those would imply some change in God, in the way He is from time to time. Mere people fall in — and out of — love all the time. Even people in love sometimes can't stand the sight of the person they're "nuts" about. God isn't like that. He just *is* love. His love is unfailing. It never varies.

What a comfort and joy it is to have this truth! I never have to worry that God doesn't love me! The great 19th century preacher, Charles Spurgeon, was out walking one day when he saw a weather vane on top of an old mill. Over the weather vane, the text was carved: "God is love." Spurgeon knocked on the door. An old miller answered politely. When Spurgeon asked him why he had put the verse up there, the old man replied, "That it might speak to the people at all points of the compass and say to them, 'God is love — whichever way the wind blows!' "

I want you to know that today: God is love — no matter how the wind blows. It's so easy to let the kinds of events and circumstances you face influence how you think God feels about you. When things are going well, it's natural to think that God is "smiling" on you. When things get rough, it seems that God is just trying to "do you in." It seems that He just doesn't care. Oh, nothing could be further from the truth. I want you to know that no matter what you're feeling or thinking, God loves you today. He *is* love — He can't do otherwise!

Today, believe with all your heart that God's love for you is a fact. You don't have my word on it. You have God's Word. And listen: He'll love you, even if you doubt it!

Whosoever Will!

" ... And let him that heareth say, Come.
And let him that is athirst come. And whosoever
will, let him take the water of life freely."
— Revelation 22:17

Oh, how I love this verse! It doesn't leave out anybody, does it? The fountain of God, overflowing with the water of life, is there for the drinking, to anyone, old or young, weak or strong, smart or dull, large or small, who learns about it, thirsts for it, and is willing to take it! I'm so glad, aren't you, that as an old country Gospel song says, "That 'whosoever will' included me!"

I never preach a Gospel message and not give an invitation. I believe I should always give a chance for people to respond and receive Jesus. I thank God that He's promised never to turn away anyone who comes to Him.

There are those who say that a little child or a mentally retarded person can't know and love Jesus. But God's Word says "whosoever will." It doesn't say you have to have been to seminary. There's no minimum I.Q. requirements for the kingdom of God. The Bible says that John the Baptist was "filled with the Holy Ghost, even from his mother's womb" (Luke 1:15).

One of my secretaries has a son who's considered retarded. But my, does that boy love Jesus! He watches the PTL Club every day, and in fact, was used by the Lord to tell his mother that she should come to work for PTL!

God is interested in saving souls today — big souls and little souls, old souls and young souls, all souls! Is there anybody you could tell about Jesus today that you haven't given the Good News that Jesus loves them? Talk to them today — you may never know how thirsty they are for the Water of Life.

Heal Me, O Lord!

"Heal me, O Lord, and I shall be healed, save me, and I shall be saved: for thou art my praise."
— Jeremiah 17:14

TAMMY: Over the years that Jim and I have been in the ministry together, we have seen God do many, many miracles. But somehow, when He heals someone we love, it is even more precious.

Last year, at the Labor Day dedication of the Heritage Hall, one of our employees, Nancy Hawkins, was having a terrible, terrible time. She had fallen down about five months before and broken both bones in one of her legs.

Because of that accident, one of her legs was shorter than the other by about an inch. (She could have had it operated on, but she remembered Cheryl Prewitt's testimony of how God had healed her leg and caused it to grow about two inches. Nancy decided God could do that for her, too.)

That Labor Day, she was hobbling about on her cane, and her leg was hurting really bad. Well, Charles and Frances Hunter "just happened" to see her and ask what was the matter. Minutes later, they were praying down the healing power of God, and they watched in awe as her leg grew out to its normal length.

The funny think about all of this is that when the Hunters called her over, Nancy thought to herself, "Oh, no Lord . . . I haven't got time to be prayed for . . . " But God knew what He was doing!

Today, Nancy is wearing high heel shoes again and testifying to the healing power of our Great God!

Whatever your need is today, God wants to meet that need. If you are like Nancy and don't think you have the time or have the faith or whatever . . .

Take the time to give your problem to Him!

Do It Anyway

"But I say unto you which hear, Love your enemies, do good to them which hate you, Bless them that curse you, and pray for them which despitefully use you."

— *Luke 6:27-28, 31*

I can't think of any commands in the Bible that are harder to obey than those above given by Jesus. It's part of a wisdom and a warfare that is going to win the world — whether it seems to make sense or not. Believe me, when you step out to do good, you're going to make enemies, people are going to hate and mistreat you. I've found that if you just love them anyway — you'll win!

An unknown, but very wise person said the following words. Ponder them today — and put them into action!

(1) People are illogical, unreasonable, and self-centered. Love and trust them anyway. (2) If you do good, people will accuse you of having selfish motives. Do good anyway. (3) If you are succussful, you'll win false friends and true enemies. Succeed anyway. (4) The good you do today will be forgotten tomorrow. Do good anyway. (5) Honesty and frankness make you vulnerable. Be honest and frank anyway.

(6) The biggest men with the biggest ideas can be shot down by the smallest men with the smallest minds. Think big anyway. (7) People favor underdogs, but follow only top dogs. Fight for the underdogs anyway. (8) What you spend years building may be destroyed overnight. Build anyway. (9) People really need help but may attack you if you do help them. Help people anyway. (10) Give the world the best you have, and you will get kicked in the teeth. Give the world the best you have anyway!

Jesus give us the strength to do your will and love others.

Believe And Receive

"Therefore I say unto you, what things soever ye desire, when ye pray, believe that ye receive them, ye shall have them."

— *Mark 11:24*

Certain he'd been called by the Lord to preach in a foreign country, an evangelist made preparations to go. Someone asked him, "Do you have the money for your airplane ticket?"

The preacher answered, "I sure do — I've got it by faith!" And it wasn't long before he had the money in his hands, coming from unexpected sources. He understood the meaning of faith.

One of the most important faith principles in all Scripture, that we can apply to our lives, is to believe that we've received the things we ask God for — *when we pray!* We don't believe God when we see the thing itself, we believe Him when we ask Him. There's a difference.

An old preacher's saying goes, "Seeing isn't believing, believing is seeing." That's what faith is all about. The Bible teaches that it was faith that built the whole universe we see today, faith brought into being what we have now. When God wanted to create something, He simply spoke it into being, with faith that it would appear (Hebrews 11:3).

Prayer is an echo of the creative power of God. God has given us prayer so that we, too, may call into being things that would glorify Him and bless others. In prayer, we do exactly as He did: We speak the things into being that we desire, and believe that as soon as we've spoken them, we already have them. Then, we keep confessing that those things are ours, and the manifestation will always follow, because God always stands behind His Word.

You can practice this in your own prayer life. State the specific things you need to God, then take God at His Word that you have those things in the *now.* Then, keep confessing that they're yours — and your believing will soon become seeing!

Our Eternal Hope

"Let not your heart be troubled; ye believe in God, believe also in me. In my Father's house are many mansions: if it were not so, I would have told you. I go to prepare a place for you. And if I go and prepare a place for you, I will come again, and receive you unto myself; that where I am there ye may be also. And whither I go ye know, and the way ye know."
— *John 14:1-4*

Everyone wonders, at one time or another, about the question, "What's going to happen to me after I die?" For the non-Christian there is only speculation about what they can expect. But, for the true believer, there is the comfort that Jesus has a beautiful home ready for us when we leave this world.

This promise is quickly forgotten by many Christians when they are faced with death themselves or the death of a close loved one. We must remember that death is not an ending, but a glorious beginning. It is so important that we know, by faith, our salvation is promised, so we can share the hope of eternal life with people who don't know what awaits them.

It is really a time to celebrate and look forward to, for ourselves and those we love, who know Jesus, because our real home is in Heaven.

I'm not saying that it is wrong to feel a sense of sorrow with the loss of a loved one. We should not grieve when someone special leaves this world, but rather rejoice that they are now with our Father, and look forward to our reunion in Heaven. Our loss is our loved one's gain, just as it will be our gain when we die.

As Christians, we can face the future with hope and expectancy of great things. We need to share our hopes with others so they, too, can know the saving knowledge of Jesus Christ.

Forcefulness

*"And from the days of John the Baptist until
now the kingdom of heaven suffereth violence,
and the violent take it by force."*
— *Matthew 11:12*

God likes forceful people. I'm not talking about the kind of "fools who rush in where angels fear to tread." I'm taking about people to whom the kingdom of God is worth so much that they'll hold onto it like bulldogs to a pants leg, will fight for it like wildcats in a corner, with a hunger and thirst for God so great that nothing will stop them.

There's been a commercial on television that says, "Go for it!" Well, that's how I've felt about winning ground for the kingdom of God. For a while, when so many newspaper articles about PTL and myself were being printed, I got discouraged and almost gave up. Then God began to speak to my heart and say, "Jim, you've got to take it by force. You've got to fight. Don't take all this lying down. Get up and start swinging!"

So I pulled myself up by my bootstraps. I said, "Devil, you're a liar. I resist you in the name of Jesus. You've had your day. I'm not going to listen to your gossip and accusations anymore! I know I'm a part of the kingdom of God." Once I started to fight back, all the bills started getting paid, the accusers stuck their tails between their legs and took off the other way! PTL's had the greatest time in its history in the midst of recession. We've built, we've stayed on the air in forty-two nations, and we are not only expanding here at home but all around the world for His glory.

So many things in this world — in ministry, in business, in entertainment, are there for the taking. God is looking for people to reach out and lay hold on them for Him. Will you be, wherever you are, a forceful servant of Christ today?

We Are All Sinners

"Even the righteousness of God which is by faith of Jesus Christ unto all and upon all them that believe: for there is no difference: For all have sinned, and come short of the glory of God."

— Romans 3:22-23

God doesn't lie. He has told us that "all have sinned" and this is true. Whether it is by thought, word, or action, everyone has sinned.

Think about Adam and Eve. Because of their disobedience, we are all born sinners. When you were a child you were constantly doing something wrong. Many times you may have thought what you were doing was right, but by using our own children as examples we know we were wrong.

Children don't have to be shown how to do things that are bad. They are part of their way of life. Instead, we have to show them what is good.

There probably isn't a child alive who hasn't stolen some candy while passing through a room or taken a cookie when they weren't supposed to eat. These acts were wrong, so the children have sinned. We scold them and tell them they were wrong. Here, we have just taught them the way to be good.

Or, how many have ever told a little white lie? That lie may have been small, but you were never taught to lie, it came naturally. Instead, our parents tried to teach us to speak only the truth, and by the way, a lie is a lie!

Man sins by choice because he is a sinner by nature. From that very first sin in the Garden of Eden, all mankind have been born sinners.

We don't tell our children to go out and steal and lie, but no matter how hard we try, they will experience lying and stealing. You have to teach your children, and remind yourselves, that goodness and truthfulness are the ways of God. And accepting Jesus Christ as our Savior is the answer to sin!

Freedom Produces!

"... The laborer is worthy of his hire...."
— Luke 10:7

Thank God that in America a person can own his own house, farm, or business. This is a blessing that is part of our heritage as well as a principle spelled out in the Bible. God recognizes that people need to enjoy the fruits of their labor.

Did you know that in countries where private ownership is allowed there is more prosperity?

Look at the conditions of agriculture in Soviet Russia. During the Russian Revolution, the state seized more than 98 percent of all land used for farming. The Communists killed many of the big land owners or sent them to prisons in Siberia. Then the state took over management of the farms, putting the workers into barracks and keeping all the profit for Kremlin use. Only 1.6 percent of the land was left in the hands of private citizens.

But that 1.6 percent owned privately produces 64 percent of Russia's potatoes, 35 percent of the milk, 50 percent of the eggs, and 35 percent of the meat. Half of all the agricultural products produced in Russia overall are produced by the 1.6 percent of the land that belongs to individuals! Again, the principles of God have proven true!

God didn't make people to be numbers on a statistics sheet or living robots. He created us for freedom and abundant life in Him. And because we're made for freedom — freedom produces!

Thank God today that you live in a land where you can still work for your family and enjoy the fruit of your labor. Won't the world be great when Jesus comes back and all the earth will be free to grow and thrive with Jesus as Lord — and his Saints living in perfect liberty!

Rest And Wait

"Rest in the Lord, and wait patiently for Him...."

— *Psalm 37:7*

These are really two sides of one principle that describe our leaning on Jesus and which result from trusting, delighting, and committing. One side is REST, from the Hebrew "daman," meaning "to quiet self, to stand still."

Rest is our reaction to our enemies. We just keep silent to the fear, bitterness, and resentment that arise when circumstances or other people come against us. When we fight back or judge others, we only get the same judgment back on ourselves. Rest means to let God fight our battles. He can do it better. If we commit our enemies to God and rest, He will thrust them out, even turn them into friends. Many people have called me and apologized for things they said against me — because God has fought my battles when I didn't get involved and just committed them to Him.

The other side of rest is to "wait patiently." This means literally to "twist or intertwine." It was used to describe the way a strong rope was made by twisting together four strands of hemp. Waiting on the Lord, therefore, is not a passive thing but an active expectancy of involving yourself with God to bring about His will. Solomon describes this in Ecclesiastes 4:12: "If one prevail against him, two shall withstand him, and threefold cord is not easily broken."

As your little cord of faith becomes intertwined with the cords of the Father, Son, and Holy Spirit, it suddenly takes on a great new strength and power that accomplishes the impossible every time. This is leaning on Jesus.

TRUST, DELIGHT, COMMIT, REST, and WAIT. There you have them — they're what the PTL ministry was built on. They make up a good foundation for your personal walk with God. Learn them, practice them, and God will bring you out also to a place of success and victory!

Pressing On

"By your standard of measure it shall be measured to you; and more shall be given you besides. For whoever has, to him shall more be given; and whoever does not havea, even what he has shall be taken away from him."
— *Mark 4:24-25*

No Christian can live on past spiritual victories, and remain vital and alive in the Lord! It seems to be a natural law governing the Christian's life that he is either growing in the Lord, or he's losing ground.

Of course, we can't skip stages of growth in our spiritual development! But, when we don't use the truths we've been given, we stand still, and then most likely move back a few stages.

I don't know about you, but all of my victories came with a battle, and they are far too dear for me to lose them. I'll fight to keep every inch of ground I've gained, and I'll struggle to apply every principle the Lord has taught me. That is how I keep moving on in the Lord.

People sometimes accuse me of being a dreamer and reaching for the stars. But I'll tell you one thing — a dreamer is so busy scrambling to make his vision a reality that he doesn't have time to get that complacent, self-satisfied outlook on life that will rob him of his desire to grow further in the Lord!

If you want to be effective for the Lord, you have to keep moving on in Him. The more you use what God's given you, the further you'll move and the more He will give you.

If you feel like easing off a little today, resist that temptation, and press on. I'm, sure your victories have come with a battle, too, and it would be terrible if you fought them for nothing.

A Risen Standard

" . . . When the enemy shall come in like a flood, the Spirit of the Lord shall lift up a standard against him."

— *Isaiah 59:19*

Oh, I'll tell you that's one of the greatest scriptures in the whole Bible for me, today, yesterday, and the day before! I don't know whether you've ever had circumstances where you thought the devil was coming in like a flood but if you have, you appreciate this promise as much as I do.

One time, I was speaking at a meeting in Alaska. My host put me up in a mobile home, but during the summer in Alaska black flies are all over the place. They just kept flying into our trailer. We closed the doors and all the windows, but flies kept coming in by the hundreds. I don't care if you had every crack in that entire trailer sealed, I think the flies would have found a way to get in.

This is the same way the devil is at times. Sometimes you think you have defeated him at the front door, only to look around and find him knocking at the back door. You try and close off the back door, and lo and behold, if he isn't coming in the window. I don't care if you have covered all windows, doors, and chimneys in your house, if you have the slightest crack he will come through that. Just like a flood coming over the sides of a dam, the devil will seep through every crack and crevice he can find to get through and attack you.

But, the Bible tells us not to worry because the Spirit of the Lord will lift up a standard against him even when he invades your house like a flood. Hallelujah! No matter how hard his attack is, regardless of what your enemies and neighbors do or say, God's word will stand fast. God isn't going to leave you stranded in the middle of the flood, He will bring you through. Keep your eyes on Jesus, and He will make you victorious.

"Nowhere" or "Now Here?"

"Whither shall I go from thy Spirit? or Whither shall I flee from thy presence?"
— *Psalm 139:7*

I'm always amused when I hear about someone "running from God." That doesn't mean that I think backsliding is funny. I just know that running from a God, who's everywhere, isn't possible. There may be times when you don't feel His presence or communicate with Him — but He's always there.

I used to enjoy watching Jamie Charles as a toddler playing by himself. He'd get wrapped up in his own little world with his toys, completely unaware that I was keeping an eye on him, sometimes chuckling quietly to myself at the cute things he said and did. If he suddenly turned around and saw me standing there, sometimes he'd laugh. But some times he'd be a little upset and shocked — especially if he were doing something he shouldn't have been.

God is always close by us, too. And perhaps He enjoys watching us play in our little corner of the world, just as we do our own children.

There is a story of a bedfast atheist who sent his little daughter to live with friends, who taught her to read. When she came home, she burst into her Dad's room and cried, "Daddy, I've learned to read!" Well," he smiled, "let me hear you read the sign I wrote on the foot of the bed." Printed there, in large letters, were the words, *God is nowhere.* "Oh, Daddy, that's easy," the little girl said gleefully, "It says *God is now here!* " That unbelieving father was stunned. He couldn't get that thought out of his mind. God used it to get hold of his heart and save his soul!

Yes, God is "now here," wherever "here" is for you right now. Always remember that, especially when you don't sense His closeness and love. For no matter how you feel, His love and concern for you will still be there — and will never change.

Happy Father's Day!

"Furthermore we have had fathers of our flesh which corrected us, and we gave them reverence . . . . "

— *Hebrews 12:9*

TAMMY: With all the commotion the women's libbers have raised about what women should be doing and what men should be doing, there is one thing they have left out, (and it's probably because this is scriptural and most of what they believe isn't) — modern men need to spend more time with their kids!

Today is Father's Day, and I think any of us gals that have a man who truly takes an active part in disciplining the kids should be very grateful — for those kind of fathers are a rare breed!

In the past, the children were with the father almost from sun up to sun down as they planted the fields together, and took care of the farm. Back then, the Dad was always there to teach, encourage, and discipline. And the kids were more well behaved than today.

But times have changed. Almost all fathers work outside the home and are away anywhere from nine to twelve hours each day — and sometimes more. Thus, the burden for raising the kids falls on the mothers, and many of them work, too.

In so many homes, and even in many Christian homes, the dads need to re-evaluate their priorities between work and home, and then take corrective action.

But if you are one of those rare, blessed dads that take plenty of time with your youngsters — then Praise the Lord! You are truly hearing from God, and He is using you mightily in those young people's lives.

And, to my Jim and all the dads, Happy Father's Day!

Forget The Past

" . . . This one thing I do, forgetting those things which are behind, and reaching forth unto those things which are before . . . . "
— *Philippians 3:13*

Anyone who knows me very well is aware that I practice this truth with great faithfulness. I say that sort of "tongue in cheek" because it's more the result of my nature than something I've worked at: But once something's past me, it's absolutely over. I just can't be bothered with it.

People react in a strange way to this attitude. They have a hard time understanding it. Rather than forgetting the things behind them, a lot of people tend to hold onto them, as if somehow they might be able to change what happened, after all.

There's nothing you can do about the past. The only thing you can affect is what's right in front of you. If you set your car in reverse gear, you can't expect it to go forward, can you? And setting your life in the "reverse gear" of thinking about the past won't advance it either.

Paul's life was probably so productive because he'd learned this lesson. He certainly had a lot of "past" to hang him up, if he had let it. How would you like to have been a murderer and a persecutor of the church before you were saved? That's a lot to think about living down and forgetting. But Paul didn't waste his life making excuses for what he'd been. He just forged ahead, bringing the Gospel to as many people as he could. He became so involved with the calling that God had for his life that he didn't take time for self-pity or concern about past mistakes.

Have you been fretting over a past error? Have you let something in your past hinder you from really stepping into the calling that you know God has on your life? Try getting so involved in God today that you forget it. If you do, I doubt if you'll ever want to remember it again!

But, Lord . . . . . .

". . . Ah, Lord God! behold, I cannot speak: for I am a child. But the Lord said unto me, Say not, I am a child: for thou shalt go to all that I shall send thee, and whatsoever I command thee thou shalt speak."

— *Jeremiah 1:6-7*

Isn't it just like us to greet God's call on our life as Jeremiah did — with negative words about our capabilities tumbling out among all the reasons we "can't" do as God directs us.

Isn't it just like God to remind us that He's not asking us to serve Him with our own capabilities — He already knows very well that we'd fall flat on our faces if we tried. Instead, He merely jogs our memory with a small detail we seem to frequently forget — *He's* going to be our wisdom, our words, our way.

God doesn't call us to tasks He hasn't first equipped us to perform, and won't guide us through.

We can either tell the Lord (and others) what we're capable of doing — which in all reality usually turns out to be a long list of the things we can't do, complete with the reasons why — or, we can let the Lord tell us the things we're going to capably accomplish through Him. You'd be amazed at the difference that choice will make in your life.

The child of God who will quietly listen for the Lord's call, and then step out confidently in obedience rather than try and persuade God He called the wrong person, is the child of God who will grow into a spiritually-alive adult.

Trust God's call on your life to be the right one for you. He'll strengthen the talents He's given you and stand in place of the ones you don't have. If you'll just start obeying and walking today, God will do the rest.

Worth It All — For One

" . . . I will receive you, and will be a father unto you, and ye shall be my sons and daughters, saith the Lord Almighty."
— 2 Corinthians 6:18

A wealthy man gave generously to help build a home for orphan boys. At the dedication ceremonies, he got up and said, "You have put a great deal of money and energy into this home. But if it results in the salvation of only one boy, it will all be worthwhile."

After this gathering, a man came up to the speaker and asked skeptically, "Weren't you stretching it just a bit when you said it would be worth it if only one boy was saved?" The answer shot back: "Not if he were my boy!"

Probably Satan tries to get on God's back with the same type of sarcasm: "Look what a waste of time it was to send Jesus to die for mankind! So many don't want Him. Look at all the people refusing to accept Him right now!"

But, I'll tell you something. If you had been the only sinner ever born on this earth, Jesus would have come to die for you. That's the kind of love God has for you. Do you know why? Because *you're His child.*

God made men to love and serve Him. Though man disobeyed Him from the beginning, God had made him to be His child. Back there in the Garden of Eden, God promised to send His own Son to be the way of salvation through the shedding of His precious blood. While you were a sinner, God set His saving love upon you and drew you to Himself. He really loves you!

Will you let God really get involved with you today? You are worth it to Him, worth every stripe, every nail print, every drop of blood that Jesus suffered. Show Him the gratitude right now of letting Him love you completely. He can't love you more than He can love you this very moment!

Partners With God

"For My yoke is easy, and My burden is light."

— *Matthew 11:30*

God wants to be partners with His people, in every area of life. As you may know, a yoke was made for a pair of oxen, so they could pull a plow or a load together. Believe me, having Jesus to help pull your load can make it a lot lighter. That's why it makes sense to put on His yoke.

Some years ago, a man decided to make Jesus a partner in his business and put to the test the Bible's teachings on tithing. He started an experiment by planting one cubic inch of wheat which contained three hundred sixty kernels. It grew, and he harvested it with a sickle, and after threshing it, came up with a crop of fifty cubic inches. He gave a tenth to his church and planted the remaining forty-five cubic inches. The next year, his yield was fifty-five fold or seventy pounds! Again, he gave a tithe of the wheat, and replanted sixty-three pounds on the land.

Four years later, as the experiment continued, forty-five combines were sent out to thresh the wheat, which had grown to 5,555 bushels from two hundred thirty acres! After the wheat was sold, the tithe went to the church, which gave it to a hospital. Now here's the amazing part: The five thousand bushels of seed left over were sold to 276 farmers, representing thirty religious faiths, who planted it on 2,666 acres, agreeing to tithe the crop to their churches. On the day of that harvest, the yield was 62,150 bushels of wheat! Most of the tithe went to help starving people at the end of World War II in Europe.

The man who started it all, Perry Hayden, said, "I recommend taking God into partnership. He has blessed my business, my family, and me, spiritually, physically, and financially." Do you need any more encouragement? Make God a full working Partner in everything you do, say, or give today!

No Way Around God's Laws

*" . . . Cursed is every one that continueth not
in all things which are written in the book of the
law to do them."*

— *Galatians 3:10*

No man is saved by obeying the Law, but being saved can't erase the effects of disobeying God's Law. No one is above God's laws, whether saved or not.

If you stand at the bottom of a snowy mountain, and an avalanche comes rushing down on you, do you think you can make it stop in mid-air? If you go out to sea in a boat eaten up by termites, with the rudder broken and the spark plugs sputtering, and sail straight into a storm, will the waves take it any easier on you?

No if you act contrary to natural laws, you'll suffer for it. If you bang your head against a solid rock, it's gonna hurt!

It is no different with God's moral laws. If you commit sin and deliberately break God's laws, certain results are going to follow, none of them good. In fact, God's Word promises that curses of all kinds will befall you and your household and your property. No one can get away with living a sinful life.

That's why it's important, if you profess the name of Jesus, to live what you say you are. God demands obedience to His commands, and if you don't mean business with God, you're going to find yourself in trouble.

These are hard words today. But I'm urging you to submit to God's will. Obey God. Don't try to knock your head against a rock. Don't try to sail life's ocean with a boat full of holes. With the help of the Holy Spirit, it's not hard to follow God. But it's hard — very hard, to try to live the Christian life, saying you're His, and not obeying Him! So let's live the abundant and joyful life with Jesus!

Trust Or Bust?

"Thou wilt keep him in perfect peace, whose mind is stayed on Thee: because he trusteth in Thee."

— *Isaiah 26:3*

Imagine that I walked into a bank one day with some money to deposit in my account. I went up to the teller and said, "Would you please put this into my savings account?"

The teller answered, "Of course. Did you make out your deposit slip?" I said, "Yes, but before I give you the money, I want to ask you a question. Do you really think my money will be safe in this bank?"

"Well," the teller answered, "we've never had a robbery here, and our vault is the best kind made." "All right," I said nervously, "I just wanted to make sure." So I handed her the money, the deposit slip, and bankbook. She credited me with the deposit and gave back my book. "There you are, Mr. Bakker," she said cheerfully.

I walked toward the door, but suddenly ran back in a panic, knocking three customers out of the way. "Wait a minute," I panted, "Are you sure that money will be safe?" "Mr. Bakker," the teller replied, somewhat annoyed, "your money is perfectly safe!" "Well, all right," I muttered and turned to go.

This time I got to my car, but suddenly went running back again for more reassurance. Then I got in my car again, got scared again, drove to a telephone booth and called the bank. "Is my money still there?" I shouted into the phone. "It's still here, Mr. Bakker, and even if we're robbed, your money is insured. Stop worrying!"

Now, that would be kind of foolish, wouldn't it? You wouldn't say I trusted my bank very much, would you? Yet, isn't this how we treat God, supposedly trusting Him with our lives, but constantly worrying about whether He can take care of us and keep us? If you really trust a bank, or a repairman, you have peace in your heart, don't you? Start giving God real trust today. He's faithful — your soul will never "go bust" with Him!

A Cry of Danger!

"Cry aloud, spare not, lift up thy voice like a trumpet, and shew my people their transgression, and the house of Jacob their sins."
— *Isaiah 58:1*

Nothing comes more naturally to a preacher than lifting up his voice. A teacher can remain cool, calm, and collected, but there's an urgency in calling sinners to Christ that's just got to be there — and we preachers feel that very deeply and tend at times to cut loose and get all excited.

If an eternal soul's at stake, it's well worth it even to make yourself look silly to get someone's attention. For most sinners have no idea that they are in trouble.

I heard a story of a man who was walking down a dark road at night. He came upon another man, who said, in a very relaxed and jolly tone of voice, "I don't think you should go on to the river. The bridge is broken, and you just might fall in." Well, our man shrugged his shoulders and took no notice because the warning didn't sound serious.

On he went, and soon met another man, who said to him, very gravely, "Don't go any further. The bridge ahead is out, and you'll never cross it alive!"

"You can't fool me," the traveller answered, "I know that's just a joke — a while ago, another guy told me the same thing, and he was almost laughing."

He took a step to go on, but the man stood in his way. "Let me by!" the traveller cried.

"No!" the man exclaimed, grasping the traveller by the shoulder, "I won't let you go — I just barely escaped death myself, and I tell you, your life's at stake!"

"You know," the traveller said wonderingly, "now I'm beginning to think you're telling the truth!"

When you share the Gospel, do it with urgency. Remember, that soul in front of you may end up in Hell if you don't keep him from going his own way. Ask God right now to give you a heart that really cares for lost souls. Then don't be silent — tell a perishing world that Jesus saves!

The Dream Treasure

"But that no man is justified by the law in the sight of God, it is evident: for, The just shall live by faith."

— *Galatians 3:11*

While passed out in a gutter, a bum had a dream. A huge quantity of money lay before him on a table in large bags. In his dream, he got up to count the money, his joy growing greater and greater as he thought of the riches that were his.

Passing by, at that time, was a wealthy man who saw the bum lying in the gutter, and took pity on him. He knelt down and shook the bum, saying, "Wake up, mister, I've got some money for you."

As people often do in dreams, the bum, not wanting to wake up from his beautiful vision, blended the voice he heard into his dream. Without opening his eyes, he growled back, "Get out of here! I don't need your miserable couple of bucks. Can't you see I've got piles of money here? Leave me alone, and let me count my money!" He kept mumbling on like that and finally struck the hand shaking him gently by the shoulder, causing his helper to get up and leave.

When he awoke and looked around, he realized with great sorrow that he had nothing. He had driven away a chance for real help.

This is like any person who is hoping to be saved by good works. All their good works piled up together are nothing more than dreams. None of them are pure and sinless enough to please God. Jesus comes by and says, "I've come from heaven to save you. If you had any truly good works, I wouldn't have had to come and die for you. But since you were poor and blind and hopeless, I shed my blood for you — here's your pardon, receive it!

Don't ever tell Jesus, "No, I don't need you. I've got plenty of good works to keep me going for a while." You need Jesus today — a dream of riches can't save you, but Jesus can!

God's Mirror

*"Their trouble is that they are only compar-
ing themselves with each other ... Our goal is to
measure up to God's plan for us ...."*
— *2 Corinthians 10:12-13 (LB)*

Christians often get complacent because they compare
themselves with other Christians. They begin to build standards for
themselves rather than looking to God's standards. Sometimes
they look at someone else and say, "Well, I might do a lot of things
wrong, but So-and-So is worse than me, so it's all right for me to go
on the way I am." Let me tell you, that attitude of looking at yourself
through the flaws of other Christians can get you into a lot of trouble. It could even make you miss heaven!

God recognizes only one way to measure yourself — one true
scale, one sure yardstick — the Bible. If you want to see yourself the
way you really are, the Bible is the mirror. Only in God's Word will
you learn what He expects of you and find His plan for your
redemption. The church has got to get back to God's Word. It's the
only security, the only hiding place, the only firm foundation on
which we can stand.

It's not what Jim Bakker says. It's not what Oral Roberts says.
It's not what Billy Graham says. We're just mortal men. It's "Thus
saith the Lord!" His Word is the true Word.

I believe the reason many are beset today with sin problems is
that they've ignored God's Word and begun to build a doctrine unto themselves, justifying everything they want to do. They've
justified gossip, justified slander, justified their meanness, justified
adultery, and all the other sins. But outside of our justification
through the blood of Jesus, there is no other. "The wages of sin is
death, but the gift of God is eternal life through Jesus Christ ..."
(Romans 6:23).

Let's get our eyes off of people and onto Jesus and His Word.
Start being guided by the Bible — and you'll always measure up!

Jim and Tammy Bakker, and their children, Tammy Sue and Jamie Charles, share together on a PTL Club broadcast.

TOP: *Jim is the President and host of the PTL Club, which is shown daily across the United States.* **BOTTOM LEFT:** *As Pastor of Heritage Village Church, Jim shares with the congregation each Sunday morning.* **BOTTOM RIGHT:** *Jim is often called upon to deliver messages from God at meetings throughout the United States.*

TOP: *Tammy Faye Bakker ministers to audiences at Heritage USA and on the PTL Club through word and song. She has several albums on the market including her latest hit, "The Lord Is On My Side."* BOTTOM: *Tammy is also a very gifted writer. She has two best-selling books,* I Gotta Be Me *and* Run To The Roar.

TOP: *The PTL Club was broadcast live from Heritage USA during the summer of 1980. Jim and Tammy declared a "camp-in" at Heritage USA until the completion of the great Heritage Hall Auditorium.* BOTTOM: *And, completed it was! Dedication ceremonies for the huge Auditorium were held Labor Day weekend with thousands of PTL Partners and friends attending the ceremonies hosted by Jim and Tammy Bakker.*

TOP: *The beautiful Williamsburg inspired Heritage Village houses the studio facilities and offices for the PTL Television Network.* **MIDDLE:** *Hundreds of visitors crowd the Heritage Village Studio daily to be a part of the live PTL Club broadcast.* **BOTTOM:** *During the PTL Club broadcast, and 24-hours a day, the PTL Phone Counseling System is in operation taking hundreds of calls each day for prayer.*

TOP: *A "Victory Day" parade was held September 1, 1980 to celebrate the completion of Jim Bakker's vision — Heritage Hall Auditorium.* MIDDLE: *The massive and elegant Heritage Hall is a vital part in the continuing ministry of PTL and Heritage USA.* BOTTOM: *Thousands of people can attend services and telecasts each day in the huge facility and witness the work PTL is doing all around the world.*

TOP: *Oral Roberts supports Jim and Tammy Bakker at a telethon during construction of Heritage Hall.* MIDDLE LEFT: *World Outreach Center — Heritage USA — key to more efficient and economical operations.* MIDDLE RIGHT: *Earth dish, core of the PTL Satellite Network, sends signal around the world.* BOTTOM: *Phones at campsites in Heritage USA allow counselors to work on the 24-hour PTL Phone Counseling System.*

TOP: *Jim leads a rally with Nigerian host, Benson Idahosa.* BOTTOM: *Forty-two nations are reached through the PTL World Missions project. The programs are hosted by native countrymen.*

TOP: *The Japanese PTL Club is reaching a country where less than one percent of the population is born again.* BOTTOM: *The French version of the PTL Club, "Entr' Amis," is a lively talk show in a contemporary setting.*

TOP: *Host of "Club PTL" Juan Romero is also an accomplished singer.* BOTTOM: *PTL is helping Mark Buntian feed thousands of children in India every day.*

TOP: *The PTL Club telecast in Thailand is reaching hundreds of souls for Christ daily.* BOTTOM: *Bob McAlister hosts the program in Brazil.*

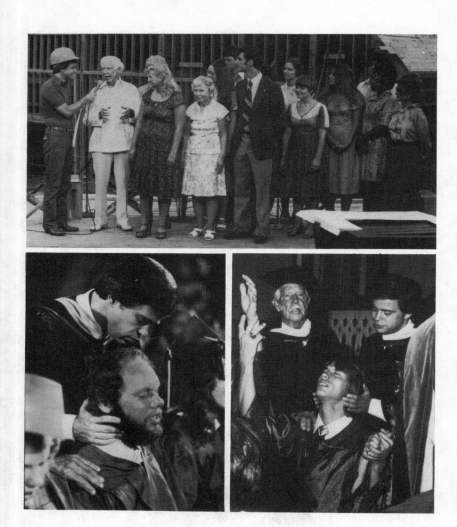

TOP: *Dr. Maynard Ketcham and eleven Heritage School Missions students were given a fond farewell on the PTL Club prior to their departure on a two-month tour of such countries as India, Korea, and Japan.* BOTTOM: *Jim delivered the graduation address at the first Heritage School graduation ceremony.*

TOP: *Tammy and the PTL Singers are regular musical guests on the PTL Club. Their talents blend together for the glory of God.* RIGHT: *Little Jamie Charles helping his Daddy host the PTL Club.*

Jim Bakker and President Ronald Reagan met prior to the election for an interview and discussion of President Reagan's views and opinions on various topics. Following their interviews, Jim and President Reagan relaxed and enjoyed a time of casual conversation.

TOP: *Jim asked President Reagan some very pointed questions concerning ERA, foreign policy, and his beliefs in Jesus Christ.* BOTTOM RIGHT: *Jim and President Reagan shake hands following their informal interview in President Reagan's California home.* BOTTOM LEFT: *Former President Jimmy Carter met with Jim on several occasions during his term in office. Here, they shake hands and share smiles after a meeting in Washington, D.C.*

TOP: *Roy Rogers and Dale Evans visit with Jim and Tammy at PTL. BOTTOM: Donna Douglas, better known as Elly Mae Clampett on the Beverly Hillbillies series, shared with Tammy during the Labor Day Heritage Hall dedication ceremonies.*

Only Against God

"Against Thee, against Thee only, have I sinned, and done this evil in Thy sight . . . ."
— *Psalm 51:4*

King David cried out these words to God, when Nathan the prophet came to him and confronted him with the adultery he had commited with Bathsheba and the murder of her husband, Uriah the Hittite.

They are curious words, when you consider all of those who had been affected by David's sin. First, there was Bathsheba, who had been drawn into sin, probably by the glamour of the king's power and position. Surely, David had sinned against her. Then, David had sinned against Uriah, in arranging his murder, one of his most faithful "mighty men." David had forced his general, Joab, to be an accomplice to this murder, and thus sinned against him. David had hidden his sin and thus sinned against all of the nation of Israel.

And yet David cried, "Against Thee only have I sinned," to God. For he knew in his heart that as much as he had injured each one of those individuals, and the nation of Israel, he had injured God with every one of his sins. No matter who else was affected, God was always involved — He had been sinned against every time.

There is no sin any of us ever commits that does not grieve the heart of God. No matter who we injure, including ourselves, we injure God first and foremost. David realized that there was no sacrifice he could make that could atone for his sin. The only sacrifice he could give was a broken heart, and a spirit willing to repent. The sacrifice that saved David, and saves you and me, was made on Calvary's cross, where Jesus shed His blood for all our sin.

You have sinned against God. Yet, for your every sin, He paid. Let your heart ring out in gratitude to Him today, for the love He has shown in forgiving each sin — for they have all been against Him — and are all under His blood.

Love Never Fails

"Charity never faileth: . . . And now abideth faith, hope, charity, these three; but the greatest of these is charity."
— *1 Corinthians 13:8,13*

If you have an unsaved loved one, whether it be a friend or a member of the family, that you've been praying about for years and years, and you feel like you just want to give up on them — *don't!*

Keep praying in faith for them, keep hoping in God for them, but most of all keep loving them — it's that never-failing love that's going to finally do it.

Love makes you hang in there when your faith wavers and your hope is about spent. Love makes you call out to God with just one more prayer. Love just won't let you give up, no matter how discouraged you are!

My brother Bob ran from God for years. It looked like he'd never come back to God.

But every single meeting I went to, my stubborn love for my brother had me raise my hand when the preacher would ask if we had unsaved loved ones. And every time there was prayer for the unsaved, love urged me to pray once again for Bob.

Just before he died, my brother finally stopped running from God. Finally, he came back to Jesus.

If my family and I had given up on Bob, he might not have been with the Lord in Heaven today. As it is, his story is an awesome testimony to the staying power of love and to the faithfulness of God in answering persistent prayer that claims souls for His Kingdom.

Hold fast to your claim on that special person's soul — God is working, even today, through your unwavering love.

It's All In His Hands

*"And we know that all things work together
for good to them that love God, to them who are
the called according to His purpose."*
— *Romans 8:28*

In my life, there have been times so dark that I have hardly seen the light of God's face at all. I was sustained only because I knew the truth of this verse.

I think of all the times that I have had to call on this verse to help me through rough days. All the articles the newspapers wrote about me and PTL, all the threats that have been made on Tammy, Tammy Sue, and Jamie Charles, and the anguish we went through when we were building Heritage USA were hard times.

But, in all these times, what a comfort and assurance I found in that promise. It's easy in the natural to think that only the good things in life can work together for your good. But thank God, His Word doesn't say that. It says, *"all things."* I've hung onto that promise through lies, opposition, doubts, fears, and everything else Satan had to throw at me. Only our God is great enough to twist the devil's arm and turn all his evil devices into good results for the beloved of God.

I've found more than comfort and assurance here, I've found victory. I could hardly stop weeping with joy the day I saw Heritage Hall dedicated. Tears just kept flooding my eyes as I looked at my family and thought of how God had kept and strengthened us all. I shouted, "Hallelujah!" again and again to God for putting the enemies of the Gospel to flight and vindicating the ministry of PTL.

That's why I can tell you to cling to this promise of God today. No matter what you face, grit the teeth of your spirit and hurl God's Word at the devil and anything he tries to do. Friend, God won't quit on you. He's got it all in His hands — and He always has the upper hand!

Never Too Dark For The Son

"But God commendeth His love toward us, in that, while we were yet sinners, Christ died for us."

— Romans 5:8

I'll bet you never said to yourself on a dark winter morning, "Ah, it's not a fit time for the sun to come up — it's too dark out! The sun makes everything light — it's got no business coming into this pitch black morning — the day's not worthy to have the sun shine on it!"

I'll bet you've never said after a long, cold winter, "The world's not fit for spring. Let spring come where it's beautiful and fresh, let it come into a setting delightful enough for it."

No, you welcome the light where it's dark and cold. You welcome spring when the depressing bleakness of winter has been with you too long. Light and spring are just what are needed to change dark and cold situations.

If this is true, why do we ever shut God out because we insist that we're unworthy to receive Him? Isn't His presence exactly what we need, to drive away the spiritual darkness and warm the cold heart? Isn't the melting power of the Son of love the only thing that will loose you from the icy shackles of sin and despair?

Then why worry about your worthiness? No, a cold dawn isn't worthy to receve the sun, a dragged-out winter isn't worthy of the warmth of spring. When you were in darkness and sin, you weren't worthy to receive Christ, yet He loved you, and He came, like the sun and the spring, into your heart.

You weren't worthy then, and you are unworthy now. But let the Son drive away the darkness, and let the spring of gladness melt your cold heart. Let Him live in the temple of your heart, even though you are not worthy that He should come under your roof. Isn't He just what you need, right now?

A Thirst For God

"As the hart panteth after the water brooks,
so panteth my soul after thee, O God."
— *Psalm 42:1*

When the Bible paints a picture, it is remarkably life-like. Hunters, who have trailed deer to near-dehydration, can tell you why God chose to use a thirsty deer to describe the thirst He wants us to have for Him.

The panting of a thirsty deer is something terrible to see. Its whole body seems to be thirsting, from its swollen tongue to its snorting nostrils, its glaring eyes, and all its pores, as it gasps for breath.

If a person, who loves God, feels in any way separated from the Lord, the agony in his spirit will be just as great.

Thirst is a desperate thing. Men have fasted for many days and lived, and even thrived during the period when they had no food. But no man can live long without water. Severe thirst must be satisfied, or death will follow soon.

Jesus once stood up on a great feast day of the Jews and cried out, "Is anyone thirsty? Let him come to Me and drink!" (John 7:37) On this day, a priest drew water with supposed healing properties and brought it into the temple in a golden vessel. When the morning sacrifice was on the altar, this water, mixed with wine, was poured over the sacrifice, while all the people sang and shouted. But Jesus knew that the people would go away from this ceremony still thirsty for God. Only Jesus can quench the thirst of man's spirit.

Jesus said, "He who believes in Me . . . from his innermost being shall flow rivers of living water" (John 7:38).

That is His promise for us today, those rivers which are the powerful movings of the Holy Spirit, refreshing and ever-new. Are you thirsty for God today? Does your whole soul cry out for His presence and His love in your life? You can drink deep of that love right now, by bowing your head and asking God to bathe you in that living water, until your thirst is quenched.

The Way Of Holiness

*"And an highway shall be there, and a way,
and it shall be called The way of holiness; the
unclean shall not pass over it; but it shall be for
those: the wayfaring men, though fools, shall
not err therein."*

— *Isaiah 35:8*

Somebody once said, "Christianity never fails — it's just hardly ever really tried." God hasn't made the highway of holiness difficult. We make it hard, by not following Jesus in childlike faith.

But as I sometimes stumble along the road to heaven, I find a lot of assurance in verses like this one. When I find myself losing my footing or unable to see the road ahead, it's not hard for me to indulge feelings of foolishness and get down on myself. That's when this verse really speaks to my heart. For God says here that there's hope for me even when I've been foolish. If I'll just turn to Him, I'll find my way down the road.

Have you ever felt like you've really "blown it?" Ever had something unkind come out of your mouth and then regretted it? Ever come up with just the right words of guidance or love for a needy person — too late, because you were tongue-tied when the need was there? Ever make a really bad decision or study the wrong things for an exam at school? Are you punishing yourself right now for some mistake you've made?

Listen to me! God doesn't want you to sit in that mess of bad feelings. He wants you to know right now that even if you are sitting in a rut on the highway of holiness, you still haven't blown it so badly that He doesn't love you! He wants to take you by the hand right now and lead you further along.

Let Him! "God is on our side."

Growing Up In God

"Not as though I had already attained, either were already perfect: but I follow after, if that I may apprehend that for which also I am apprehended of Christ Jesus."

— *Philippians 3:12*

Faith in Jesus Christ is the way to eternal life. But, there is more than having eternal life — Christ came so we might also have an abundant life. To achieve the abundant life you must have passed through the four stages of spiritual growth in the Christian life.

The first stage is the baby stage. Here, self is thought of exclusively. Think of how a newborn baby acts. If you don't feed a baby the minute it decides it is hungry, it will pitch a tantrum. The baby's feelings are sensitive and it is very jealous of your affection to others. A baby wants only to be served — not to serve. Many people have been born into a Christian family, but they haven't developed spiritually, so they are still spiritual babies.

During the little child stage, the person is often untruthful, envious, and cruel. They are little talebearers because they repeat everything they hear. Little children will create a scene because they don't like the way things are going, but they love praise and don't care about its source. They want only the things that appeal to them.

The Christian, who has reached the young man stage, is strong and able to overcome his enemy. He has put away the "childish things" and has grown into a man who can tackle the future.

The adult stage can be reached by all, but very few obtain it. The spiritual adult has peace with God and he recognizes the peace of God. He is content in all situations and he knows that the Lord is the source of all strength. He doesn't sulk over the past, but rather looks toward the future. But, above all, he enjoys the abundant life now and will enjoy it in the life to come!

Bowing The Knees

"For this cause I bow my knees unto the Father of our Lord Jesus Christ."
— *Ephesians 3:14*

When I was visiting the Orient, I was told that the lower the bow, the more humble you are. When we get way down on our knees, on our faces before God, as we pray, we are saying, "God, I admit that you're God. I am your servant, and I am at your disposal. I'm here, God, and I humbly commit myself to you."

The Bible was written in the Middle East, and bowing and kneeling had the same significance there. I'm not saying that you can't pray in any position. When you're driving along a highway, you can't get down on your knees before God — although sometimes that's when you need help the most! Yet there comes a time, when it comes very naturally to get down on your knees and humbly bow before God.

We need to admit that God is God and worship Him. When a group of PTL vice presidents went away on retreat for a week, we prayed together and had a communion service. At the end, the Spirit of God came down in such a beautiful way. We all just knelt in a circle on the floor, and some were on their faces before God praying. There is something about even the physical attitude of humility that's conducive to hearing from God.

A Sunday school teacher once explained the raising of hands in worship to God this way: "When I lift my hands to God, I'm like the fellow in the cowboy movies who drops his gun and 'reaches for the sky.' I'm saying to God, 'I've got nothing in my hand, I'm giving up!'"

Kneel before the Lord today. Lift your hands to Him. Tell Him that you are glad He's your God — and that you "give up," and submit to Him.

Warfare In The Heavens

"Then said he unto me, Fear not, Daniel: for from the first day that thou didst set thine heart to understand, and to chasten thyself before thy God, thy words were heard, and I am come for thy words."

— *Daniel 10:12*

At the time that Daniel had this encounter with the Angel of God, he was in captivity in Babylon having been brought there by King Nebuchadnezzar. Daniel had retained his relationship with the God of Israel even in the midst of the heathen culture of the Babylonians.

In today's scripture, Daniel had been fasting and praying for three weeks, or twenty-one days. The Angel appeared to Daniel and told him in the scripture that he had heard his prayer the first day he prayed, but that the prince of the kingdom of Persia, or Satan, had hindered his bringing him the answer to his prayer.

The Angel, Michael, came in as reinforcement to help get the answer to Daniel's prayer through.

If you, as a child of God, have prayed earnestly and have not received an answer to your prayer, do not give up. Your prayer, too, may be hindered by one of Satan's cohorts. God loves you just as much as He did Daniel and the answers to your prayers are just as important to Him. But remember, when Adam fell he delivered unto Satan the control of the airwaves and Satan does everything in his power to hinder, not only the answer to your prayers, but also the spreading of the Gospel.

Be persistent in praying for your loved ones and for your needs to be met. Remember, Jesus conquered Satan on the cross and when He said, "It is finished," every need you will ever have as a Christian, was met. Rejoice! Jesus always hears and answers your prayers.

In The Valley

*". . . In the world, ye shall have tribulation:
but be of good cheer; I have overcome the
world."*

— John 16:33

In this verse is one promise of God that a lot of folks wish He'd
never given, and that is that we're going to have tribulation. Notice
also that there's only one condition that is attached — that you be in
the world. As long as you have your feet planted in the soil of this
life, tribulation is going to come. But there's great victory in the last
part of the verse, because we have the Overcomer in Jesus Christ,
and He's going to make it work out for our good.

I thank God that through the tribulation in my life, I've grown
more than any other time. During the worse tribulation PTL has
grown and grown and grown! When you're a new Christian, you
don't want to accept that. We have had much teaching that
everything should be glory and light and happiness. We all should
be living on the mountain top. But it doesn't always work that way,
does it?

Not a thing grows on a mountain top? Things grow in the valley.
The view is great from the mountain top, but food that tastes good
is cultivated in the valley.

We grow in the valley. We all like the mountian top experiences. But you can't live there for long — the air's too thin!
Thank God for the good times and the victory times. As Andrae
Crouch's song says, "Through it all, I've learned to trust in Jesus."
Through the valley and up the mountain, we can trust Him. One
thing I've learned these last few years is, there's a Rock under my
feet. Take everything away, there is Jesus, "The Rock."

Father, bless these precious friends today. If they're on the
mountain top, refresh them with a vision of you. If they're in the
valley, cause them to grow and flourish for your glory today. Amen.

The God Who Carries

"Fear thou not; For I am with thee: be not dismayed; for I am thy God: I will strengthen thee; yea, I will help thee; yea I will uphold thee with the right hand of my righteousness."
— Isaiah 41:10

Almost everybody, at one time or another, has gone through a period in their life when they felt utterly forsaken by the world, and even misunderstood by family and friends. It's hard to fight back the terrible loneliness that threatens to overwhelm you, when you feel you're facing your problems alone and no one cares.

God, however, isn't fickle like people sometimes are. Isn't that great! God loves us with a perfect love — a constant love. I heard a story once that illustrates this beautifully:

A man fell asleep one night and dreamed he was walking along the shore of an ocean. As he made his way down the beach, he could see clearly the various events that made up his life sketched in the sand before him. The further he walked the more puzzled he became over a curious detail he didn't quite understand. It seemed that for most of the walk, there were two sets of footprints embedded in the sand along the course of his life. But during times of painful crisis or periods of bleak despair, there was only one set.

"Lord," the man finally asked, "What do these footprints mean?" The Lord answered him, saying, "My child, those footprints are yours and mine, for I've been walking beside you all the way." This baffled the man even more. "But Lord, why weren't you there when I was going through the hardest times of my life? Look! There's only one set of footprints beside the roughest periods. Why did you leave me when I needed you most?"

The Lord laughed gently and replied, "But you don't understand, my son, I was still there. True, there is only one set of footprints at times, but those were the times I carried you."

If you're going through some personal crisis now, and you only see one set of footprints in the sand, remember — those footprints belong to God, not you. You are never alone!

Our Steps Are Ordered

*"The steps of a good man are ordered by the
Lord: and He delighteth in his way."*
— *Psalms 37:23*

TAMMY: When you go with God, you can't go wrong!

Again and again Jim and I have looked back on a situation
we've come out of or have narrowly missed plunging into, re-
garding them as mistakes. But when we looked more closely, we
have seen God's hand in each step we've taken. When God is order-
ing your steps, there are no mistakes — just a perfect walk toward
Him!

Early in our ministry, an evangelist came to our church,
describing his burden to reach the South American people along
the Amazon for God.

Jim and I felt that was where God was calling us, so we asked
the evangelist if we could join him. He agreed that if we could raise
our own support money, then we could be a part of this exciting
adventure. Eagerly, Jim and I began to make plans.

A pastor, who took an interest in us, suggested we come to his
church in North Carolina to preach a revival, and raise support
money for our missionary trip at the same time. We were off, enthusiastic about the things the Lord was laying before us.

Shortly after we finished our ministry in that North Carolina
church, however, bad news reached us — the evangelist, we were to
accompany to South America, had skipped with all the money raised for the venture. We were so disheartened.

It was a dear pastor friend, though, who pointed out that the
Lord had used the evangelist, and the need to raise money for the
trip, to get us out of our "nest" in Minneapolis, and onto the road of
evangelism!

We have a tremendous security in knowing that our steps are
ordered by God. Spend some time thanking God today for the times
He's used one situation in your life to lead you into another one.

Powerful "Foolishness"

"For the preaching of the cross is to them that perish foolishness; but unto us which are saved it is the power of God."
— *I Corinthians 1:18*

People in the world don't understand the preaching of the Gospel of Jesus Christ. Once we have accepted Christ as our Savior, everything becomes so clear. When many people look at the ministry of PTL they only see dollar signs.

I'm always asked the question, "Isn't it wrong for Christians to become big business? Well, nobody wants Christian ministries to become big business, but there's no other way, my friend. If you're going to buy air time on two hundred or more stations, your bill is millions of dollars and that is big business to the world. If you're going to produce professional television, you have to have studios and cameras. It takes business. You can't do what Oral Roberts, Billy Graham, or Rex Humbard are doing without paying bills.

The world criticizes us if our business is run sloppily, and then they criticize us if we run a big, efficient machine. The world won't ever be content with what we do. No matter how hard we try, we can't please everyone. I've come to the conclusion that the best thing to do is what God has called us to do, and, as the old saying goes, "let the chips fall where they may."

Whatever you try to do for God, the world isn't going to like it. They're never going to think your motives are sincere. They don't see the sense in spending time, money, and energy in trying to save souls. The world doesn't believe souls can be saved. Whatever you have to do for God, do to the best of your ability and look to Him for approval. If the power of God looks foolish to the world, don't worry. It might be foolish enough to make some of them "wise unto salvation" one day.

Put Him First

*"And thou shalt love the Lord thy God with
all thine heart, and with all thy soul, and with
all thy might."*

— *Deuteronomy 6:5*

A while back, I was in a grocery store. I saw a little boy about
five years old studying the cereal boxes to see what prizes were in
them. Suddenly, looking around and realizing he was alone, the little boy dropped the box and began to run, crying, "Daddy! Daddy!"
From the next aisle I heard a man's voice, "I've already gotten you
the best cereal. If you'd stayed with me, you wouldn't have gotten
lost. It's all right now, I'm here."

Isn't that how God has to deal with us sometimes? We get so interested in what we want that we forget to stay near Him. Whether
it's a prize in a cereal box or a new car, we can get so wrapped up in
our desires that we get ourselves out of step with God and suddenly
discover we're lost.

It's easy to get taken up in "doing your own thing." Like the little
boy, you may hear, but not reply to your Father's request to stay
close to Him. You may end up even holding the thing you want, but
without the joy of sharing it with God.

When that little boy got to the cash register, his Dad had the
money to pay for what he wanted. When you get to the point of your
need, it's God who will provide for you. As that Dad got the very
best for his boy, God is that way with you. He wants to give you the
desire of your heart. He just asks you to delight yourself in listening
to Him and loving Him as He loves and cares for you. It is nice to
know that when you drop what you think you want, and go find
God, He will already have the very best that you need waiting for
you.

Satan And Drugs

*"... For by thy sorceries were all nations
deceived."*

— *Revelation 18:23*

A lot of people think that since the days of the hippies in the "sixties" have passed, drug use among teenagers has passed also, and that drugs are not a problem we have to worry about any more.

Unfortunately, that's just not true. In fact, according to the latest surveys, just the opposite is true. More high school and college students are using marijuana, for example, than at any previous time, and now alcoholism has become a serious problem in many high schools. Use of "soft" drugs like marijuana and cocaine has even become a fad among many young professionals these days. Hair styles may be a little shorter nowadays, but drug use is wider.

Did you know that the Bible talks about drugs? Today's verse speaks to drug-related problems directly. The word used here for "sorceries" means "enchantment with drugs" in the Greek. This passage is saying that in the end times, there will be people who will use drugs to perform witchcraft and cast spells that will deceive many throughout the world.

I used to be a rock and roll disc jockey when I was a teenager, before I made a serious commitment to the Lord. I didn't know it then, but many rock performers live a lifestyle of constant drug use. Many of these "artists" are deeply involved with the occult. One group in particular, called by many "the greatest rock and roll band in the world," has written several songs dedicated to the devil.

Of course, God also tells us in Revelation that He will destroy the sorcerers and their drugs, eventually. But for now, we need to thank God for raising up ministries like Teen Challenge that expose drug use as a dangerous deception that opens up young minds to the enchantments of Satan, and provide young people with a real alternative to drugs — the power of the Holy Spirit.

A Blessed Friend

"And it came to pass, when Moses held up his hand, that Israel prevailed; and when he let down his hand, Amalek prevailed. But Moses' hands were heavy; and ... Aaron and Hur stayed up his hands, the one on the one side, and the other on the other side . . . . "
— *Exodus 17:11-12*

Sometimes when PTL is going through a battle with Satan, I tell you folks, I start to feel like Moses must have felt in this verse, straining his weary body in order to keep his arms raised to God so the battle would go well. But, just as God gave Moses two men to stand at his side and support him by holding his arms high when they grew heavy, the Lord has also graciously brought people into my life who have helped me from time to time bear some of the burdens that come with giving your life to full-time ministry for the Lord.

Uncle Henry has been one of those people who's faithfully stood beside me, lifting me up and encouraging me when I needed it the most. In fact, Uncle Henry believes that's what his ministry is — holding up the hands of God's children.

One day, Henry was standing between Pat Robertson and me in the prayer room at CBN, and he was holding both my and Pat's uplifted hands. Suddenly, he heard the voice of the Lord speak to him, "Son, this is your ministry, to hold up the hands of these my servants." As Pat's co-host, and later mine, and by both praying with and for me, that's exactly what Henry's done, and I'll always praise God for him.

God never asks you to go through a battle with no help — He will always bring someone into your life who will share your burdens with you. If you're going through something right now, and could use a friend, ask God, and wait for Him to bring that person into your life! Or be willing to be that kind of friend to someone else going through a battle. Either way, you'll find a blessing.

What's In Your Hand?

"And the Lord said unto him, What is that in thine hand? And he said, A rod."
— *Exodus 4:2*

After spending forty years on the back side of the desert tending sheep, Moses saw a burning bush on a mountainside that just wouldn't go out. He went up to investigate, and lo and behold, God spoke to him from the bush and told him to go back to Egypt and lead out the people of Israel.

You remember that Moses had had to flee Egypt. He had been raised as Pharaoh's son, and had all the learning and power of Egypt at his disposal. But, he knew that he was a Jew. He went out to see the plight of his people, and he killed an Egyptian who was mistreating a Jew. He fled for his life across the desert and ended up being a shepherd.

Here he was an old man, all of his pride and glory gone, with nothing but excuses for why he couldn't do what God was directing him to do. First, he said he was a nobody. Then, he said he couldn't speak well — in all, he had eleven complaints to offer God.

Then God asked him a strange question: "What's in your hand?" Moses must have looked down and wondered, "Well, what's that got to do with anything?" It might have crossed his mind that if God wanted to use him, why hadn't he done it sooner, when he had the authority of Egypt in his hand, the strings of power to make something happen? Why now, when he had nothing but a shepherd's staff? Moses didn't know that God was going to turn the Nile to blood with that rod, part the Red Sea with that rod, gobble up snakes with that rod.

You may feel like Moses today. You may say, "God, if you were going to use me why didn't you do it before I got too old or too deep in debt or too dry spiritually?" God is asking you today: "What's that in your hand?" You've got something, and God can use it. Will you turn it over to Him, right now?

Be Armed With The Word Of God

"For the builders, every one had a sword girded by his side and so builded."
— *Nehemiah 4:18*

God had charged Nehemiah with the important task of building the wall around the city, but evil kept trying to stop him at any cost. His carpenters and builders had to keep armed at all times to fight off any attacks.

All through the Bible, and up to modern times, any time that God tells man to do something, Satan is going to try and stop it. I don't care what it is, if God wants it, Satan doesn't.

I know when I was trying to complete Heritage USA, every possible attack that could have come — it came. I had the soothsayers prophesy my doom and PTL's destruction. I had the newspapers attack in the most vicious way. In the middle of everything else, the finances began to drop off. Then the Federal Government came in on us.

But just as Nehemiah's builders were armed with swords, I was armed with the believer's sword — the Word of God! I wore a medallion around my neck engraved with the scripture, "No weapon formed against thee shall prosper," (Is. 54:7), to remind me God had promised me the victory. I stood firm on His promise, even when it didn't look as though things could possibly work out.

For two years, Heritage USA stood silent. The very sight of it was like Satan himself mocking the work of the Lord. But you know, God had the victory in the end. He breathed life back into the project, and it is to His glory that it stands completed today.

It's not always easy when Satan is fighting you, in fact it is never easy. But as long as you stay armed with the mighty Word of God, you will have the victory.

That's a promise from God!

Don't Be A Wreck-Watcher!

"Look straight ahead; don't even turn your head to look."

— *Proverbs 4:25 (LB)*

People seem to be fascinated by wrecks and accidents. Did you ever notice how traffic almost stops in both directions on a highway if there's been a wreck? Cars slow to a crawl just to get a look at the damage.

One of our employees recently had an accident in just such circumstances. While passing a wreck, he was trying to get a peek and ran up on the median, demolishing his own car.

I think there's a lesson there for some of us in the Body of Christ. God's people have their share of "wrecks" in life. We're living in times when it's not easy to maintain a steady Christian walk. And occasionally a brother, sister, or family falls by the wayside.

I thank God for Good Samaritans. God is pleased when we reach down and offer help to one who's fallen or troubled. All too often, someone makes it his business to be an eager spectator of other people's problems without being any sort of help. He's not really concerned with the problem, he's just excited by the wreck!

God wants you to be sensitive to the needs of others. If you can be a part of meeting those needs, enter in. But if you can't be of help, move on. Don't tell your pastor how he ought to minister to a certain person. Don't insist on being "up on" everyone else's problems. Don't get excited by others' misfortunes — you may get your eyes off of God and end up a "total wreck" yourself!

Heavenly Treasures

"But lay up for yourselves treasures in heaven, where neither moth nor rust doth corrupt, and where thieves do not break through nor steal. For where your treasure is, there your heart will be also."

— *Matthew 6:20-21*

Experts differ as to what the best investment is in the recessed economy of today. The Bible is clear in saying that this world offers no real security, so you'd better have Jesus Christ. "Trust in the Lord and do good, and verily thou shalt be fed." The only superior investment is in God.

It's best not to put your hope and faith in money, gold, land, or anything else. You may remember what happened during the Great Depression. People jumped out of windows because they couldn't face the panic of losing all of their stocks and money. Those who had their faith in God were able to be happy, no matter what.

My financial advice would be, put your trust in God. Remember, you can't take your money or fame to Heaven. The only thing you can take with you, to Heaven or hell, is another person. Did you know that? Think of someone you know right now and plan to take that person with you to Heaven.

As you give of your substance, your time, and your love, the Bible says, you're building treasures in heaven; therefore, the most important thing is people.

Have *you* done everything in your power to see that the person *you* thought of is going to Heaven? If not, begin today to win that soul for Christ. It will be nice to get up there and have some friends who can show you around. Share Jesus with others today — and get rich in God!

Truth In God's Word

"For the Word of God is quick and powerful,
and sharper than a two-edged sword."
— Hebrews 4:12

I am constantly amazed at how seemingly intelligent, educated people can say the Word of God is not true. The Bible affects everybody in our country whether they realize it or believe it.

Just think about all of the cliches that come from the Bible: "To wash one's hands of something" (Matt. 27:24), "A labor of love" (Heb. 6:10), "A fly in the ointment" (Ecc. 10:1), "A thorn in my side" (Num. 33:55), "To see the handwriting on the wall" (Dan. 5:5), "Pearls before swine" (Matt. 7:6), "The nature of the beast" (Rev. 19:20).

I could go on, but I think you see my point. And not only has our speech been affected by passages from the Bible, but just think of the effect of Biblical holidays. People celebrate Christmas from Thanksgiving to New Years (whether they acknowledge it as Christ's birthday or not).

Then, there is Easter and the celebration it brings — American culture is married to Christianity. We are one nation under God — regardless of what some atheists try to do!

Why have these days and the sayings become part of our culture? Because the Bible is truth, and these sayings ring of truth that can apply in many areas of our lives. They are nuggets of wisdom that even the "world" can't deny.

Our holidays are a great time of celebration, and the world is jealous of that. I guess that's why Satan has tried to ruin these special days with the emphasis on Easter baskets and eggs, and spending money on expensive Christmas gifts rather than emphasizing the Biblical occasions they represent.

If you have Jesus in your heart, keep Jesus in your celebration and in your speech.

Your Weakness — God's Strength

". . . Most gladly therefore will I rather glory in my infirmities, that the power of Christ may rest upon me."

— *2 Corinthians 12:9*

People have said to me, "Jim, I'm so weak. Can God use me?" I'll tell you something: God delights in using weak people. I believe each one of us has a weakness. Maybe yours is a tendency to gossip. Maybe you've had a problem with nicotine or alcohol and still have to fight to control it.

Let's be honest. As the bumper sticker says, "Christians aren't perfect, they're just forgiven." It's about time ministers, churches, and religious groups stopped putting on the phony front that says everything is perfect when you have Jesus. It's not. We still have a bunch of problems, maybe even more than before. But we've got a God to solve them for us one at a time. That's the difference!

I have a hard time relating to people who fly two feet off the ground and never have problems. There's something phony somewhere. Even the apostle Paul had a thorn in the flesh that kept him humble. In my own life, there have been problems that I've asked God to remove and heard Him answer in love, "I'm going to let you live with that because I want to show my glory in you and let people know Jim Bakker isn't perfect or any sort of god."

Are you bogged down in thinking about your weakness? If you will take that thing and lay it on the altar before God, He can move through it. Don't say you're too weak. Give God all you've got and slap the devil in the face by glorying in your weakness. When God is through with you, your weakness will be your strength. That's what Paul meant. In His good time, God will use you — old or young, weak or strong.

Loving and Sharing

"Be ye therefore followers of God, as dear children, and walk in love, as Christ also hath loved us."

— Ephesians 5:1, 2

We laugh at the story of the new Methodist preacher that moved to a little town. The ministers of the other two churches in town invited him to go fishing with them one Saturday.

They were all sitting in a small boat fishing in a nearby lake. After a few hours, they ran out of bait. "No problem," said the Baptist preacher, "I'll go get some more."

He stood up, stepped out of the boat, and the Methodist preacher watched wide-eyed as he tipped toed across the top of the water to the lake edge. A few minutes later, he returned with the bait.

A few more hours passed and they ran out of bait again. This time the Pentecostal preacher volunteered to go get some. Once more, the new preacher watched amazed as the Pentecostal pastor walked across the water to the shore.

The next time they ran out, the Methodist preacher volunteered. "I've got just as much faith as they do," he thought to himself. He took one step out of the boat and sank to the bottom.

The Baptist turned to the Pentecostal preacher and said, "You reckon we ought to have told him where those stepping stones are?"

It's a funny illustration, but it was a point. We have to share with the others in the Body of Christ!

Part of loving is sharing. And that love has to oversee the denominational boundaries we set up. If we truly profess to love the Lord, we have to love our brothers and sisters in Him.

And that, my friend, means sharing.

Saltiness

"Ye are the salt of the earth: but if the salt have lost his savor, wherewith shall it be salted?...."

— *Matthew 5:13*

Until explorers brought back spices from the Orient, people in Europe ate a bland diet. Lack of refrigeration and food preservation, along with poor sanitary conditions, made eating meat risky for even the wealthy. Salt and spices were among the greatest treasures laid at the feet of kings. Salt and seasonings, and the know-how to use them, made eating both savory and safer, with salt to preserve foods and season for taste.

No wonder Jesus called Christians "salt." To a world sick of a monotonous diet of fear, hate, guilt, and suffering, a Christian, who's really tasty with the love of God, is great seasoning. Christians are the only sprinkling of true joy, hope, and encouragement in a bitter world.

A Christian's words or actions, sprinkled on a situation, can preserve like salt, too, helping to retain truth and justice in the midst of confusion and corruption. The witness of born-again believers is the only thing that's keeping the world from total decadence and destruction.

Christians are the only answer to this lost and dying world, but, like salt, we're only effective if we get out of the "shaker." Christians shouldn't keep to themselves. Jesus told us to go into the highways and hedges and mingle with unbelievers and compel them to come to Him.

Let your love and joy in God make others thirsty for what you have. Share freely with others what Jesus has done for you. As a Christian, try to "taste" like Jesus in your conversation and all that you do. The only sample of heaven's flavor some people may get will be what your lived and spoken testimony adds to their lives today.

The Only Way

"Thy word is a lamp unto my feet, and a light unto my path."

— *Psalm 119:105*

During the past decade, road maps have become a must for every driver. They help you find the most direct course to your destination. Relying on your intuition to get from place to place can be an exasperating experience. By refusing to consult a road map, a person will likely get lost.

Life has been called a "journey" or "road" that has to be traveled. But, God has provided a road map for the Christian to follow. When the Bible is read and its truths practiced daily, it will steer you clear of many a dead end street and assist you in making decisions at dangerous intersections of your life.

Like unpredictable weather conditions and driver carelessness, there are experiences and problems we face unexpectedly. Christians aren't promised an accident or problem-free life, but rather a peaceful and free assurance of salvation. You can also refer to the Bible as a traveler's first aid kit with its promises of God's help in every situation we find ourselves.

When we read how God intervened for the men and women in the Bible on their behalf and granted them the wisdom and strength they needed, we also see His promises to do the same for us.

It would be foolish for a lost person to refuse a free map with clear directions. Likewise, it is foolish for a person, who is lacking direction and purpose in their life, to refuse the Word of God to help them.

Know the assurance of God's love and concern for you. It will move you in a positive direction to help you weather storms and avoid eternal disaster. Make your destination Heaven by accepting Jesus Christ into your heart today and using the divine road map — God's Word.

The Happy Woman

"And blessed is she that believeth: for there shall be a performance of those things which were told her from the Lord."

— *Luke 1:45*

TAMMY: I believe that there are no happier women in the world than Christian women! I know saying that is like holding up a red flag to feminists, but even they might be a little embarrassed over the results of a survey taken a few years ago.

Redbook, a non-Christian women's magazine, conducted a survey to determine the attitudes of women towards themselves, their husbands, their jobs, their children — their lives.

In nearly every category, Christian women expressed the most satisfaction. The lowest, on the scale of personal satisfaction, were feminists and career women without families.

The interpreters of the survey had no explanation for this, because they expected the results to be a lot different. Those who said that the Christian way of life for women is "old hat," and needs to be abolished along with other social evils, had some pretty fast talking to do.

Of course, we ladies who belong to the Lord could have explained it to them — the reason Christian women are the happiest is love!

We love our husbands and our children. We lavish love and care on our homes. As we give and serve, God multiplies it all back to us!

Ladies, God has given us so many precious promises. And if we will believe them and obey God, we'll continue to have the contentment and satisfaction feminists are still searching for.

I'm glad the world's surveys are proving God's ways are best. Not that we needed proof! We've known all along the way to happiness is through God.

The Present Help

"God is our refuge and strength, a very present help in trouble."

— *Psalm 46:1*

It seems like whenever we're in trouble, we begin thinking God's "out to lunch." When times get rough, we sometimes can't imagine that God's still there. That's because we think God's only present when we have certain feelings. You've heard people say "Oh, how I feel the presence of God in this place!" But they rarely say it when the place is a hard one.

God is everywhere, and He's promised never to leave us or forsake us. In fact, today's verse says that He's not only present when we're in trouble, He's *very* present! We may not "feel" Him, but He's there. The presence of God isn't a feeling, it's a fact, and one on which we can depend.

Often times, the problem that looms in front of us is the thing that generates the most feelings. And if we let those feelings get the best of us, before long, they overwhelm all our vision of the Lord. A pile of bills can seem bigger than God. A sickness can seem all-powerful. A fear can look bigger than King Kong! And we panic and wonder, "Where is God?"

Well, He's right there, if we'll only call out to Him. No problem is bigger than He is, no sorrow is greater, no need is beyond His supply. God is always with us in trouble, to help, as only He can.

If you've got a tough problem, a dire need, or a feeling of depression or hopelessness you can't conquer today, I urge you to look to God right now. Don't wait to feel His presence or hear a voice from heaven. Call out to Him this moment, and He'll hear you. He's ready to answer. Turn your eyes from what's troubling you. Let God take care of it, and the problem will be "out to lunch!"

A Living Letter

" . . . Ye are manifestly declared to be the epistle of Christ . . . not written with ink, but with the Spirit of the living God . . . . "

— *2 Corinthians 3:3*

"I'll believe it when I see it," the skeptics always say. Today, you have to prove everything. Words aren't enough; people demand absolute proof.

Today, the word "Christian" is so loosely defined it carries little punch in the world. To some it means simply having their name on a church roll book. To others, it's going to church on Sunday. Some people think they're Christians just because their parents were.

But like everything else today, unless there's evidence to support your claim to being a Christian, it won't mean anything to others. Paul called Christians "Living epistles known and read of all men" (2 Corinthians 3:2). Saying "I believe" does not convince other people to believe. The world needs to see a living Bible. Its verses have to be people alive in the Spirit of God, who radiate the reality of His love working for good in the lives of those who trust and believe in Him.

Every Christian ought to live a daily sermon before his or her co-workers, classmates, friends, and especially their own family — not a solemn one, or the "fire and brimstone" type, but a living testimony of Christ inside that backs up the outward witness. That's the only sermon a lot of people will ever receive. The people around us will take notice only when they see God's love and the likeness of Christ in our actions, as well as our words.

What kind of life will people "read" if they watch you today? God wants you to live your faith vibrantly every minute. Make Jesus Christ your lifestyle. You never know who might be reading today's page of your life.

Raw Material

" ... All things are possible to him that believeth."

— Mark 9:23

Just about any product on the market today started out as raw material. Right now, men and machines are transforming the basic ingredients from animal, mineral, and vegetable substances into goods and products you use every day.

But there's another type of raw material that can't be seen: time to organize, and talents and abilities to be developed. That kind of "raw material" is in your own hands.

The final value of any type of raw material depends on the use made of it. Consider a bar of steel. As raw material, it's worth only ten dollars. But if you make watch springs out of it, the same piece of material is worth a total of $500,000. What a vivid contrast in value with increased usefulness!

God has equipped you with the raw materials to become the person He's designed you to be. You're probably aware of a lot of them, and no one has more time than you do each day to develop them. But that's going to take self-discipline, work, and some concrete goals. Once you've got these in focus, you can start to use your time and abilities to fulfill the vision you have for your life.

That refinement process won't be painless. It hurts to discipline yourself, and it takes self-confidence to be the best you can. But the molding will make you a better person.

God can help you put it all together, if you'll ask Him. Maybe you don't see how you can fulfill your goals and dreams with your abilities or background. Well, God wants you to know right now that, though with men it looks impossible, with Him, all things are possible. Don't give up that dream or goal. Don't lose sight of what you are — don't lose confidence in what you can be! You may think you're nothing but raw material now. But remember: God and you can do anything!

God Knows Even Before We Do!

"But when ye pray, use not vain repetitions, as the heathen do: for they think that they shall be heard for their much speaking. Be not ye therefore like unto them: for your Father knoweth what things ye have need of before ye ask Him."

— *Matthew 6:7-8*

I love to preach on God's perfect timing, because I can think of so many instances in my own walk with the Lord where He supplied an answer to a prayer before I even asked.

In 1977, when the idea of a Christian campground — a Total Living Center — began to form in my mind, we began to look for land.

We *just happened* to find some beautiful acreage that already had its own water sewage treatment plant on the property — all for the price we would have had to pay to install the plant ourselves!

When I began searching for the right man to design the Fort Heritage campground, I discovered there was a man who'd just come to work at PTL as a janitor — a janitor who had recently graduated with a degree in campground design and management, and couldn't figure out why God had brought him here.

Months earlier, when he'd been hired, there was certainly no campground around, and the vision for Fort Heritage wasn't even born yet. He just *knew* that he was supposed to be here. Sam McLendon is now my Vice President in charge of Fort Heritage!

We Christians can take great security in knowing that even now God is arranging circumstances and bringing things about in our lives in answer to yet unspoken prayers.

Today, take comfort in knowing you don't have to say just the right words or speak the proper amount of sentences to have your needs met. God has already answered yesterday your prayers of tomorrow.

Everlasting Comfort

"Now our Lord Jesus Christ himself, and God, even our Father, which hath loved us, and hath given us everlasting consolation and good hope through grace, Comfort your hearts, and stablish you in every good word and work."
— *2 Thessalonians 2:16, 17*

You may go out into the world to make money and make a lot of it, by virtue of a lot of hard work. That money might be quite a comfort and consolation to you. But it can never be an "eternal comfort." You may spend it all or lose it. You might invest it in the stock market and watch it shrink into nothing. You might get sick and spend it all on doctor bills, or you may die, and leave it all behind.

You may decide to go to college or a university and get all the knowledge you can. You might acquire a lot of doctorates and college degrees that might give you a lot of satisfaction. But if a heartache comes, or you get depressed or soul-sick, there's no comfort in a handful of sheepskins.

You can go out and exercise and become a famous athlete and win medals. But you might walk half-way across a street and get struck by a car or grow old and feel your vigor and youth slip away. What comfort will your medals be to you then?

None of these earthly satisfactions, or any others you may imagine, comfort you forever. But the comfort God gives to His people lasts forever. The joy and peace that come from knowing you're a child of God can survive shocks, trials, persecutions, aging ... even death itself!

Because there's an eternal comfort in Jesus Christ, look today to find opportunities for good works and good words. There's a true and enduring investment in God's business — because God has a true and eternal investment in you!

God Or Baal?

"And Elijah came unto all the people, and said, How long halt ye between two opinions? If the Lord be God, follow Him: but if Baal, then follow him . . . . "

— *1 Kings 18:21*

In this passage, Elijah was challenging the prophets of the idol Baal. The people of Israel had forsaken God to worship this idol, and Elijah had set up a challenge: Two stone altars were set up with sacrifices on them. Both Elijah and the prophets of Baal would try to pray fire down from heaven to consume the sacrifice. Well, in spite of the fact that Elijah soaked the sacrifice and altar, the fire of God came down and licked up the sacrifice, the altar, and the water!

At a difficult time in the ministry of PTL, a psychic magazine did my horoscope. They predicted that within a short time, the PTL ministry would collapse and that Jim Bakker would be dead. But God led me to this scripture. He said, "Go on television and challenge the devil." I began to research old Baal and found out that there was a male and a female Baal, and they were related to the stars and planets. I began to see a connection. God was telling me to challenge the prophets of astrology and the psychic predictors and their predictions.

And that's what I did. I challenged the prophets of doom, and God began to go to work. That very month was the greatest month for PTL ever financially. The editor of the psychic magazine started watching PTL and ended up calling and getting saved! He folded up his magazine, while PTL lives on for God.

Friend, if God's enemies speak against you, if prophets of doom are saying you don't have a chance, if the devil seems to be laughing at you and waiting for you to go under, you can challenge them today. Stand on God's Word. Yes, God is God! Serve Him with all your heart — and you'll see your enemies put to flight!

A Friend For All Times

"A friend loveth at all times, and a brother is born for adversity."

— *Proverbs 17:17*

"You look like you just lost your last friend." Has anyone ever made that remark to you? It makes me think of a sad and lonely picture, like a child sitting at a window looking out on a dismal rainy day.

Everybody understands loneliness. I know the feeling. As a teenager, I worked as a disc jockey for school dances, yet I was empty inside, feeling like no one cared. I guess we all suffer loneliness at times.

People need each other more than they think. A psychologist once told me that seventy percent of mental problems today could be solved if each patient had a close friend to trust and share with. Having a friend is the best prescription for many ills.

The verse above talks about lasting friendship. It's worth more than money. If that fails, real friends won't disappear. A friend can know the best and worst about you and still believe in you, trust you, and love you. I hope you have friends like that to depend on in times of trouble. I've been grateful that through PTL, I've been able to be a friend to so many.

Jesus Christ is the pattern for all friendship. He "sticks closer than a brother," says Proverbs 18:24. His friendship goes beyond a blood relationship. He loves you, in every situation of life, and He'll help you with every problem and supply every need you have. And praise God, Jesus forgives and forgets your past failures and gives courage for facing each new day. He came to understand your loneliness by hanging in agony on the cross.

Jesus, if there is emptiness in the heart of this reader today, fill it right now with your joy and peace. In your precious name, Amen.

Small Things

"For who hath despised the day of small things?...."

— *Zechariah 4:10*

We're living in "big" days. Government is big. Businesses are big. We have the "Big Three" television networks. Sometimes it seems as though the "little people" don't have much of a chance any more. But I'll tell you something: God hasn't forgotten the little people, and He doesn't want anyone despising little things, or "little people," either.

Don't ever forget that God has a special feeling for the "small things." Jesus Himself knew a lot about them. After all, He was born in a stable and raised in a small town up in the hills by folks of no great repute. The Bible doesn't tell us that from age twelve to age thirty He accomplished things of great significance. I think it's one of the glories of the Gospel that Jesus knew how to be "ordinary." That's why He was able to relate so well to the needs of people. And it's one of the reasons why He was both loved and hated so much.

Think of all the "small things" God used in the Bible: a rod, five stones from a brook, a donkey's jawbone, a ram's horn, five barley loaves, and two little fish. Nobody despised those small things on the day God did big things with them!

Some people might say that PTL is a "big ministry" today. But it didn't start that way. When we opened up in Charlotte, we broadcast on just one station, with a handful of people, from a room above a furniture store. But we didn't despise those "days of small things." Instead, we did our best to make the very most of them. And as a result, God gave us the increase.

You know, God hasn't built PTL on big donations — He's used small ones. It's "little people" who are faithful who make the great things happen for God. No matter how "small" the thing you do for God is today, God thinks it's great!

A Way Of Escape

". . . But God is faithful, who will not suffer you to be tempted above that ye are able, but will with the temptation also make a way to escape, that ye may be able to bear it."
— *1 Corinthians 10:13*

From the history of the Old Testament to the New, every man of God who has faced an impossible situation, God has given a way of escape. Let me name a few of them for you.

There was a preacher of righteousness called Noah, and when he faced the world's worst flood, God made a way of escape for him. Abraham was about to kill and sacrifice his only son Isaac, but God made a way of escape for him. Joseph was thrown into a pit and sold into slavery, but God made a way of escape. Moses came up against the Red Sea with Pharaoh's mighty army behind him — and God made a way of escape.

David came up against a giant, but God made a way of escape. Mordecai was framed and facing the gallows, but God made him a way of escape. Daniel was thrown into the lion's den, but God made a way of escape. Jonah ran from God and messed up his life — and God made a way of escape. Even baby Jesus was plotted to be destroyed with the newborn babies, but God made a way of escape.

And I want you to know that the enemy came into PTL like a flood, but God made a way of escape! I was called by some atheists the most dangerous Christian on earth. We were millions of dollars in debt. The newspapers attacked us. I was tempted to give up. But I hung on, and God made a way of escape!

You may be facing a problem today that you just don't know how to handle. You may be tempted to pack up and run from it. But don't fall for that line from the devil. Hold on — and watch God make a way of escape — and snare the devil with it!

God Cares About Everything

"Behold the fowls of the air: for they sow not, neither do they reap, nor gather into barns; yet your heavenly Father feedeth them. Are ye not much better than they?"

— Matthew 6:26

TAMMY: The Lord has taught me many lessons in faith over the years — some of them hard, some strange, but some truly delightful.

One of the more delightful lessons in believing God as my source came early, when Jim and I were just kids starting off our ministry together. I learned an important thing about God — He not only cares enough to provide for our every need, but He also cares about meeting the desires of our hearts at the same time.

I had asked Jim to buy me a shawl. He knew how badly I wanted one, but we just couldn't afford it, so he had to say no to me.

A few weeks later, we were holding a meeting in Florida. Although it was autumn, we felt like there was a heat wave going on. But in the middle of this Florida heat wave, a woman came to the door carrying a white shawl! This lady said it probably seemed silly to us, but she felt the Lord had told her to make the shawl and give it to me. Little did she know that God was teaching me a precious lesson in faith.

So many times since then, God has met one of my needs with a desire of my heart. God is so good to His children. He just wants us to know that we mean so very, very much to Him. Today, think back over the times God has shown you His love by proving your faith in Him is well-placed, and thank Him for it.

The Schoolmaster

"What shall we say then? Is the law sin?
Nay, I had not known sin, but by the law . . . the
law was our schoolmaster to bring us unto
Christ . . . . "
— *Romans 7:7, Galatians 3:24*

A recent Gallup poll showed that 84 percent of Americans claim to believe the Ten Commandments are still valid today. However, more than 50 percent couldn't even recall five of them! Folks, no wonder we see morality falling apart in this country! Without knowing what God's Commandments are, a lot of people are doing wrong and don't even know it!

Some of our Heritage School evangelism interns have found this out in trying to witness to young people. They'll go up to a teenager in a shopping mall and say, "Jesus died for your sins. He's the answer to your need."

And the kid will answer, "Hey man, what sins? I'm not hurting anybody. And you know what I really need right now? An ounce of 'pot.' "

That's really sad.

People need to know what right is and what wrong is. That is what the law of God is all about. We don't get right with God by obeying the law — that's impossible, with our sinful natures. Only Jesus obeyed the law fully. But the law can actually "take us by the hand" and lead us to Christ to be saved.

The "schoolmaster" this verse talks about was a special slave whose job it was to take a Roman child by the hand and make sure he got to and from school. When school days were over, the "schoolmaster" was no longer needed. God's law leads us to Christ, because we know we can't keep it, and we cry out to Jesus to have mercy and save us. Then, if we get off the track, the law through the Holy Spirit takes us in hand again and points us back to Christ.

Get to know God's law. Roy Rogers, who's been a highly successful father, thinks every child ought to know it by heart. And I agree. You're never too old to learn. Write God's law in your memory today — it'll keep you from "playing hooky."

Looking Back

"Remember Lot's wife. Whoever shall seek to save his life shall lose it; and whosoever shall lose his life shall preserve it."

— *Luke 17:32-33*

In the Dead Sea region of Israel today stand curious pillars of salt the Arabs call "Lot's Wife."

They are referring to the story of a woman who started to flee reluctantly, the imminent destruction of her city, Sodom, for a place of safety the Lord provided.

Lagging behind her husband and daughters, she looked back towards the wicked city, and was instantly transformed into a pillar of salt.

Bible scholars say the word "looked back" in Hebrew means something more like "looking intently." In other words, Lot's wife was longing to return to the home and lifestyle she loved. In seeking to hang on to her life in evil Sodom, she lost her life when the city was destroyed.

Often, the Lord will try and remove us from a place of danger we've settled into. It may be a world of materialism that's endangering our spiritual growth, or an atmosphere of decadence that slowly drains our vitality for the Lord from us.

Whatever the particular pitfall we're making our home in, we can resist the Lord's urging to flee, turning back instead, with longing eyes, toward the comfortable lifestyle we prize. But, in that very act of trying to preserve our cozy life, we face the risk of losing our true life in Jesus Christ.

Has God been warning you about a dangerous lifestyle you're holding on to? If so, my friends, I most strongly urge you to flee that life, without backward glances, for God has said that only in losing our life do we preserve it. Run to His place of safety, today.

Ask, Seek, and Knock

"Ask, and it shall be given you; seek, and ye shall find; knock, and it shall be opened unto you: For every one that asketh receiveth; and he that seeketh findeth; and to him that knocketh it shall be opened."

— *Matthew 7:7-8*

How many of us talk to God on a daily basis? Do you just kneel down to pray when you have an urgent need or request? Prayer does answer needs, but prayer is also asking, and receiving, seeking and finding, knocking, and opening.

Prayer is talking with God. When you pray, you shouldn't tense up and be scared of what you say for God is your Father and your friend. You should talk to God like you would talk to your closest friend.

When you make your request known to God, He acts on it. Whether your need is material or spiritual, you can ask God and receive if you know the will of God.

If you aren't sure of God's reaction to your request, you aren't seeking and finding. You are to seek His will in prayer about your need until you find the answer.

On the other hand, if you know the will of God but your prayer reached a closed door, you need to knock until the door is opened. I think of this prayer as mountain-moving faith because it is miracle working prayer. A "knocking prayer" keeps knocking until the impossible becomes possible.

All things are possible when you ask, seek, and knock. God wants us to grow in Him and through prayer we grow both spiritually and emotionally. By asking for God to help us we are relying totally on Him. By seeking, when we pray, we are learning more about God's will. And, by knocking, when the door is closed, we are seeing miracles happen. Don't be afraid to ask, seek, and knock.

I Am

"And thou shalt call his name Jesus."
— Matthew 1:21

Mike Adkins sings a powerful song of ministry with these words, and Oral Roberts has preached anointed sermons quoting them. Let the names of Jesus and the Word of God minister to you today:

PRINCE OF PEACE (Is. 9:6), MIGHTY GOD (Is. 9:6), WONDER-FUL COUNSELOR (Is. 9:6), HOLY ONE (Mark 1:24), LAMB OF GOD (John 1:29), PRINCE OF LIFE (Acts 3:15), LORD GOD ALMIGHTY (Rev. 15:3)

LION OF THE TRIBE OF JUDAH (Rev. 5:5), ROOT OF DAVID (Rev. 22:16), WORD OF LIFE (I John 1:1), AUTHOR AND FINISHER OF OUR FAITH (Heb. 12:2), ADVOCATE (I John 2:1), THE WAY (John 14:6), DAYSPRING (Luke 1:78), LORD OF ALL (Acts 10:36), I AM (John 5:58), SON OF GOD (John 1:34), SHEPHERD AND BISHOP OF SOULS (I Peter 2:25), MESSIAH (John 1:41), THE TRUTH (John 14:6).

SAVIOR (2 Peter 2:20), CHIEF CORNERSTONE (Eph. 2:20), KING OF KINGS (Rev. 19:16), RIGHTEOUS JUDGE (2 Tim. 4:8), LIGHT OF THE WORLD (John 8:12), HEAD OF THE CHURCH (Eph. 1:22), MORNING STAR (Rev. 22:16), SUN OF RIGHTEOUSNESS (Mal. 4:2), LORD JESUS CHRIST (Acts 15:11).

CHIEF SHEPHERD (I Peter 5:4), RESURRECTION AND LIFE (John 11:25), HORN OF SALVATION (Luke 1:69), GOVERNOR (Matt. 2:6), THE ALPHA AND OMEGA. (Rev. 1:8).

As I read these words, now on a popular poster in one of my employees offices, I was blessed again with the greatness of the God we serve.

Worship Him today!

A Monument To Death

"O death, where is thy sting? O grave, where is thy victory?"

— *1 Corinthians 15:55*

One of the greatest discoveries in the history of archeology was a monument to death. In the early part of this century, explorers digging in Egypt came upon a mound of dirt. As they dug, they came upon a building, made of huge bricks. They recognized its shape as that of an ancient Egyptian tomb.

This was a remarkable find. Most known Egyptian graves of that date had been broken into by robbers, and all their treasures had been carried off. But here was a tomb untouched!

As they broke through the entrance and shined their lights inside, they gasped at the amazing treasures: gold, silver, precious jewels, and fine garments beyond measure. And in a glorious gold casket was the mummy of the great young king for whom the tomb was built — Tutankhamen.

You may have seen "King Tut's" treasures when they toured the United States several years ago. They are indeed spectacular — but they are nothing but homage to a dead man.

There was another tomb sealed up many years ago in the Mid-East. No treasures were placed in it. It held the body of a crucified criminal, for whom it was not even made. It is empty today. But not because it was plundered by thieves or unearthed by archeologists. It is empty because the man buried in it is now alive! He lay in that tomb for three days and then rose from the dead! He, too, was a great King, but unlike "King Tut," Jesus is alive and still King!

King Tut's treasures are locked away in a museum. But the treasures of King Jesus are in heaven and walking this earth, the redeemed souls of men. Thank God as Christians, we don't look in admiration to a monument to death, but in wonder to a living Savior who triumphed over death! May Jesus be truly victorious in your heart today!

The Power Of The Written Word

"And the Lord answered me, and said, Write the vision, and make it plain upon tablets, that he may run that readeth it."
— *Habakkuk 2:2*

I'm very proud and delighted that Tammy Faye Bakker has had not one, but two books (*Run to the Roar* and *I Gotta Be Me*) among the top ten Christian bestsellers at the same time. We're really rejoicing in God over this new dimension in ministry that He's given Tammy. Alongside the rapid growth of Christian television and recordings, the Christian book business is booming, and millions of souls are being reached right now through the printed word. Christian tracts, newspapers, and magazines are finding their way around the world with the Gospel message. Praise God!

A few years ago, a minister in England told the following story: He was ministering at the deathbed of an elderly Christian woman, and he asked her how she had met Jesus. She reached over and found her Bible on the night table. From it, she took a piece of paper torn from an American journal, which contained part of a sermon by the great English preacher, Charles Spurgeon.

She explained that this scrap had been wrapped around a package that came to her from Australia. As she was unwrapping the package, those few words caught her attention and were the means of leading her to Christ.

Imagine that: God used part of a sermon preached in England, printed in America, wrapped around a package in Australia, sent to England, to save this woman!

That's only one example of the power of God's Word as it has gone out in print. Thank God today for the Bible you have in your home. There are nations where it's breaking the law to own religious books. Allow yourself to be ministered to by Christian literature. God has great treasures for you in the writings of His servants who minister in print.

The Deadly Pastime

"A gossip goes around spreading rumors,
while a trustworthy man tries to quiet them."
— Proverbs 11:13 (LB)

Few people can do more harm than a gossip. Rumor-mongers have tried to destroy PTL again and again. In fact, I've come to recognize a certain tactic of the devil: just before a real milestone in God is about to be reached, just as some much-needed facility is almost completed, the devil starts up the rumor mill. I've had to learn to ignore these sowers of discord and press on with God's business.

Gossip almost seems to have replaced baseball as America's national pastime. The newsstands are filled with gossip magazines. New biographies, about the seamy side of great public figures' lives, flood the bookstores every day. There are few newspapers today that don't carry a gossip column.

The Bible doesn't even talk about most of the things church people wag their fingers at as sin. There's no scripture that says, "Don't smoke or wear makeup or go the movies." I'm not advocating any of these things. But I do know that the Bible speaks out strongly against gossiping. Yet even Christians ignore those verses and spend much of their time gossiping about who's committing all those other "sins" the Bible never mentions!

A PTL employee once told Uncle Henry Harrison, "You know, in all the time I've been working here, I've never heard anyone say anything bad about you." Uncle Henry smiled and said, "Well, that could be because I don't pass on anything bad about anyone else." That's something I really love about that man — I can trust him to keep his ears and lips pure.

Take a hint from Uncle Henry and today's verse. Don't listen to gossip, and don't pass it on. If someone tries to burn your ears with gossip, just say, "No thanks, I don't want to hear that." Be trustworthy in your ears and your tongue today.

To Do Or Not To Do

"Great peace have they which love thy law: and nothing shall offend them."
— *Psalm 119:165*

Shakespeare asked the question, "To be, or not to be?" But I think a far more important one is, "To do or not to do?" The consequences of your answer to this question will affect not only the quality of your life but also the very course your life will take.

In the garden of Eden, Eve faced the temptation to sin. She chose to give in to that temptation — "to do." Her life changed drastically from that moment, and the lives of millions of people yet unborn were altered at the same time.

God could have made things easier for Eve by programming all the right choices into her. God did not want a world full of puppets because they could not have satisfied the desire He had for the special kind of fellowship He wanted with man. God wanted a communion that required a voluntary commitment of man to love Him and follow His laws freely and willingly.

Now, God didn't put you on earth and require the right decisions of you without giving you any guidelines. He has given you His Word. When you study the Bible, and meditate on its teachings, you tuck away God's guidelines for the lifestyle He wants you to live, deep within your heart. Then, when a situation arises that requires a choice of action on your part, you know what God says you should do. Knowing the right thing to do is half the battle. The other half, and the victory, is in setting your will to do it!

You have a choice today. You can choose to follow God or to give in to temptation and sin. To choose sin is death. To choose God is eternal life. Decide today to make the Bible the guide to your every action. Get to know it really well. For that book will make all your other decisions a whole lot easier.

You've Got To Take It All!

". . . they have no knowledge that set up the wood of their graven image, and pray unto a god that cannot save."

— Isaiah 45:20

There is a story about a man who came up to an evangelist after a service and said, "I'd like to buy about $5.00 worth of God."

"Uh, how's that?" replied the evangelist.

"I want to buy about $5.00 worth of God. Let me explain, my life's not all that bad, you see, and I think just a little bit of God will be enough to clean up the spots that aren't quite right. If I give you that much money, will you give me that much of God?"

"Listen friend," the preacher answered, "you can't buy just a piece or two of God. If you want Him at all, you've got to take all of Him."

"But I don't need that much of God," the man protested, "If I did, I'd buy more."

"Well," the preacher said, "that's your first mistake — you can't buy God. If you don't know, that all of you, needs all of Him, you'll never have Him at all."

"Disappointed, the man shook his head and walked away.

A lot of people want a God they can manage rather than one who will manage them. They want a "god" they can buy, instead of the living God who bought men with His precious blood. That's why false gods and idols have always been so popular. You know, you can still go into a store today and buy an idol. You can buy a Buddha or an African idol or a Hindu idol. And you can pray to it, just the same as you can to the true God. But I'll tell you something — it'll never save your soul from hell.

No, you can't buy a little bit of God. There's no price tag on Him. There's nothing you've got that could ever be worth all He is. And yet, He gave all He is for you! His shed blood was price enough to buy you out of the clutches of the devil. Make sure today you're worshipping the God who can't be bought! But who gave Himself freely for you and me.

Three Steps To Righteousness

"Wherefore, my beloved brethren, let every man be swift to hear, slow to speak, slow to wrath."

— *James 1:19*

This one verse holds the key to living a righteous life as a Christian.

Be swift to hear. How many of us are quick to receive new revelations from God through His Word. The easy thing to do is to read the passages we become used to — that don't threaten our lifestyles. Thus, we become stagnant in our relationship with God.

God wants us to grow in Him, and the only way to do that is to be swift to hear from Him.

Be slow to speak. We get ourselves into more trouble talking than almost anything else! In the third chapter of James, verses 3-7 we read:

"Behold we put bits in the horses' mouths, that they may obey us; and we turn about their whole body. Behold also the ships, which though they be so great, and are driven of fierce winds, yet are they turned about with a very small (rudder). . . . Even so, the tongue is a little member, and boasteth great things. Behold, how great a matter a little fire kindleth!"

It is easy to see why God wants us to be slow to speak. Each thing we want to say, we'd better think about first. Like the kids used to say, "Make sure your brain is in gear before your mouth is in motion."

Be slow to wrath. When we are mad, we are very apt to say something we don't mean or to hurt someone we love. Even Jesus got mad in the temple when the money-hungry people were selling their wares in God's house. But it's easy to lose our temper for no good reason, and that's what God is saying here. Be slow in getting mad.

If we ever get to the place where all of these are working in our lives, we know God will be pleased!

Live That Vision

"... Your young men shall see visions."
— Joel 2:28

You're never too old to serve God, or too young, either. This verse talks about young people, and this is surely a day when God is not leaving out the young people. Just look around. Evie Tornquist Karlsson, the number one sacred music artist in America today, began recording when she was just a little girl. She made her first major record when she was only thirteen years old.

Debbie Boone has had one of the best selling hit records in history. The Humbard kids are all being used of the Lord. If it wasn't for the youth, we could never have built the PTL Television Network. (That's because, if you had experience, you would never have dared to go into an operation like PTL!)

God has given these young people a vision. Some of our camera men, directors and artists didn't know a lot about TV when they started. They were willing to work hard and learn, because they had a vision.

No long ago, the PTL Television Network was just a dream in the hearts of a small group of us. We'd lost everything we had except our vision and our faith in God. With only a few dollars between us, our young people began to design remote trucks and studios. Today we have a multimillion dollar remote truck that can televise broadcasts to millions around the country.

Now, many of our Heritage School students are coming up with visions of their own which will some day make valuable contributions to the future of Christian television.

No matter what your age, if you will live your vision, God will bring it to pass. You might be mired down at a detour right now. You might not be able to get anyone else to share your vision. Never mind: Hold to it, have faith in God, and you will see it happen.

As He Is, So Are You!

"Herein is our love made perfect . . . because as He is, so are we in this world."
— *1 John 4:17*

In the name of Jesus, you are God's extension in this world. You are the one that God wants to show His love through to your companion and to your neighbor. God wants you to reach out and touch people for Jesus' sake. To listen to the cries and hurts of others.

Jesus is in the caring business, and He put all of us into it, too. Love is something that has to be demonstrated. Love isn't love until it's demonstrated. Many people get "spiritual," and recite the Word and sing the hymns loudly. But they don't have any love, and that's not spiritual — that's wickedness, a religion without God.

Do you know that people are dying in this world because nobody will touch them? People are scared to even hug each other. Christians don't even hug each other any more. But it's not "dirty" to hug somebody. Somebody might need you to hold their hand and say, "It's going to be okay. I care about you." People have left all the caring up to the preachers. I want to tell you something: The preachers can't do it all. There's not enough time — not enough energy for one man to love everybody. God has told us that we are to love one another. What's standing in our way?

It's going to have to start in our own marriages or our own families and our own relationships right where we are. One of the nicest things you can do for somebody is to sit down and listen to him and hear his heart's cry. Jesus did a lot of that. Right now, ask God to release that mental block, that something inside you that keeps you from being that caring person you want to be. Then, step out in faith and bring compassion and love to that person near you who needs it most.

Feed His Sheep

". . . And he said unto Him, Lord . . . thou knowest that I love thee. Jesus saith unto him, Feed My sheep."

— *John 21:17*

I feel like every time we care for a Partner at PTL, we're caring for God's people. These are the "sheep" that write us and support us — and they deserve our very best.

If our Partners don't get the book or Bible they write for, we're not feeding the sheep. An old preacher's saying is, "You can shear the sheep a lot, and if you feed them, they'll give you wool. But you can only skin them once." You can't claim to love Jesus and not do everything you can to feed His sheep.

That's why when a guest or a Partner comes to visit us, they are special, honored guests, and we've pledged to feed them, and not to hurt them in any way at all. We want to care for and give them love. PTL isn't here to turn a profit. As we run this ministry right, it takes care of itself. We try to balance good business with good ministry, because good business is Biblical. All good business principles are in the Bible.

It is worth while for every child of God to give that some thought. Every one of us has a ministry. Every one of us has at least one "sheep" in our life who needs feeding. You may work in a business or a ministry. You may teach school, be a student or a housewife. You may even live in a nursing home. But there is someone near you, or within writing or calling distance whose life you touch. Ask yourself, am I feeding that person?"

A word of encouragement, a verse of Scripture — a gift of money, or something you've made special — a prayer or a kiss or hug, even a thank you for a service well-rendered — a bit of good advice or sound instruction — a cup of coffee or a delicious meal — a bunch of flowers — All these are "food" for someone near you. Make sure they get it today.

Mental Junk Food

"Finally, brethren, whatsoever things are true, whatsoever things are honest, whatsoever things are just, whatsoever things are pure, whatsoever things are of good report; if there be any virtue, if there be any praise, think on these things."

— *Philippians 4:8*

TAMMY: Have you ever heard the expression, "You are what you eat?"

Well, I'll tell you something else, you are what you think, too!

Most of us know someone who is caught up in the health food craze. Jim is. He starts his day out with whole grain cereal and fruit and munches on raw vegetables and fruit juices all day long. He goes to a lot of trouble to avoid sugar and white flour, and I must say, it has paid off for him. He has kept his weight down and in many areas, his health has improved.

But, are we that careful about what we take into our minds? A lot of us have a steady diet of "mental junk food" — and like too much of any type of junk food — we have to pay a price for it.

If we fill our minds with soap opera problems instead of the good things of God — if we constantly dwell on the problems in our lives instead of the joys — if we spend more time reading the bad news in the newspapers instead of the good news in the Bible — then people, we are going to find our Christian joy is gone.

The Bible tells us to dwell on the good, the pure, and the lovely. God was very exact about what He wanted His children's mental food to be.

If you are feeding on mental junk food, make an effort to improve that area today. You'll be happier for it!

The Fraud

"Knowest thou not this of old, since man was placed upon earth, that the triumphing of the wicked is short, and the joy of the hypocrite but for a moment?"

— *Job 20:4-5*

Satan is a fraud. He's not what he cracks himself up to be. Sometimes I wish he did look like the popular idea of him, with horns and a tail, warts on his face, and a villainous look. Then nobody would be fooled by him. That's not how he comes on, though. He tries to imitate the most beautiful thing you can imagine. He'll pretend to be whatever you think is best for you. And it's not always easy to see through his disguise!

In the great Metropolitan Museum of Art in New York City, a huge bronze statue of a horse stood on display for almost forty years. It was hailed by art experts as one of the finest examples of ancient Greek sculpture. It was written about in books and admired by thousands of passersby.

But in 1967, the art world and the public was shocked. Special photographs taken with gamma rays proved beyond the shadow of a doubt that this "great" exhibit was a fraud. A clever sculptor had created it and sold it to another man who then claimed to "discover" it in some ruins. It was then sold to the museum for a large sum of money and dated back to the year 470 B.C. How embarrassing it was for the museum to have to admit that it had been made in the twentieth century!

The consequences are far worse for those who fall for the devil's tricks. You need the special "discernment" of God's Holy Spirit to help you unmask that old snake! Pray right now that God will re-fill you with His Holy Spirit if you haven't had a fresh anointing in a while — and fill you, for the first time, if you've never been filled before!

Real Faith

"But without faith, it is impossible to please God . . . . "

— *Hebrews 11:6*

A famous aerialist named Blondin once rode a bicycle over a tightrope stretched across Niagara Falls. The watching crowd was eagerly cheering for him, one man more loudly than the rest. Fixing his gaze on the man, Blondin asked, "Do you think I can do it again?" "Without a doubt," the man answered confidently. "Good," smiled Blondin, "Get on my shoulders and I'll ride you back across!" "Not me!" cried the man and quickly disappeared.

Faith in God requires more than being an enthusiastic spectator. It means climbing up on God's shoulders at times and trusting Him to carry you across troubled waters. However, like the man in the crowd, there are Christians who'll boast of their faith in God but balk when put in a position to act it out. It's sad that many Christians don't understand what faith in God really means. In daily living, they don't trust God to help or direct them in decision making. Instead, they fret and strive and flounder with their problems, thinking they have to work them out for themselves. They never learn that God won't just take us over the troubled waters, He'll also carry us through the mainstream of daily life.

You can't please God without trusting Him. He's very willing to help anyone who asks: "Cast all your cares upon Him, for He careth for you" (1 Peter 5:7).

Now, asking God to help you doesn't mean He wants you to lean back and let Him do all the *work*. But He does want you to leave all the *worrying* to *Him!* Whatever the problem, He can deal with it and show you what to do in the situation.

If you want more faith in God, begin today to exercise what faith you do have. God's shoulders are broad enough, and His love is great enough to carry you — and your problems.

Be Profitable For God

"So likewise ye, when ye have done all those things which are commanded you, say, We are unprofitable servants: we have done that which was our duty to do."

— *Luke 17:10*

Did you ever kind of "pat yourself on the back" because you did something for God? It's easy to want to take credit for having done a good job isn't it? But if you're ever in danger of getting a swelled head while working for God, read this verse. Jesus is saying here that even if you've done everything that God considers your duty, you've only earned the title of Unprofitable Servant.

If that's God's idea of an unprofitable servant, what is profit to Him? God wants us to be using our imaginations constantly to think of good things to do for others.

God is sovereign and takes such good care of His business. If He depended only on us, His profit margin wouldn't be very high. Somebody once asked an old country parson how many active members there were in his congregation. He replied, "They's all active. Half of them are active for the Lord and the other half for the devil!" He was luckier than most preachers, a lot of whose members don't seem to be active for anybody or anything!

God wants every member of every church and ministry to get into action for Him. Maybe it's time we started taking the teachings of Jesus seriously. Everybody pays lip service to them: "Oh, yes, I think the Sermon on the Mount is great. Jesus was a great teacher!" Well, He wasn't teaching just to be teaching, he meant us to do what He said. So let's do it!

"Jim," you say, "that's a tall order!" Well, it's no taller than Jesus' words. Yes, you'd need the strength of God Almighty to begin to measure up to all that Jesus taught. But that's the point, to get you to pray for that strength. Ask God right now to help you make your life *show a profit* for Him today.

Redeem The Time

"See then that ye walk circumspectly, not as fools, but as wise, redeeming the time, because the days are evil."

— Ephesians 5:16-17

Did you know that there are 168 hours in every week?

How much of that time do you spend seeking God? Well, if you go to Sunday School, church twice on Sunday, and once on Wednesday, that might add up to four to six hours a week. That's 2 percent to 4 percent of your time!

What about that other 162 hours?

Researchers say that in the average American home, the television is on at least five hours a day. By itself, that's a thirty-five hour chunk of time — 20 percent of the week! If you spend time reading "junk" books and gossip magazines, running around shopping centers, "hanging out with the boys," talking on the telephone, and spreading your time out on other God-less pursuits, is it any wonder if your life is short on victory in Jesus?

Try a little experiment. Take a glass and an eyedropper. Put in 164 drops of clear water. Then put in four or six drops (or however many hours you spend on the things of God every week) of ink or food coloring. You'll notice that a few drops will hardly change the color. But if you start putting in a bigger percentage of colored drops, soon, the water will take on that color strongly. Start adding prayer, Bible study, and rich fellowship with others who love Jesus, and it won't be long before your life with God, and before the world, takes on a different color, too.

Make up your mind today to stop putting "drops" of the wrong color into your life. Replace some of those hours that don't glorify God — and add some more time and activities that will show your true colors in Jesus.

Dream Tramplers

" ... Be ye steadfast, unmovable, always abounding in the work of the Lord, forasmuch as ye know that your labor is not in vain in the Lord."

— *1 Corinthians 15:58*

One night, I had a dream so vivid and real that I had to get out of bed and make a sketch of what I saw: a beautiful church building where families from all over the world would come to share and pray for souls to be won to Jesus. For years, I held on tightly to that vision.

It's amazing, though, how many people seemed determined to do all in their power to take it from me. They told me it was impossible. They told me it wasn't really God's will. They told me to give up and get practical. They tried everything they could to steal my dream.

I call these people the dream stealers. They're like the people who try to sap your strength by stealing your joy. I think these people are the greatest thieves in the world.

God tells us to stand firm. So, I stood steadfast and picked up the tattered pieces of my vision again and again. I wouldn't be swayed. Today, that Church building I saw in my dream is the same church building that's at Heritage Village. Families from all over the world do come, and thousands of souls have been won for the Lord through PTL Club telecasts that originate there — just like in my dream.

Many servants of the Lord have faced ridicule and persecution before they realized the dream God had given them. When Joseph shared his dream with his brothers, they mocked him, plotted to kill him, and sold him into slavery in a foreign country. But even when he had been cast into prison, Joseph held fast to God and to his dream. And one day, he saw his dream fulfilled.

You can too, if you'll just keep your eyes steadfastly on the dream God has given you — if you'll just keep your eyes on Him!

Who's Got The Most?

*"And he answered, Fear not: for they that be
with us are more than they that be with them."*
— *2 Kings 6:16*

The prophet Elisha's servant thought he had a right to be frightened. The Syrian army was ready to attack with a great host of horses and chariots, surrounding Elisha at the city of Dothan. How could they possibly escape?

But Elisha had eyes to see what his servant couldn't. He could see horses and chariots of fire surrounding him! And soon he asked God to show his servant what he saw! With help like this, it wasn't long before Syria was driven out of Israel.

Today, we can get disheartened, also, if we look only at the adversaries around us. At times, they seem exceedingly strong, informed, and situated in powerful places. But we have no cause for fear. God has forces, seen and unseen, on the side of His people, that will reveal themselves at the right time.

Remember, when God threw the devil out of heaven, only a third of the angels went with him. God has double the number of "agents" the devil has, and His own Omnipotence to back them up. How can you beat a combination like that?

You may be in a fierce battle today. It may seem like there is trouble everywhere you look in your life, or in the life of someone you love. But, I want to tell you that wherever you see trouble, God has greater forces than you see arrayed against Satan and his hosts.

I pray today that if your heart is troubled with the savagery of the enemy of your soul, God will open your eyes to see the forces of good arrayed on your behalf. I pray that you will see "the horses and chariots of fire," and take heart: God always has more going for you than the devil has against you!

Talebearing

"The words of a talebearer are as wounds, and they go down into the innermost parts of the belly."

— *Proverbs 18:8*

When I was a kid, we used to say, "Sticks and stones will break my bones, but words will never hurt me," when we were teased. But that's just not true. A gossip's words most certainly can and do hurt, as this verse points out. Gossip causes wounds. If you gossip about a person, you wound him with words that, like knives, cut deep and long.

You can choose to talk about your neighbors' shortcomings, or you can talk about their good points. You can spread dissension, or you can spread love and peace. Several years ago, there was a cartoon movie about a young deer and his life in the forest. One of his friends was a little rabbit who was in the habit of gossiping about the other animals. Finally his mother heard him and took him aside and told him, "If you can't say something nice about someone, don't say anything at all!"

It's a shame that so many people forget that kind of common decency. For just as a little match can burn down an entire city, a little tongue can destroy a whole business, church or family.

If you have trouble getting along with others, then perhaps you need to take a look at yourself. You may be causing the strife yourself by your talebearing. It's not enough to simply do unto others as you would have them do unto you. You must also say about others what you would have them say about you! Remember God's Word in Proverbs 22: "Cast out the scorner and contention will go out; yea, strife . . . shall cease."

Today, make a decision that you will not gossip — you will not be a talebearer. And decide that you won't listen to any gossip about others, either. Cast this sin out of your life, and truly, your own "strife and reproach shall cease."

Generosity

*"But the liberal deviseth liberal things; and
by liberal things shall he stand."*
— *Isaiah 32:8*

A church once rejoiced greatly because the town miser came to a meeting one day and met the Lord. A few weeks later, he went down to the river to be baptized. The preacher was waiting for him out there in the water. The miser got about knee-deep and then stopped.

"What's the matter, John?" asked the pastor.

"Well, I've got to go back," the miser replied, "I forgot to take my wallet out of my pocket."

"Get on out here this minute," the pastor snapped, "Your billfold needs to get baptized, too!"

God does everything He can in His Word to discourage His children from being misers. Did you know that the words "miser" and "misery" come from the same root? And that root means "extremely poor and unhappy."

Poor? How can a miser be poor? It makes me think of those stories I read ever so often in the newspapers of some wretched soul who's been living for years in a broken down building, in a room filled to the ceiling with junk, and when he dies, they discover a million dollars hidden in the middle of all the rubbish. That's a truly sad and poor end.

God promises His blessings to generous people. Generosity is a sign of faith. It's saying that the money I have is really God's, not mine, and it's not money that makes me what I am, it's God. I can affort to be generous because I've got a giving and generous God.

Have you let God "baptize" your billfold or pocket book? You'll never know the blessings you may be missing until you do. God puts goodness and generosity together in today's verse. Let your goodness be sure to extend itself as a free hand in giving to God's people and God's work.

The New Birth

"... Verily, Verily, I say unto thee, Except a man be born of water and of the Spirit, he cannot enter into the kingdom of God. That which is born of the flesh is flesh; and that which is born of the Spirit is spirit. Marvel not that I said unto thee, Ye must be born again."

— John 3:5-7

When Jesus met Nicodemus face to face, Jesus knew Nicodemus as he knew all men, but Nicodemus knew Jesus as "a teacher from God."

Although Nicodemus was a very religious man, he wasn't a child of God. Can you imagine the shock he had when he learned his religion wasn't enough! Religion is never enough.

Nicodemus needed more than religion, he needed regeneration. He needed more than the law, he needed life. And, he needed to know Jesus, not as a teacher, but as his Savior.

The flesh birth produces an old, sinful nature. It produces a nature that makes every unsaved person a child of the devil.

But, the new birth produces a sinless nature. A person born again is righteous and it is against their nature to sin.

Yes, every born-again person has two natures. The old was from the old birth where we were children of the flesh and the new birth were we are the children of God.

We can be children of God because Jesus died for our sins on the cross. God so loves his children that you can exchange your sins for righteousness. Calvary is proof that God loves you and wants to have you born again!

Love One Another

"That there should be no schism in the body; but that the members should have the same care one for another. And whether one member suffer, all the members suffer with it; or one member be honored, all the members rejoice with it."
— *1 Corinthians 12:25-26*

The carnal man will eventually always destroy one another when equally sharing and working together. The solution for Christians is simple — we have to be motivated by love.

Since the carnal man becomes jealous of others who are blessed, we, as part of the Body of Christ, should take others' blessings in the Body as part of our own family being blessed. When someone hurts, we can help share that hurt by listening, consoling, and sharing. The Church could win millions to Christ overnight if we all really cared for one another.

Tammy and I have recognized the need to minister to the masses through television, but we also see that individuals need to be touched in other ways. When close friends have problems that they feel are beyond hope, like divorce, I have pledged to them, before God, that I am going to work, talk, pray, love, and listen to help keep them together.

How many Christians have sat back and seen some marriage ruined or a divorce in the church and not lifted a finger? Many have seen pastors in trouble, but when it happens, instead of lending a helping hand, we point the finger and condemn. The biggest indictment against the Church today is that we "kill our wounded."

We can't continue to let this happen. Jesus came to heal the brokenhearted and bind up the bruised. Today, God wants each of us to befriend and help the bruised and wounded among us — to give them the "wine and oil of the Holy Spirit," so they can be restored in soul and body.

It is going to take the WHOLE Church to nourish and care for each other in these days. We all have a part, and a job to do. Start today to do your job!

All Things Are Possible

"But Jesus beheld them saying, With men this is impossible; but with God all things are possible."

— *Matthew 19:26*

Looking back over the years, I can't help but chuckle to myself at all the times people have frowned at me and said, "Jim, that's impossible."

When PTL first came to Charlotte and began broadcasting out of the little furniture store, people would hear my dream for a two-hour daily Christian talk show all over the country and they would shake their heads. "Jim," they would say, "Nobody will sell religious programs those kinds of hours. It's impossible."

Then, when we began expanding into every state in America, God began to speak to my heart about using television as a mission's tool in other countries. We started making plans to go into Latin America. Then those same people came up to me and said, "Jim, you don't have enough money to do that, just concentrate on America."

Well, today we are in forty-two nations. Why? Because I wasn't willing to listen to man when I knew I had heard from God.

Those things really were impossible in man's eyes. Television stations really don't like to see the kind of time we buy, and we really didn't have the money we needed to expand into other countries.

But it was possible with God!

Whatever your vision, whatever your dream, if it is God's will for your life, it will happen. It's not always easy, but there is never a victory without a battle. So, thank God for the battle, even in the midst of it, and keep looking for the fulfillment of your dream.

Because with God, all things *are* possible!

The Plank In The Eye

"How can you say to your brother, Brother, let me take the speck out of your eye, when you fail to see the plank in your own eye? You hypocrite, first take the plank out of your eye, and then you will see clearly to remove the speck from your brother's eye."

— *Luke 6:42*

If you've ever gotten a speck in your eye, you know that it feels as big as a log, doesn't it? It's difficult to keep your mind on anything else but that thing in your eye, and you've just got to get it out, one way or another.

If only peoples' souls were as sensitive as their eyes! We find it all too easy to ignore the "specks" of wrong that creep into our souls. They annoy us, but instead of working at getting rid of them with the Lord's help, we go around looking to find other peoples' wrongs. When we think we've found something wrong with someone else, we meddle in their lives and only confuse things more.

It's pride that puts a hard shell around our hearts and we just don't feel the effects of sin in our lives sometimes. Too often we think we're in a good place spiritually, and we want to imagine that nothing can touch us. Before we know it, we're excusing sin. The guilt of sin is going to come out one way or another. Thus, we go out and "get tough" with others for the same sins we're ignoring in ourselves.

Oh Lord, make our hearts tender towards you! When sin enters into our hearts, make us so sensitive that we feel it immediately. Help us today not to be slow to pluck that sin out of our lives, before we try to minister to others. Let our "specks" truly feel like "planks," and fill our hearts with love for you, and a sincere desire to help others. Amen.

Put On The Armor And Stand!

"Wherefore take unto you the whole armor of God, that ye may be able to withstand in the evil day, and having done all, to stand."
— *Ephesians 6:13*

This may be an "evil day" for you or for someone you know. You or that person may be in the thick of a problem that just doesn't seem to have a solution. You may be saying right now, "Jim, I've done everything I know to do. I've obeyed God. I have prayed. I can't do any more."

I say to you today, hold on! Stand firm! The answer's on the way!

Over the last few months, I've talked with many men of God, as many as I've been able to, and I've asked them all the same question: What have you done when the things have gotten really tough?

Robert Schuller, what did you do when they tried to stop you from building the Crystal Cathedral? Oral Roberts, what did you do when you were building the University and trying to finish the City of Faith and opposition came and money ran low? Demos Shakarian, of the Full Gospel Businessmen — what did you do when enemies came against you, when you were trying to build your building and couldn't get it done, when some of the roof beams collapsed, and other men tried to push you out of your ministry?

Each of these men, I've asked them all, what they do when they've done everything? Do you know what every one of them has said so far? They've said, "Jim, we've stood. When we've done all, we stood and saw the deliverance of our God!" Hallelujah!

No matter how difficult the problem is that you're facing, if you've done everything you can to solve it, if you've prayed and wept, and obeyed God and searched His Word — if you've done all you can do — God hasn't even begun to do all He can do! Stand now! Stand, and let God bring the victory! Don't budge from your place. The victory is sure in Him!

Our Children Need Discipline

*"Train up a child in the way he should go:
and when he is old, he will not depart from it."*
— *Proverbs 22:6*

TAMMY: I did a program for ladies once, and one of the women on the program was sharing how she disciplined her kids.

This smart gal always carried a wooden spoon in her purse when her children were small. The little ones always knew that spoon was there, so she only had to use it a few times. But, anytime they started to act up, all she had to do was to start pulling the infamous spoon out, and her children instantly started behaving. So, I started carrying a spoon in my purse when Jamie was with me. He called it the "panking poon."

I think it is time parents started disciplining their children more. In the wake of all the controversy about spanking youngsters, we have raised a generation of ill-behaved, ill-mannered children. And the fault lies totally on the parents for not having the backbone to discipline our kids.

The Bible says that if we spare the rod, we're going to spoil them and that they are going to come to naught. The responsibility for them is on our shoulders!

Now, don't get me wrong. Children need praise, too. We have to love them and praise them when they are doing their best. But, there has to be a balance.

It's time we got back to the "Old-fashioned" methods of raising children. Our mommies and daddies and grandmas and grandpas, they knew the Bible and knew what it was talking about; and we should, too.

Love your children enough to discipline them. It's the only true way to raise them to be the Christian men and women we want them to grow up to be!

Dry Bones

"And He said unto me, Son of man, can these bones live? And I answered, O Lord God, thou knowest."

— *Ezekiel 37:3*

"Dem bones, dem bones, dem dry bones," the old spiritual goes. Puts into your mind a rather grisly scene, doesn't it? Well, in this passage of scripture, the prophet Ezekiel faced a whole valley full of them. It wasn't a very lively sight.

God took Ezekiel up to this valley in a vision and had him walk all around, gazing at one skeleton after another. And you thought the last Halloween procession was ugly! Ezekiel noticed that these bones were not only dry, they were *very* dry, without an ounce of sinew or meat on them. Just when Ezekiel must have begun to feel a bit creepy, God asked him a question: "Can these bones live?"

I don't think anyone, who didn't know the Lord, would take that question seriously. After all, once something's dead, it's gone for good, right? But notice Ezekiel's answer: "O Lord God, thou knowest." Now, there was a man who knew God! He didn't doubt that God could do it. God went on to tell Ezekiel to prophesy over those bones and bring them back to life. And in this vision, Ezekiel did exactly that. Those bones grew flesh and sinews, and the wind came and blew breath into them, and they stood up as a mighty army.

God let Ezekiel know that those bones represented the nation of Israel, which had lost its hope and been carried off captive. God was saying through this vision, "Yes, I can make dry bones live. I can revive a people whose hope is gone and raise them up again as a mighty people for Me."

Your life may seem dry right now. You may not be experiencing a vibrant sense of God lately. But God can restore you! He can revive your hope and put spiritual muscle in you and re-fill you with His Spirit if you ask Him. "Can these bones live?" Yes they can, and they will — by the power of God!

Rest In God Today

"So don't be anxious about tomorrow. God will take care of your tomorrow too. Live one day at a time."

— *Matthew 6:34 (LB)*

So many people live life with their minds on next year's problems. They're so busy worrying and planning their future that they never stop to enjoy today.

A man got sick and went to his doctor. The doctor told him "You're about to die. Think about that and live the next day accordingly. I'll see you again tomorrow." When his shock wore off, the man went home and lived the next day to the fullest. He went back again to see the doctor. Again, the doctor said, "You may have only one day to live. If you make it through, come in again tomorrow." This went on for several days, and the man finally said to the doctor, "I guess I'm lucky to still be alive." "You sure are," the doctor said. "Your real problem is trying to live ahead of yourself. From now on, you may plan for the future — but try to live one day at a time!"

That's a lesson I learned when I first began building PTL. I tried at times to do too much too soon. God slowed me down, and then PTL began moving faster than I'd ever planned. Every day I see people squinting from tension headaches and carrying bags under their eyes from worry. No wonder — we weren't meant to lug tomorrow's troubles around. Yes, you ought to have some goals to work towards. But don't make gods out of them.

Today has all kinds of opportunities that won't be here tomorrow. So, instead of rushing around like the proverbial chicken with her head cut off, stop trying to do tomorrow's work and solve tomorrow's problems today. Get off tomorrow's treadmill. Rest in the Lord today — He won't leave any of tomorrow's loose ends undone.

No Substitute For Victory

"But thanks be to God, which giveth us the victory through our Lord Jesus Christ."
— *1 Corinthians 15:57*

General Douglas McArthur led his troops with a rallying cry: "There's no substitute for victory!" That's a good philosophy for winning wars — and a good one for our personal lives as well. The Bible says we're all in a spiritual warfare, but God wants to help us win that war. If you've been wounded and you're down in the trenches and stepped on, don't lie there any longer. It's time to get up, re-arm, and go forward.

Most nations have been devastated by war. Many have risen again to restoration. Look at Japan: Though defeated, they refused to give up. They've rebuilt and are now industrial leaders in the world. What a tragedy had they been content to live on in the rubble of war!

There are people who do that — they grovel in the ruins of their past mistakes, thinking about the horrible things they've gone through, looking with fear and despair at the turmoil of their lives. If you're among these, listen to me! Do you see the verse above? You don't have to fight the battle yourself. You don't have to save yourself. You don't even have to earn the forgiveness to start over.

Why? Because Jesus paid the price of your sins at Calvary. "For He has received us out of the darkness and gloom of Satan's kingdom and brought us into the kingdom of His dear Son, who bought our freedom with His blood and forgave us all our sins" (Colossians 1:13-14).

God wants you to have that victory today. It's yours for the asking as a gift of God. God loves you so very, very much, and He wants to rebuild you. Reach out right now for the victory He offers, for truly, there is Victory in Jesus!

Gossip Hurts

"For there is nothing covered that shall not be revealed; neither hid, that shall not be known. Therefore whatsoever ye have spoken in the darkness shall be heard in the light; and that which ye have spoken in the ear in closets shall be proclaimed on the housetops."
— *Luke 12:2, 33*

There is an old joke where one lady comes up to the other lady and says, "I don't repeat gossip — so you'd better listen carefully the first time."

I really believe that gossip has hurt the church more than any other sin. I'd rather have a person that smokes in my congregation than a gossip. At least the smoker is hurting his own lungs.

Gossip hurts everybody. It hurts the bearer, first and foremost, because it's a sin. Whether it is true or not, if you spread terrible things about your neighbor, it's a sin.

It also hurts the person you tell. Then they are put in the situation of temptation. Should they tell old so-n-so about this?

Then there is the victim of the tale — the person that supposedly did this terrible thing. Do you think talking about it to other people would bring them to repentance any sooner?

In almost every case, sooner or later, the tale goes back to the talebearer — the one that spread the gossip in the first place. You'll find what you whispered being shouted out loudly, and everyone will know that you were the one that started it.

Gossip sows discord among the brethren in the church. No wonder God hates it so!

The next time someone comes up to you and says, "Boy, have I got a great piece of gossip!" turn and walk away. Don't even listen, and then you won't be tempted.

Just like my Grandma used to say, "If you can't say something nice about a person, don't say anything at all!" Remember, the spoken word can't be recalled.

Unity In The Church

"Behold, how good and how pleasant it is for brethren to dwell together in unity! It is like the precious ointment upon the head . . . as the dew that descended upon the mountains of Zion: for there the Lord commanded the blessing, even life for evermore."

— Psalm 133:1-3

The Labor Day celebration here at PTL last year marked not only a victory for this ministry, but also a victory for the Body of Christ. In fact, one of the things that really overwhelmed me about that weekend was the gathering together of so many ministries in an effort to reach out to people in a spirit of cooperation and love. It still thrills me when I think about it.

You have to understand that when Tammy and I were young, we used to look up to famous evangelists like Oral Roberts. I've admired him and his tremendous ministry for years. You can't know what it meant to me to have him come all the way to PTL to share in the celebration!

The Lord is doing such an exciting work in the Church! He's bringing ministries together like never before, and you can just feel the Lord at work as He binds together the hearts and souls of the top leaders of today's biggest ministries.

I tell you, it's something when a man, as great in the Lord as Oral Roberts, comes to me and says the only thing he is here for is to assist me in any way he can. I feel like I should be at his feet, and he's coming to help *me!* That's got to tell us something about how the Lord is working!

I think this new spirit of cooperation among ministries is going to be one of the keys for reaching the rest of the world for Jesus, ushering in His second coming! I just praise God for men like Oral who are behind this great move in the Spirit. Today, help me pray that this unity in the Body continues to grow, along with our love for one another.

Doors Of Direction

"I am the door..."

— John 10:9

A well-known television game show has the contestants pick one of three doors behind which is a grand prize. People in the audience dress in crazy costumes to try to get the host's attention so they can be contestants and make that decision.

Life involves a lot of choices between alternatives, too. Each "door" or direction we choose has an affect on our future. In making decisions, success often hinges on timing — being in the right place at the right time.

Most people see time and opportunities as all their own. They dart in and out of life's doors, finding emptiness behind one and barging into another. But man doesn't really own time. God does. Trying to make things happen in "our own" time can create all kinds of problems for us and those around us. That's why a Christian needs to learn to follow the leadership and timing of God in making decisions and accomplishing goals.

One thing I've learned is that God will close a door if He doesn't want you to go through it. And if you trust God with your life, you won't have to push doors open. If one shuts before you enter it, you don't have to be frustrated. Another will open, and you can walk through it by faith.

If God prevents you, don't resent His intervention. He only steps in to stop you from making mistakes that would cause you sorrow. Never hesitate to ask Him for wisdom. No matter how small or insignificant your decision may seem, God has the time in His hands and the desire to help you choose rightly.

The way to discover God's timing is to ask Him to help you make decisions. "In all thy ways, acknowledge Him, and He shall direct thy paths," Proverbs 3:6 promises. Yes, He can direct you to the right door, in the right time. And the right door will always have "Jesus" written on it.

Not A Job For Angels

"... The things, which are now reported un-
to you by them that have preached the Gospel
unto you with the Holy Ghost sent down from
heaven; which things the angels desire to look
into."

— *1 Peter 1:12*

God might have given angels the job of preaching the Gospel, but He didn't. He might have worked out a plan for salvation that the angels could have brought to earth, but He didn't. Instead, He sent His only Son as a man to purchase our redemption, and sends us out, as flesh and blood people, to win others to Jesus.

Angels, who were pure and sinless, might have proclaimed God's Word without taint or error. But they could never have entered into the feelings of those burdened with the heaviness of sin and the cares of life. With their minds in perfect tune with God, and without bodies to suffer, they would have been unable to have compassion on those whose hearts and eyes were dim to the things of God.

Jesus might never have come to earth in human flesh and known hunger, thirst, pain, and death. But then, He never could have truly wept with those who wept. He could never have sensed in His own body the torment He came to redeem.

There is a story that when Jesus ascended to heaven, an angel greeted Him and asked, "Lord, what did you do there on earth?" Jesus answered, "I brought the kingdom of God into the hearts of a handful of human beings and told them to spread it throughout the world." "And what if they fail?" the angel asked. Jesus answered, "I have no other plan — but they will not fail!"

You may feel inadequate at times to be a vessel for the Good News of God. But God knows that in your weakness, you can make the Gospel message real to others, who in their weakness, need Christ, too. Let God use you to spread His Word of salvation — something an angel will never do.

Being A Good Steward

"Moreover it is required in stewards that a man be found faithful."
— *1 Corinthians 4:2*

God has blessed PTL's ministry by letting us operate out of a studio equipped with the finest machines we need to put a high-quality, first-rate show on the air. The studio itself is housed on the beautiful grounds of Heritage Village. The campground facilities at the Total Living Center are excellent, and every addition to Heritage USA seems to increase its beauty.

But God hasn't just reached down and handed it to us all in one fell swoop. We had to prove ourselves as good stewards, first, and then God gradually gave more into our care. Operating a ministry for God is a responsibility!

The first studios we had in Charlotte were in an old furniture store. Even when we finally moved to Heritage Village, we had to use every nook and cranny before God would allow us to expand.

One of my employees, Richard Scarborough, had an office right outside the door of a ladies room, because we didn't have space for him anywhere else. One day Richard was sitting in his office holding an important meeting with some utility officials. Meanwhile, one of the lady staffers decided she needed to visit the restroom. She walked through Richard's office into the bathroom and closed the door. As she did, she started singing! She sang so loud, the men had to stop the meeting!

But we faithfully used what God provided, trying never to waste anything. (Not even office space!) God blessed our efforts, and kept allowing us to grow. We've learned a very important principle through this, and we're determined that God will find us as faithful stewards with the good things He's given. Concentrate on being a faithful steward with the things God has placed in your life today, whether it be a house, family, or job, and watch God add more to your responsibilities!

God Is Our Source

". . . for every beast of the forest is mine, and the cattle upon a thousand hills. I know all the fowls of the mountains: and the wild beasts of the field are mine. If I were hungry, I would not tell thee: for the world is mine, and the fullness thereof."

— Psalm 50:10-12

God is the source of everything in our world, from the air we breathe to the paycheck we bring home!

It's a shame, but some of God's children have gotten a little confused and believe it's *their* drive and ability that's putting food on the table. As their bank account grows larger, so does their feeling of security in themselves.

Well, I may not have as much faith in my ability to provide for myself as they do, but nothing this side of Heaven can convince me to trade places with them. You see, I recognize God as my source, and I think I'm getting a much better deal because of it!

I'm not sitting up burning the midnight oil, trying to figure out how to pay my bills — I simply hand them over to my Father. He never seems to have any problems coming up with the money to pay them.

And I don't have to worry about building a huge savings account, for "emergencies," either. I've discovered that my Father always has enough to cover any emergency that comes up.

I found out a long time ago, that the more I held on to money and material things, the less I had to guard. But the more I gave out, the quicker God added to my supply.

Since God is the source of everything to begin with, I'm just going to keep acknowledging Him as my provider. If all of those "self-supporters" just knew what kind of a deal they were missing! Try making God your source today.

Cast All Your Cares

"Casting all your cares upon Him; for He careth for you."
— 1 Peter 5:7

Have you ever had the impulse to walk out on life? Just leave the room and slam the door on your problem? At times, that seems like the only thing to do. But when you have to get back to the job of living, that problem is still waiting on the other side of the door. So what can you do?

Some people take a fire escape (alcohol, an affair, overeating, etc.). Others stay in their room and go through the motions of living, ignoring the problem as it knocks on the door of their conscience. A few fearless ones open the door and ram into the problem with all the logic and strength they know, only to realize that the problem is too big to unravel or batter down. There's got to be a better way to deal with life and solve problems — a single, if not simple, answer to life.

If you ever go white-water canoeing, you appreciate a strong man in the stern. Without a skilled person steering the canoe, the paddling of the person in the bow doesn't amount to much in dangerous rapids. It's that way in life. In rough waters, you need someone strong in the back of your boat. Well, the single answer to life's problems is the person you'd better have steering it — Jesus Christ.

If you're letting Jesus help you handle your life "canoe," you can rest assured every expedition you take will be planned, insured and skillfully directed by the best teacher and friend there is — God Himself. He's been down the river before and successfully negotiated every peril.

So don't take the "fire escape," hold up or punch the problem in the nose. Launch out and ride it like the rapids — with Jesus at the steering oar.

Freely, Freely Give

"And as ye go, preach, saying, The kingdom of heaven is at hand. Heal the sick, cleanse the lepers, raise the dead, cast out devils: freely ye have received, freely give."
— *Matthew 10:7-8*

We usually hear only the last part of this verse and think of it only in terms of financial giving. But as you can see, when you include the whole passage, Jesus' idea of giving was all-inclusive.

Jesus' disciples had seen Him do all of the things above, and they had also been the recipients of some of those blessings. Now Jesus was sending them out to do likewise. Notice that they were to give what they had received.

You may not think that you have a whole lot to give to others. But think about it. Have you ever had the Gospel message preached to you? Did you receive it? Then you have something to give — you can give the Good News to someone else. Has God ever spared you from death? Then you can share Him as the keeper of your soul and the Lord of life with others.

Have you ever had a healing in your body? Then healing is something you can give to others, through prayer and the laying on of hands. Has God ever driven despair of depression or anger from your life? Then you can be used of Him to take authority over the devil and his ravages in the minds and spirits of others troubled with emotional problems or fears.

Whatever God has blessed you with, you can now give as a gift to someone else in need. Right now, take a few moments to think of all the comforting, healing, and delivering God has done for you. Then consider each of those things, not only in terms of what they've meant to you, but what if you "gave them away," they might mean to others. You've received freely, now freely give!

God's Gifts

"For every good gift and every perfect gift is from above, and cometh down from the Father of lights, with whom is no variableness, neither shadow of turning."

— *James 1:17*

TAMMY: It delights us to be able to delight loved ones with gifts we know they'll enjoy. God feels the same way about giving us, His beloved children, presents too.

God's gifts don't always come with His name on the tag, so sometimes we don't recognize Him as the giver. The little granddaughter of one of our employees, though, will always see God in every present she receives.

As this little girl lay dying in a hospital bed, she looked up to see the faces of angels who quickly swept her up to Heaven for a brief visit. There she gazed into the loving eyes of her Lord.

The Lord showed her a shimmering vision of her next Christmas. Under a glittering tree lay several packages with her name on them.

"See your Christmas presents, Shanna?" the Lord gently asked. "They're really all from Me, because I love you so much. I often choose to give to you through the people I've placed in your life, but every good gift that reaches you is first thought of, then hand-picked by Me."

When the vision faded, Shanna found herself back in the hospital bed. After that she recovered quickly and was soon back at home.

Shanna, and those of us who have heard her story though, will always see God behind every surprise present from a friend, every sticky hug from a child, every wilted flower given shyly.

The next time someone gives you a gift, thank your Lord who first picked it out for you, along with the person giving it.

God's Unsearchable Wisdom

*"O the depth of the riches both of the wisdom
and knowledge of God! how unsearchable are
his judgments, and his ways past finding out!"*
— *Romans 11:33*

Only a few months before, the young mother had lost her husband. Now her only little son was on the brink of death with an "incurable" disease. Her pastor came to visit at her son's bedside. "It doesn't make sense," she burst out. "When thousands of women are happily married, with small children, why me and my son?"

Her pastor thought for a moment, then told her this story.

Some years ago, a group of Christian businessmen donated a light airplane to a missionary in the heart of Africa, so he could bring the Gospel to an isolated tribe living in a deep jungle area.

After a number of flights, the missionary contacted the tribe. They took to this kind stranger and helped him clear a crude airstrip for his "giant bird," as they called it.

One day, a tribesman from a distant village happened upon the airstrip. He walked across it, examining it carefully. "This is strange," he remarked to himself. "Here is a road in the middle of the jungle. But it doesn't go anywhere at all! What a stupid tribe must live near here!" Shaking his head in bewilderment, he went on his way.

In the tangled confusion of some of life's darker moments, there are "landing strips" of God's mercy and grace that we cannot recognize as such. Would be that we could fly above it all and know all of the purposes of God.

But I'm glad today that I have a God whose mind can unravel even the most difficult problem, who can solve any mystery. I don't have all the answers to life. But I can trust the One who does, right now, and every moment — and so can you.

Don't Ask Amiss!

"Ye ask, and receive not, because ye ask amiss..."

— *James 4:2*

When you pray, you need to be specific with God. When you pray for God to bless missions work, don't just say, "God, bless all the missionaries around the world." Say, "God, help brother Mark Buntain with that hospital in India," or whatever person or project you want to see God bless. You need to be specific in making your requests known to God, even for the smallest things: Say, "God, this particular thing is what I need." Otherwise, you'll be asking amiss — you'll just miss God with your prayer.

Tammy taught me this years ago, when we were just starting out in evangelism. She had such a child-like faith in God. She'd believe God for every little thing, and then she'd write it down in the margin of her Bible. And it wouldn't be long before we'd see God start to do amazing things for us, down to the tiniest details. People who didn't even know we had needs would walk up and give us just what we needed: A tape recorder, or tires for the car, or unusual things that they wouldn't have expected we'd need.

Out of that I learned one thing: God doesn't want us to pray amiss, but be specific. Dr. Cho of Korea has shared that praying specifically brought most of the materials and equipment that went into making the world's largest church that he pastors. He wouldn't just ask God for a table or desk; he'd ask for exactly the one he wanted — and God would give it to him.

Housewife, do you need a new washing machine? Pick out the model and ask God for it. Young lady, are you looking for a husband? Maybe you should try picking a young man you think would be right. Business man, do you need a new copy machine? Find the one you want in the catalogue and ask God for it. Then commit it to Him and thank Him for the answer. Try it today, and just watch what God will do!

God's Question

"And should I not spare Nineveh, that great city, wherein are more than sixscore thousand persons . . . and also much cattle?"
— *Jonah 4:11*

Jonah is the only book in the Bible that ends with a question. And I'd like to have seen the expression on that old boy's face when God asked it!

Poor old Jonah! He seems to have missed the point at every turn. First, he tried to run from God, then he was thrown overboard, swallowed by a whale, who ferried him to where God wanted him anyway. Then he failed to understand why God had sent him.

You see, God sent Jonah, not because He wanted to destroy Nineveh, but because he wanted that city to repent. But then, when Nineveh repented, Jonah got mad! To Jonah it was more important that God destroy the city, as he prophesied, than for people's lives be saved. So he went and sulked in the shade of a gourd vine. God sent a worm that ate up the gourd, and then Jonah got mad at God! That's when God, with this question, reminded Jonah that saving souls takes priority over a prophet's being right!

Jonah's problem was that he really cared more about his own comfort and reputation than he did about people. How many churches are filled with people who want to be comfortable and right?" "Let all those souls who don't agree with us go to perdition! We've got the truth, and let the devil have everyone else." Even a lot of preachers would rather show people why they're going to hell than show them how to get to heaven. How they've misunderstood the love of God!

God is *for* people, not against them. Even if God threatens, it's just to wake people up so they'll turn to Him. Don't be a Jonah today. Don't run from God or wish people ill. Be truly right — start developing the kind of heart God has for saving people.

Resist the Devil!

". . . Resist the devil, and he will flee from you."

— *James 4:7*

How many times have you been going about your business, doing the job God has called you to do, when suddenly a little voice inside you begins to whisper about some secret fear? "Psst! You know that pain you've been noticing lately? I'd call and make a doctor's appointment right away if I were you. It could be some terrible disease!" Or else: "You really haven't been performing too well on the job these last few weeks — not like that new person they hired. You'll probably lose your job. A shame, too, all those years you've given the company."

Before you know it, you're in a panic, dialing the doctor, trying to save your job, fear and resentment growing in you, fear robbing you of your ability to concentrate on the task God has laid before you.

The power of suggestion is one of the devil's greatest weapons. He has a whole collection of suggestions like those above. But you don't have to go through all that panic. God has provided a way for His children to deal with the devil's awful suggestions. First of all, if a thought that causes fear tries to grip your mind, recognize that it comes from Satan. Then tell him to get lost and just don't listen to it. You can save hours of agony and stress in your spirit and your body if you will refuse to listen to the devil and go to God instead.

I've never begun a single project without Satan slyly suggesting failure. But I've learned to turn a deaf ear to him and listen only to the voice of God.

When Satan whispers his suggestions to you today, resist him. Use the authority God's given you. Turn to the Word and stand firmly on His promise — resist the devil's lies, and he'll flee.

Empty-Handed

*"For what is a man profited, if he shall gain
the whole world, and lose his own soul?"*
— *Matthew 16:26*

A newborn baby is born empty handed, naked, its tiny body
helpless and dependent on its mother. Have you ever noticed a
baby's hands? They clench and unclench, trying to find something
to grasp. Ever feel how tightly they'll grip your finger if you give it to
them?

Babies learn quickly to hold on to a bottle or a favorite blanket
or toy. It seems to signal security to a small child. As we grow older,
hands become among the most useful parts of our bodies. Without
them, we couldn't dress, drive, or write. But many people go on acting like children, going through life searching for something to
hold for security. It may be a handful of money, or a college diploma
for career advancement, or it might be a secure human relationship. Notice how a couple in love holds hands? But the physical
body withers with sickness or time no matter how tightly we cling to
it.

All of our days, those useful hands of ours hold to the prized
possessions of this life. Yet in death, stripped of houses, jobs, cars,
and families, our hands become empty as they were at birth. Jesus
knew when He said the words above that, truly, "you can't take it
with you."

The one human thing that's eternal is the soul, the part that can
communicate with God. A time will come when each of us will
answer to God for what we cling to in life.

But there is a lasting clasp, that reaches beyond the decay of
time and can't be lost in death. If your hand isn't firmly in the hand
of Jesus, put it there right now — before you enter eternity empty-
handed.

Do You Need A Friend?

"And Jonathan caused David to swear again, because he loved him: for he loved him as he loved his own soul."

— *1 Samuel 20:17*

The Lord is so gracious to us! He gives us the most precious blessings to enable us to stand in times of adversity. I consider Uncle Henry one of the dearest blessings God has ever given me, and there are times when I look back and realize I never would have made it had it not been for the unconditional love and constant support this gentle man of God has always shown me.

God must have known how much I would need Henry, because the moment we saw each other, for the first time, God knit our souls together! We were immediate friends, having the same kind of love between us that David and Jonathan had for each other.

Henry came to work at CBN when Tammy and I were still there, and we were so delighted to be together that Henry lived with us. Eventually, he became my co-host on the talk show I pioneered, supporting me in my ministry.

When God called us to Charlotte, Tammy and I both felt Henry's loss in our lives. But I held on firmly to a promise God had made me — someday Henry and his beautiful wife, "Aunt" Susan, would help me in my ministry again.

One night I just couldn't stand it anymore — I was in a motel coming back from a telethon, and I cried out to God, reminding Him of His promise to send me Henry and Susan. Well, God saw how much I needed them, because when I walked into the PTL studio the next morning to do the show, there were Henry and Susan waiting for me! God had awakened them in the middle of the night, when I was praying, and they were on the road to Charlotte that night in obedience to His call!

Today, if you need a dear friend in your life, someone you can be close to and share burdens with, ask God. He gave David his Jonathan and He gave me my Henry. He'll give you the perfect friend, too.

God And Science

*"And he that is eight days old shall be cir-
cumcised among you, every man child in your
generations, he that is born in the house, or
bought with money of any stranger, which is
not of thy seed."*

— *Genesis 17:12*

For years men of great intellect would make a practice of mocking the Word of God, using "scientific proof" of the Bible's errancy
to justify their disbelief in the Lord.

Slowly, their scorn for the Bible and for God seeped into our
school system through the textbooks and teaching our young people received. I guess we Christians often felt at a loss to fight back
against the powerful ammunition "Science" provided.

Now, praise the Lord, things have changed greatly. God has
raised up many Spirit-filled scientists who are quickly uncovering
evidence that proves God's Word as truth.

For example, the Israelites of Abraham's time probably never
understood the reason behind God's commandment that a baby
boy be circumcised on the *eighth* day of his life — they just did as
God commanded.

Nowadays, however, we know the reason God particularly set
aside the eighth day of life as the day of circumcision, thanks to a
discovery made in the field of medicine on how blood clotting
works!

The body naturally manufactures a substance called pro-
thrombin that aids in the clotting of blood — an important factor
whenever any type of surgery, major or minor, is involved. A baby
does not manufacture an adequate supply of this essential
substance until he is eight days old!

The Bible is rich in facts like this that modern day doctors and
scientists are just now discovering. Perhaps, if all of those "great
minds" who mocked the Bible had paid a little closer attention to it,
medicine and science would be even further advanced today!

The Power Of Love

"If a man say, I love God, and hateth his brother, he is a liar; for he that loveth not his brother whom he hath seen, how can he love God whom he hath not seen?"

— *1 John 4:20*

My brother Bob died when he was only forty years old. When I went to see him, on his deathbed, I thought of something terrible that had happened to him that may have changed his life.

It was the last time he ever went to church. He had totally rebelled against God for some reason, but that night, my mother and father had gotten him to go back to church with us.

Dad was the head usher of the church, and when time came in the service for the offering to be taken, Dad looked around the back of the church for another man to help him. Bob was the only one sitting back there.

Whether it was right or wrong, Dad felt it would be a good thing, so he asked Bob to help. As he stood and took the plate from my father, the pastor's wife came running up to him and snatched the plate from my brother's hands.

"You are not fit to receive the offering," she spat out. Turning, he walked out of the church and never attended another service for the rest of his life.

My brother felt hate, and what he needed to win him back to the Lord was love.

In his dying moments, he climbed into a plane and flew to his cousin's house, to the only person he felt loved him. There he asked Jesus into his heart.

At his death, he requested that there be no funeral and I know why — because he didn't think anyone would come.

Now is the time to love. If you are truly wanting to serve God, turn away from all prejudice. Let's love each other.

In His Steps

"He that followeth Me shall not walk in darkness..."
— John 8:12

In Michigan where I grew up, there were heavy snowfalls every winter. Trudging through the snowbanks, my dad would march toward the wood pile. As I followed unsteadily behind him, the snow made the yard an obstacle course for me.

My feet and legs plodded clumsily ahead as I tripped and fell into the white wet snow blanket. Hidden tree stumps and rocks became stumbling blocks for me, too. But I found that if I followed in my dad's footsteps, I had sure footing. I could see clearly because he packed down the snow with each step.

Life is like those walks in the snow. Try to go it alone, and it's easy to get tripped up on rocks and stumps like earning enough money to pay the bills and worrying about how to get ahead on the job. Hidden dangers like unforseen illness or thorny objects like family conflicts can bog you down.

But like my father in the snow-covered yard, there is One who has traveled the road before you. There is no problem you will ever face in life that Jesus didn't experience when He was here on earth. But Jesus always knew the way, because He was the Way — and He's the Way for you.

By following His steps, you can have sure footing. He'll keep you through the rough spots and pick you up if you stumble. Walking with Him will give you definite direction in life as His footsteps outline a clear path for you, step by step in school, marriage, or career.

Before you start trudging any further in your life, look to Jesus. It's rough going it alone, isn't it? I know, I've tried it. But why keep trying that, when it's so much easier to follow Him! Also, with Him, no matter where you go, you'll never walk alone. Stay in His steps all day today.

Men And Monkeys

"Professing themselves to be wise, they became fools, and changed the glory of the uncorruptible God into an image made like to corruptible man, and to bird, and four-footed beasts, and creeping things."
— *Romans 1:22-23*

You won't read about it in most high school science books, but Charles Darwin, the naturalist who made popular the theory of evolution, met the Lord near the end of his life and repudiated his theory!

According to Darwin's earlier thinking, man evolved from lower forms of life. As the theory of evolution took hold of men's minds, many gladly scooped it up as a way to prove that God's Word was untrue. They made a god out of ungodly science, and began to worship man's wisdom, just as in Paul's description in today's verse.

But Darwin himself found God, and in a very unusual way. In his travels, he encountered some primitive tribes so savage, that he was certain they had not even become fully human. To a missionary about to go to these tribes in the New Hebrides, Darwin said, "You are wasting your time; these are not humans, they are animals." In one lifetime, the missionary, John Paton, proved him wrong. The Gospel so revolutionized the lives of those cannibals that when Darwin visited them again and saw the tremendous change, he concluded that only God could have brought it about. He accepted Jesus Christ, gave generously to the missionary society who had sent Paton, and spent his last years telling others of the glories of the Bible!

Secular historians chalk Darwin's conversion up to senility, but we can thank God he saw the light! How glorious it is to know that the pioneer of evolution knew Jesus! Now pray that God will open the eyes of Darwin's many disciples!

God's Lawsuit

"Hear the word of the Lord, ye children of Israel: for the Lord hath a controversy with the inhabitants of the land, because there is no truth, nor mercy, nor knowledge of God in the land."

— Hosea 4:1

A few years ago, a man filed a lawsuit against God! It seems that his farm was levelled in a tornado, and, as you know, the insurance companies sometimes won't pay off in cases like that. Especially if there isn't a special clause. They call them "acts of God." Well, this fellow figured that if he couldn't get any money from the insurance people, he'd go to the one responsible. So he went to court and filed a suit for damages against God.

They probably threw the case out of court because nobody could serve the subpoena. For a long time, God had a lawsuit filed against people. He charged them with being unfaithful, unkind, and without knowledge of Him. And when you think of it, He could still serve a subpoena against us on those charges — and make them stick!

Legally, there isn't a man or woman on earth who has a leg to stand on in the court of the Almighty: "For all have sinned, and come short of the glory of God" (Romans 3:23). We just don't measure up. God's given us His law, and we've broken it, every one of us.

But let me share with you some good news: God has settled the case out of court! You don't have to face Judgment Day without a case and a lawyer. Because Jesus came and took your sins upon Himself and shed His blood for you on Calvary. When He died and rose again from the dead, He settled that lawsuit with the Father. The Father gave Jesus all authority and all power in heaven and in earth, and Jesus turned around and gave us a pardon and every kind of blessing there is.

I'm glad today that God won that lawsuit, aren't you?

Grow Up In God

" . . . When I became a man, I put away childish things."

— *1 Corinthians 13:11*

There's nothing like a toy store, with aisles lined with puzzles, dolls, games, and fire trucks, to light up a child's eyes. I've watched Jamie Charles and Tammy Sue get almost wild with excitement trying to pick out Christmas or birthday presents. Well, like any parent, I buy them for my kids, knowing that some toys will soon be broken, discarded, and outgrown. I can see that as an adult — and yet I've noticed that even big people never really leave "toys" behind.

Adults have a "pretend" world, that's like that of children. We're susceptible to putting the things of this world — family, possessions, ambitions — on bright pedestals in our hearts. Getting a new car or house, having a happy family life all sound like the height of happiness. But when achieved, even these can leave an inner emptiness.

We use Jesus like a toy sometimes, too. The kind-faced man we learned about in Sunday School is just a storybook character set aside with childhood. He's like an old Jack-in-the-box whose handle we crank only when we get in trouble. As for daily living, He stays in His box, unable to meet our needs. And yet, though we don't serve Him, He's always supposed to rescue us.

That is childish, isn't it? Have you been guilty of centering your life on adult "toys" — and even made God just a boxed-in last resort in your thinking? I'll tell you, you've missed a lot, if you've dishonored Him in this way. You have not yet seen His greatness — to Him, the whole universe would be nothing but a toy — if that's how He wanted to treat it.

Instead, He's given you the choice to grow up, to be complete in Him, to set your goals on His values and on eternal treasures which nothing can destroy. He's real — can you be real enough today to experience His reality in your life?

A Merry Key To Good Health

"A merry heart doeth good like a medicine:
but a broken spirit drieth the bones."
— *Proverbs 17:22 (LB)*

This is one of Uncle Henry's favorite verses, and I guess it explains why you almost never hear of his getting sick. It has been truly discovered that one of the best ways to keep healthy is to stay happy.

Some scientists did a study that reflects on this truth. For over forty years, the health of 204 men was monitored. At the start of the study, all of the men were tested psychologically as well. Fifty-nine men were judged to have the best mental health from ages twenty-one to forty-six. Interestingly, only two of these men developed a chronic disease or died by age fifty-three.

Forty-eight of the men showed poor mental health. These were anxious, depressed, and emotionally unstable. Before their mid-fifties, eighteen became chronically ill or died.

As a factor in physical health, the researchers found that a person's state of mind plays a bigger part than alcohol and tobacco use, overweight, or how long their ancestors lived. Isn't that remarkable? I think it's about time we started using the Bible to prove science rather than the other way around!

Researchers also found that if a person were seriously ill and ready to die, if they had a birthday coming up or a holiday to look forward to, they would "hang in there" until the awaited day was over. This reminds me that Christians have the greatest day of all to look forward to — the day we meet Jesus face to face. If that isn't a reason for living and being merry, I don't know what is!

There can't be a better recipe for good health than being a Spirit-filled Christian. Think about that. Hold your head up today and whistle a joyful tune. You might spread a little of that good cheer — and good health — to others, too!

_____

The King Of Time

*"The fear of the Lord prolongeth days: but
the years of the wicked shall be shortened."*
— *Proverbs 10:27*

Have you ever said to yourself, "There just aren't enough hours
in the day!" Life seems to add job to job, responsibility to responsibility, and activity to activity, until you just throw up your hands
and say, "I just can't do it all! Lord, I just can't!"

Some people seem to get so much more done than others. Have
you ever noticed that? They don't seem to waste a second of time.
Their lives are filled with activities, meetings, and recreation — and
outstanding achievement. How do they do it?

Today's verse holds a key — a right relationship with God can
actually give you those extra hours you're looking for. How can
God do that? Well, there are several ways. 2 Peter 3:8 says that
"With the Lord a day is like a thousand years, and a thousand
years are like a day." God is the Master of time. God created time,
and He can intervene in it, just as He does in the rest of His creation.
He can move time quickly or slowly. It's not the hours you put in,
but what you put in the hours.

Plus, I think that being in touch with God saves a lot of time
because He helps you make good decisions. But you have to ask
Him first.

If you're right with God you complain less, worry less, and
argue less, and all of those things waste time.

Have you ever asked God to be Lord of your time? If you're constantly out of time, maybe it's because you haven't really turned
over the management of it to God. As today's scripture indicates, if
God isn't a part of your whole day, it's not going to produce good.
Right now, turn over every minute of this day to God. Once you let
your time go, God will give you a lot more of it!

A Kingdom, Not A Carnival

"Heaven and earth shall pass away, but My words shall not pass away."
— Matthew 24:35

How easy it is to get caught up in the bright lights and attractions of a carnival midway! With all the popcorn, cotton candy, soda, games, and rides, your pockets can soon empty if you don't watch out. You might head home with a teddy bear or a plastic necklace. But that's all you'll have to show for what you spend — just some fun and a few cheap trinkets.

A lot of people live like the world is a carnival. They spend their time and money seeking material things and pleasures, thinking they're getting the most out of life. They let themselves get drawn into the games of money, fame, or sex and go their way with nothing but their own interests in mind.

Like a carnival, that kind of life can be fun — for a while. But living life only for yourself is like spending all your money trying to toss a ring around a peg — for a prize worth only a dime. A sinful life is like that when it's finished: in the end it's just junk that can't go with you when you die and that starts rusting out even before you go.

Only things that are done for God are going to count forever. You see, God's not running a carnival, He's building a kingdom. And He's shaping it, not out of good times, big names or fat bankrolls, but out of love, joy, and good deeds. He's using the promises of Jesus His Son, which stand eternal.

You can make your life count for eternity today. Give Jesus total Lordship of your life right now. Leave the cheap trinkets behind and get hold of God. When you have Him, there's nothing so precious in the whole world that it can take His place.

Praise Through Music

"Enter into His gates with thanksgiving,
and into His courts with praise."
— *Psalms 100:1*

TAMMY: In my years of being a Christian, I have learned one thing, if I'm down and depressed, all I have to do is to start singing praise songs to Jesus, and He ministers to me.

All of my life, I've always touched God through music. There have been days when I felt like I could pray all day and still not see His face. But, if I'd just go to the piano and start singing, the praise would usher the Lord right into my living room.

Of course, not all of us can sing well, and some folks don't feel comfortable singing alone in their house. But that's no excuse for not using musical praise to get to God. Turn on a Christian radio station, or click on a record. Then sing aloud to God!

One thing you have to be careful about is to listen to the words of the songs you sing. Now, I'm not going to sing, "Lord, Don't Move That Mountain," because I want my mountains moved! So, I'm real careful about the songs I sing, either alone or on the PTL Club.

But, I tell you people, music is the key to praise, and praise is the key to bringing the Holy Spirit down. The Bible tells us that, "He inhabits the praises of His people." That means, wherever He is being praised — that's where He lives! Isn't that great!

So, whatever you are going through, no matter how dark the cloud is over you ... sing your way to praise. You'll see the difference. Believe me, I know, people!

Communication And Love

"Let all bitterness, and wrath, and anger, and clamor, and evil speaking, be put away from you, with all malice: And be ye kind one to another, tenderhearted, forgiving one another, even as God for Christ's sake hath forgiven you."
— *Ephesians 4:31-32*

There, pictured on the television set, is the husband sitting at the breakfast table, hiding behind his newspaper. His wife tries to say a few words, only to be met by grunts and moans. Finally, she gets so frustrated that she strikes a match and sets the newspaper on fire!

Sad to say, this scene is more than a far-fetched comedy skit. It's a sad part of many marriages today. The laughs come only because it's so true in many homes across America.

It's so important that mates talk to each other because it's such a major part of giving and sharing in marriage. Without intimate and regular communication, love in a marriage can't grow. Talking never seems to be a problem in courtship, does it? What happens to make it so difficult later?

First, so many resentments and irritations build up, stay unforgiven, and just get buried in angry silence. As the silences grow longer, the marriage bond grows weaker. Then, we forget that communication is not only speaking, but listening to our spouse's needs, being loving and responsive. This is really important when there's a disagreement, for communication is the "oven" needed to "bake the cake" of reconciliation. All the other ingredients may be there, but without communication, the dispute goes on, rumbling like a quiet earthquake.

Husbands and wives need to forgive one another — and then communicate that forgiveness. The verse above concludes, "just as God has forgiven you because you belong to Christ." That's the real key — realizing that God has forgiven us our sins. How can we then withhold forgiveness from others? Through forgiveness, communicate with your spouse today. And through communication, find love.

Truly God And Man

"As long as I am in the world, I am the light of the world. When he had thus spoken, he spat on the ground, and made clay of the spittle, and he anointed the eyes of the blind man with the clay."

— *John 9:5-6*

Soon after Jesus rose from the dead and ascended into heaven, false teachers crept into the church with some strange ideas. Some of these had something like this to say: "Jesus wasn't really human; He was just pretending to be human. He was a sort of super-man, really a god from another world. He didn't really die, and He wasn't really born, either."

The true ministers of God, the apostles, sent these rascals packing. For a central truth of the Gospel is that Jesus was truly man: He was carried in Mary's womb and born as every human being is born; He grew in stature, in knowledge and understanding; He got tired and slept; He ate and thirsted; He experienced real pain and died a real death; and He arose from the dead, in a glorified body, but one that was solid flesh.

Jesus was a real man, and He was also truly God. And no passage illustrates that combination better than the one above. Here, Jesus was about to heal a man blind from birth. And right after making the remarkable statement, "I am the light of the world," He spat on the ground! What a contrast! A lot of us might consider that disgusting, and I don't know how many of us would have let Jesus put that spit-clay on our eyes! Yes, Jesus was that down-to-earth. He really touched people, in the grime and grit of the *now!*

Jesus has put His Spirit into us in the *now*. As Jesus was a real human being, He wants us to be the same kind of person He was. In fact, He said of us, "*Ye* are the light of the world" (Matthew 5:14). He can work through you today, right where you find yourself. Jesus can still touch the world — through *your* touch, just as it is. Will you let Him do that today?

Rejoice!

"Rejoice evermore. Pray without ceasing."
— 1 Thessalonians 5:16-17

God wants to be able to guide our every move, and to be a part of every decision. No matter how small the detail, if it concerns you, it concerns God, too.

Of course, in order to receive God's guidance, you have to be tuned in to His voice, or in the hectic world we live in, it's possible to miss hearing some instructions the Lord may be trying to give.

It helps to be in constant communication with God, praising Him, and sharing what's on your heart. I know one "King's Kid," who visits us here at PTL, who's a firm believer in looking for continual guidance from the Lord. Harold Hill always has a story to tell about how listening to God's still voice has kept him out of some new disaster.

One time he was heading for a local bank, that was only a little way up the street ahead of him, when he felt God was telling him to go to another bank instead. Harold says he turned toward the other bank because he's "learned obedience is better than sacrifice."

But, when he remembered how inconvenient parking was at the second bank, he decided it was silly, and turned around, heading back to the bank that was his first choice.

There at the bank, he was met with a scene of total panic — the bank had just been robbed! Harold says that God's guidance, in sending him towards another bank, probably kept him from running into the arms of a gun-toting robber!

From the small, seemingly mundane decisions we make each day, to the life-changing choices we occasionally make, including God in all of them can save us a lot of trouble. Today, as you go about your work, talk to God about what you're feeling, and let Him help you make even the little decisions. You'll find this constant fellowship is indeed something to rejoice about!

Make Jesus Your Hero

"Let this mind be in you, which was also in Christ Jesus."

— *Philippians 2:5*

Did you ever have a "hero," who you thought was just great, and you wanted to be just like him? Most of us can remember having someone like that at some point in our lives. My little Jamie Charles sometimes watches television characters, and after a show is over, he'll run around the house acting just like Superman.

I remember as a boy daydreaming about famous people so much that after a while, I'd try to even think like them. Of course, as I grew older, I began to grow in my own identity, and I left those heroes behind.

God wants us to have one hero in our lives that we never stop imitating — and that's Jesus. Most of the people of God call themselves "Christians" today, and do you know how we got that title? In the early church, believers in Antioch were undergoing persecution. Their enemies made fun of them by calling them "little Christs." The believers in Antioch took that as such a compliment that they started calling themselves "Christians," which meant "Christ-like."

What a privilege it is to be able to have and imitate a "hero" like Jesus. In fact, this verse says that we can actually have Jesus' mind! That's even better than imitation. I think it's part of that child-like faith that the Bible says we should have — to let Jesus so live within us that we do the things He did, and love the way He loved, and serve others the way He did. What a blessing and a privilege!

Is your mind so full of Jesus today that people who meet you will see Him in you? Remember, that's what being a "Christian" really is. Pray that God will really let you take on the mind of Christ today, that you might bless and love others, to the honor and glory of God.

Don't Judge — Love!

"Judge not, that ye be not judged. For with what judgement ye judge, ye shall be judged: and with what measure ye mete, it shall be measured to you again."

— *Matthew 7:1-2*

Every day I meet people who seem to be carrying "the weight of the world on their shoulders." I can see it in their faces. I can see it in the way they walk. And, I can sense it in the way they talk. Sometimes, I just want to grab these people by the arms and say, "Listen, you don't need to carry this load. You can get rid of that heavy burden!"

I feel so for them, because I know what they're going through. I used to be the same way, and it nearly killed me. But, praise the Lord, God set me free. I no longer felt I had to judge everybody and it was like a ton of bricks had been lifted from my shoulders.

We put ourselves into bondage when we decide we have to judge others and worry about who we are seen with and who we help. Jesus knew who He was, so He never worried about His reputation or with whom He rubbed elbows. His love went out to the sick, the sinful, and the saint alike. He left judgements to the Father. When asked to judge, Jesus said, "He that is without sin, let him cast the first stone."

There isn't a person among us who is without sin. So today, before your burdens become too heavy, try setting your judgements aside. That doesn't mean "winking at" sin. But do love sinners! Let God's free forgiveness flow in and through you to others. I know you will experience a lightening of your load when you have God's love within yourself.

Recognizing God's Voice

"I will instruct thee and teach thee in the way which thou shalt go: I will guide thee with mine eye."

— *Psalm 32:8*

A lot of times when we talk about wanting guidance from the Lord, we want to hear Him map out exactly what He wants us to do. Maybe we'd settle for a scroll written across the sky!

We feel that if we had these easily understood divine directions for each course of action God wanted us to take, we could skip the confused "was that God or my imagination . . . " stage and pass right over the "Did God really mean . . . " questions, also.

Fortunately for us, God's guidance doesn't work that way. If it did, we'd all grow dependent on our maps and scrolls instead of having to learn to recognize that still small voice of God.

To learn God's voice, we must come to Him daily, building a personal relationship with Him in the process. It's that daily communion that forges such a strong bond of understanding between Father and child. It's that daily time together that takes away the need for any crutches we may have grown dependent upon while seeking guidance.

One of the big hindrances in learning to recognize God's voice is our appetite for instant answers. We are a generation used to fast-food and time-saving appliances. Sometimes, in order to hear God's voice, there's first a time of waiting before Him — a time our impatient natures are likely to chaff at as "holding up the proceedings."

But God, in denying us scrolls and instant signs, is wisely forcing us to grow in Him. If you're frustrated today because you've been asking God for an answer that's come slowly and isn't clear, then press closer to the Lord and ask to hear His voice again — it gets stronger and clearer every time.

Delight

"Delight thyself also in the Lord . . ."
— Psalm 37:4

This word DELIGHT speaks of confessing confidence in God. It means literally to be pliable and open up, to express your appreciation. When you receive a wonderful gift or see something beautiful, what's the first thing you want to do? You want to tell others about it. This is what delighting in the Lord is all about.

Proverbs 18:21 tells us that life and death are in the power of the tongue. By our confession, we can choose our future. Most of us are quick to talk about our needs and our problems. It's not a bad thing to let your needs and hurts be known. But telling others is not going to get those needs and hurts met. We've got to go beyond that and learn to acknowledge God in all our ways. We've got to look to Him and His great power, because He is the answer. Just as God in creation spoke all the heavens and earth into existence, we can speak abundance, prosperity, and blessing into existence by delighting in God and confessing His answer.

Several years ago, Tammy and I, by faith, spoke Heritage Village into existence. Today, it is complete and totally paid for — simply because we spoke, with delight, the desires of our heart before God. Of course, we then worked night and day to bring our faith in line with God's Word. But, it started first with speaking the word of faith. God always honors a good confession of faith. Now, we're believing God for total victory at Heritage USA. We're confessing that this soul-winning community is being established to glorify God.

If God has given you the faith for something, speak out positively, with confidence. God will honor your faith in Him. If there is something in your heart that you would like God to do, and if it's in line with His Word, start confessing it done right now — and you'll see it come to pass.

Comfort As You're Comforted

> *"Who comforteth us in all our tribulation so that we may be able to comfort them which are in any trouble, by the comfort where we ourselves are comforted of God."*
>
> *— 2 Corinthians 1:4*

Remember what it was like to fall down as a child and skin your knee? I do. Oh, how that could sting! I'd run right away to my Mom or Dad, whoever was closest, and they'd just pick me up and tell me it was all right, while they dried away my tears. Just their soft words seemed to make the pain start to go away.

Few things feel better than being comforted. The warmth and tenderness that flood through you are just what you need when you're sad and troubled. Now I have plenty of opportunities to comfort my own children when they're hurt, in spirit or in body.

As we grow older, we discover hurts a lot worse than skinned knees. Unkind words, cruel slights, betrayals, disappointments in love, at home, or at work: I'm sure you've felt deep cuts of that kind in your life. I've had plenty in mine.

In every one of these afflictions, I've had a heavenly Father to run to, who takes me up in his great arms of love, and tells me I'm going to be all right, that I'm going to make it. And that's why I've been able to comfort others through the ministry God's given me on the PTL Club. I can feel the hurts of others and minister God's love to them.

Every wound that God binds up, every word of encouragement He gives, every tear He dries, He ministers for two reasons: First to meet our need, and second, so that we might have something to give to others in need. If you've felt the comfort of God, be sure and give to others who need it that same comfort you've known. Can you think of anyone right now who might be in need of a touch from God today? You may be the one God wants to use to extend a tender hand of comfort.

The Good Ole Days

"Say not thou, What is the cause that the former days were better than these? for thou dost not inquire wisely concerning this."
— *Ecclesiastes 7:10*

There's something in our heart that causes us to harbor an occasional suspicion that the grass really is greener on the other side of the fence. I'm not sure what it is, but I have a feeling it's kin to the longing we sometimes have to return to "the good ole days," when we were happier and didn't have so many cares.

Of course, when we stop to spend some time honestly remembering the "good ole days," we suddenly gain a new perspective.

Memories of cares, worries, and times of unhappiness, just like we experience now, sometimes come to mind, shattering the idealistic image we've been enjoying mourning over.

I've heard Christians reminiscing over their pre-born again days, taking great delight in describing the exciting life and carefree existence they gave up to follow Christ. Their dissertation usually includes a long list of things they can't do anymore.

What they're forgetting to mention are the times they sat wondering bleakly if life held more meaning — and the times they cried out in despair over the empty place in their lives that no amount of excitement could fill.

They're also somehow forgetting the many times they discovered that all that glitters is rarely gold, disappointment filling their hearts.

There's nothing like a good dose of problems to cause our minds to seek sanctuary in the "problemless past" we remember in distortion, instead of dealing resolutely with the task at hand. Perhaps that's why God warns us in the Bible not to dwell on days gone by — we can't trust our memories!

Today, when a problem arises, face it squarely with God's help, and move into the future instead of making yourself miserable with clouded memories of the past.

God's Therapy

"And the peace of God, which passeth all understanding, shall keep your hearts and minds through Jesus Christ."
— *Philippians 4:7*

TAMMY: I think most of us, if we are honest with ourselves, will admit that there have been times in our lives when we have had nerve problems.

One of the worst times in my entire life was when I had Tammy Sue. I cried for hours and hours after she was born. I felt like spiders were crawling all over the room in the night, and the nurses said I tried to kill them.

Then, I thought there were mice under my bed. I didn't remember having a little girl at all. It was like a bad drug trip, and I guess, since it was an allergic reaction to the drugs, that's what it was.

The medicine had affected my emotions. For months after that, I was in such a deep depression that I doubted my own salvation.

In the middle of my despair, I finally decided to call a psychiatrist, but God stopped me. He spoke to me and said, "Tammy, let me be your psychiatrist." God spoke to me so I could not mistake His voice, and He restored my mind through Jesus Christ, just like the verse said He would. It didn't happen immediately but every day from that day I got better. He knew my breaking point.

People, no matter what you are going through today, no matter how far from God you feel, He is right there. He wants to draw you back close to Him. He loves you. He died for you. Let Him heal your mind.

Then, you will experience that great peace that surpasses all understanding . . . Praise God!

Believe In Your Answer

"If any of you lack wisdom, let him ask of God, that giveth to all men liberally, and upbraideth not; and it shall be given him. But let him ask in faith, nothing wavering. For he that wavereth is like a wave of the sea driven with the wind and tossed."

— *James 1:5-6*

Has anyone ever told you about a problem they've been wrestling with? They've tried solution after solution and wonder why God hasn't helped them yet. But many times God's already given His answer — He's just waiting for them to use it!

A famous professor of mathematics once assigned his college class a very difficult problem for homework, telling them that he expected a correct answer by next morning. Well, the students went back to their rooms and struggled far into the night. The next morning, the professor looked out over the classroom and asked, "Who has the correct solution to the problem?" One young man raised his hand quickly, "Write it on the board," the professor said. The young man did so, and the professor said, "That is not the correct answer. Who has another?" Several other students volunteered answers, all of which the instructor rejected.

Then the first young man who had stood up raised his hand once more. "Sir," he said, "I am aware of your greatness as a mathematician. But with respect, sir, you are mistaken. I worked that problem out carefully and spent hours rechecking my steps. My answer was the correct one." "Yes, you are right." the professor replied, to the shocked gasps of his class. "You see, in today's world, people will challenge your answer, even if it's correct. It is not enough to have the right answer — you must believe in your answer and stand up for it."

If you have asked God for an answer to a problem in your life, you can rest assured that He will give you the wisdom you need. Then, believe that you have indeed heard from God, and start acting on that answer. Try it today.

The Master Potter

"But now, O Lord, thou art our father; we are the clay, and thou our potter; and we all are the work of thy hand."

— *Isaiah 64:8*

One of the most foolish ideas we Christians have come up with is the belief that by sheer will-power and self-discipline we can mold ourselves into willing vessels the Lord can use for service to Him.

This misconception about "whose job involves what" has led to the manufacturing of some pretty leaky vessels, I'll tell you!

It's not that the Lord doesn't appreciate our sincere desire to help Him, I'm sure, but there is only so much a pile of clay can contribute to its own construction.

We must resign ourselves to the fact that it's God's job and responsibility to actually form us into fit vessels — it's our job to sit still and allow ourselves to be formed, bended, and molded.

Though it may not seem like it, our job is a very crucial one to the success of our transformation.

If we refuse to allow God to work on our shapeless clay bodies, plucking out pebbles, excess straw, and other blemishes as he designs us into a new shape, then we'll never be the useful or beautiful vessel God desires us to be.

Also, if we insist on trying to mold ourselves, the result is usually disaster. Because of our pride, we end up making a bulge in one side while stretching to smooth a bump in the other.

Today, allow yourself to be formed by the loving hands of the Master Potter, who is able to make you into a beautiful and perfect vessel to carry Living Water to thirsty souls.

From Crimson To White

"Come now, and let us reason together, saith the Lord: though your sins be as scarlet, they shall be as white as snow; though they be red like crimson, they shall be as wool."
— *Isaiah 1:18*

We usually think of *black* as being the opposite of *white,* don't we? Then why doesn't this verse say, "though your sins be as tar — though they be black like pitch —" Why did God choose to use *crimson* in this verse?

It's because black is much easier to cover than red. Any painter will tell you that no color is harder than red to paint over. You can apply coat after coat of paint over something you've painted red, and the fresh colors will hold for a while. But sooner or later, the red will come bleeding through. Only several coats of thick, metallic paint will bury that red completely.

One of our PTL employees tells this story: "When I was in high school, there was a big old bell on the grounds that was used to signal the start and finish of classes and breaks. It hung at ground level, and one night, some guys came and dumped a big can of bright red paint over it. For several years, the school tried to paint over that red, but nothing could stop it from bleeding through every paint they used."

God is saying to you in this verse, "Look, I've got a really reasonable offer to make you. Do you know those tough sins in your life, the ones you've tried over and over again to cover over or give up? Well, I can handle them, too. I can cleanse in a way that may seem impossible to you. Even those crimson sins, I can blot out and make you white as snow."

That's God's offer today. Do you have any such sin in your life, one you've longed to get rid of, that just won't seem to let go? If you will release that area to God in a new and deeper way today, He will make it white as snow. Ask Him right now to fulfill this Word. It's a wonderful offer — will you take it?

You'll Find Your Bread

"Cast thy bread upon the waters: for thou shalt find it after many days."
— *Ecclesiastes 11:1*

This sounds like a strange thing to do. You might think that what it means is to go out and feed the fish, and then you'll catch them later on, or something like that. But actually, it's talking about sowing and reaping in God's kingdom.

Let me give you a little of the history of this verse. In the valley of the great Nile River, there is a particular time that's ideal for planting. The farmers wait until the river overflows and floods the croplands. Then, when the water is about knee-deep, they wade through it with their seed, and they drop those seeds right into the water.

The seeds settle to the bottom and get covered up with the rich soil the river carries with it. When the waters go down, the seed is buried there. But after a while, the sun warms it, it springs up, and yields a great crop.

When the floods come in the Christian life, that's one of the most important times for determining a believer's future growth and development. It's not always easy to keep obeying God, loving people, and standing firm when the waters are high all around you. But what you do then, and what you give then, is going to determine what "crops up" in your life when the storm recedes. If you give to God in a time of need, He will take that as seed and multiply it back to you, whether in money or in love or spiritual victory — whatever your need might be. It may take a while for that crop to spring up for you. But it will— God promises it.

Living for God is a long-term investment. How much you put into it is how much you'll get out. When the waters come up around you, do you sow unto God — or do you just stop giving? If you're in a "flood time," give something — there's no better time to sow for a great harvest.

Don't Retire — Refire!

"And it shall come to pass in the last days, saith God, I will pour out of my Spirit upon all flesh ... and your old men shall dream dreams:"

— Acts 2:17

An elderly man once told me, "Jim, I'm going to *live* until I die!" I like that. There's something so exciting about an older person who won't give up on life!

It saddens me that so many older people today are tempted to just quit. I believe that our senior citizens are one of America's most neglected national resources. Our society has put such a premium on being young that just getting older is almost a sin! Well, God's Word doesn't agree with that attitude. You might have thought young people were the dreamers of the world. But this verse says that God is able to make dreamers out of the old folks!

A dear Greek lady appeared on the PTL Club not long ago. She received a call from God to go to the mission field when she was past sixty. Her friends called her crazy and told her to settle back into her rocking chair. But she had a dream, and she stepped out to make it a reality. Do you know what has happened? Now, in her seventies, she's gone to Africa. She has built not just one, but two beautiful cathedrals. She raised the money all by herself when no one would help her.

Many elderly people come to us at PTL to counsel with people in need on the telephones. God is using them mightily because they've weathered life's storms and come through. They know the faithfulness of God through long firsthand experience.

I don't believe people should ever retire — I think they should "refire" — ignite those God-given dreams and shine out like lights to a world that sorely needs their hard-earned insight.

Dear older folks, *be* the great resource God has made you today, and you young people, start to mine that source God has given you in your elders. You'll find in them riches like you've never dreamed!

A Servant Of All

"But it shall not be so among you: but whosoever will be great among you, let him be your minister; and whosoever will be chief among you, let him be your servant: Even as the Son of man came not to be ministered unto, but to minister and to give His life a ransom for many."

— *Matthew 20:26-28*

You know, we have one of the greatest teachers, I think, in America today working here at PTL. You all may have seen Judy Chavez on the show a few times — if you have, then you know what I mean!

But Judy isn't one to get all concerned about trying to be pious, or anything — she just simply goes about living the truths she teaches and serving the Lord faithfull. As a result, she's a living testimony of what God is talking about when He says, if you want to be great in the kingdom, then be willing to be the least, first.

I'll explain to you what I mean. Judy could say, "Well, God made me a teacher, so all I'll do is teach . . . " No, instead this humble woman of God comes to me when I'm the most exhausted, takes hold of my feet, removes my shoes, and then she works on my toes and rubs my feet!

One time a few years ago, I left the program so drained that I had double-vision. She worked on my feet, and it cleared my head — maybe I'm built backwards, or something . . .

Now that's what I call real love — finding out where another person is hurting and ministering to that need. That's what God is talking about in today's verse.

Today, if you see someone who needs a personal touch that will show them Jesus cares, be that instrument of humility, and reach out to that person. While the job may seem lowly, you'll be great in God's eyes, and His impression of you is really the only one that counts.

Who's Supposed To Have The Lambs?

"Go ye therefore, and teach all nations, baptizing them in the name of the Father, and of the Son, and of the Holy Ghost: Teaching them to observe all things whatsoever I have commanded you: and, lo, I am with you always, even unto the end of the world. Amen."

— Matthew 28:19-20

Somehow we Christians have managed to get the soul-winning process reversed over the years!

As obedient sheep, we dutifully scramble to church each Sunday morning to hear our pastor-shepherd teach us how to keep our wool clean, and warn us not to stray from the flock.

By Monday morning we're back at our jobs, and we assume our shepherd-pastor is back at his — adding baby lambs to the flock.

The only thing wrong with this is shepherds aren't supposed to have baby lambs — sheep are!

When Jesus handed out the great commission, He didn't hand it out to seminary graduates only. The responsibility to make disciples belongs to all of God's children. We each have a role to play in the evangelization of the world.

We don't have to be ordained ministers in order to win souls. We can reach people in our everyday life — the neighbor across the street, the teller at the bank, the guy in the next office.

A living personal testimony of what God is doing in our lives is one of the most powerful tools of evangelism with which we have to work.

If we're willing to share Jesus with those around us, soon *we'll* be bringing in the baby lambs on Sunday morning.

Today, as the opportunity presents itself, take the time to share Jesus with someone. You never know when a new lamb is about to enter into the Kingdom.

Two Ships

"Choosing rather to suffer affliction with the people of God, than to enjoy the pleasures of sin for a season."

— *Hebrews 11:25*

Moses, about whom this verse was written, grew up with a "silver spoon" in his mouth. He had been adopted by Pharaoh's daughter and raised to be a prince of Egypt. Yet, he gave it all up to suffer with God's people. Would you or I have done the same? Why did Moses?

Sometimes being on the good ship Salvation bound for heaven can be mighty rough. It seems like it seldom sails through quiet waters. You've got to work hard and be a good seaman to stay abreast of the waves. Sometimes you even have to walk on water, as Peter found out one day!

But the devil's ship is a luxury liner, a regular "Love Boat," with a jolly crew to make everything pleasant and lot of "fun" passengers along for the ride. You can do anything you want on that ship, and the more you do of it, the more the captain likes it. After all, it is a pleasure cruise, with all the trimmings. All the passengers whoop it up and think, "Hey, what a great captain! He really knows how to put on a cruise."

There's only one catch — Satan's "Love Boat" is bound straight for hell. Somewhere along the route, there is a pirate ship called Death waiting to strip away every pleasure, every dollar, and every material thing before it grabs the soul. Then there's a whirlpool up ahead, and the ship plunges down into hell — with no survivors.

The waters may be rougher with Jesus. You don't get handed everything on a silver platter. But, the Captain knows how to man the helm. He made the trip Himself the first time, and He's brought thousands home since, to a safe and lovely port called heaven. If you ever hear the "Love Boat" go by, don't "jump ship." Sail on with Jesus to the haven of rest.

Praying For The Sick

"I exhort therefore, that, first of all, supplications, prayers, intercessions, and giving of thanks, be made for all men . . . For this is good and acceptable in the sight of God our Savior."
— *1 Timothy 2:1,3*

We believe in intercessory prayer here at PTL. In fact, it's not uncommon for whole departments to meet together to pray when an emergency occurs during the day, and believe me, do they ever pray. I have some real prayer warriors on my staff, and I tell you, they don't stop praying until they've touched heaven and shaken it a few times. They really know how to be heard by God!

The reason we spend so much time in intercession here is because we know it works. God's Word said it, and we've proved it several times.

A few years ago, a little ten-year-old girl named Sarah was taken to the hospital. Sarah is the daughter of Tom Wright, one of my employees. She was declared to be in critical condition by the doctors, who said she was suffering from encephalitis, a virus that made her brain swell, and caused her to be incoherent.

News quickly spread around the ministry, and departments began to intercede for the little girl. In our offices at Park Seneca, the whole staff gathered to pray.

According to Tom, there were no miracle drugs to help her. So my staff members got in touch with a miracle working God instead. Little Sarah came home from the hospital a short time later, totally healed!

Tom says his little girl's life was saved through the intercession by his friends here at PTL. We've seen many other prayers, like that one, answered, also.

Today, if you have a need to be healed, or someone you know needs that healing touch from God, begin to intercede. Write, or call our prayer lines, and we'll intercede with you. Nothing is impossible with the God we serve, so expect a miracle!

"Wait . . . "

". . . commanded them that they should not depart from Jerusalem, but wait for the promise of the Father, which, saith he, ye have heard of me."

— *Acts 1:4*

We Christians are a strange sort. We're eager to go out and do battle for the Lord, and we're usually willing to even suffer for His sake. But all of us "mighty warriors" seem to balk when we hear the Lord say "wait."

Often we don't even hear His "wait," at first, because we're so busy conquering the world in His name.

When it finally does sink in, we try and ignore it, hoping we heard wrong, or thinking that it will go away when the Lord realizes how much we're doing for Him. After all, we're likely to reason, why would God waste all that time putting us on the shelf?

But again and again that insistent "wait" echoes from a still small voice within. So we grit our teeth, sit still, and wait.

God is never off schedule. He's always on time. Even as we sit and feel like we're watching the rest of the world pass us by, God is at work, preparing us for the next phase in our lives.

It is not until we are totally dependent on God, sensitive to His will, and content to remain at rest in Him that He can use us.

How difficult it must have been for the apostles, who had just been with the newly resurrected Jesus, to sit in Jerusalem and "wait." They must have been eager to share with the world about their Lord's triumph over death. But they waited and were given the gift of the Holy Spirit — a gift they would need in their next phase of life.

If God is asking you to wait today, then know that this time apart with Him is only a temporary time of preparation for the new thing He has ahead for you.

Hot Or Cold?

"I know thy works, that thou art neither cold nor hot: I would thou wert cold or hot. So then because thou art lukewarm, and neither cold nor hot, I will spew thee out of my mouth."
— *Revelation 3:15-16*

It's really a shame, but so many people today think of going to church as only their religious duty. To them, church is just a place where you dress up to go and hear a few nice words of philosophy and then go home.

But being a Christian is so much more than that. It's a total life commitment. It's a total immersion in the things of God. It's coming to know God as well as you know your best friend — as well as you know yourself.

How do you come to know someone really well? Suppose you came to PTL, and you wanted to get to know Tammy Faye. I could take you to our home and say, "This is where Tammy and I live." Then I might show you Tammy's closet and say, "These are Tammy's clothes." Later, I could show you her car and take you to her office. "But Jim," you would insist, "all that is great, but I want to meet Tammy!"

No, you could never get to know Tammy by seeing where she lives and works. And you can never truly come to know God by just "visiting" His house each Sunday. Instead, He wants you to be fiery "hot" to get into His Word and His works. He wants you to get involved with your church and not just attend it — and to have a burning personal relationship with Him. He can even deal with you if you are a sinner ice-cold towards Him, but there's nothing worse than being lukewarmly religious.

I believe God is shaking the church today, and the fence straddlers are going to be tumbling down. Don't be one of them! God doesn't want you sitting on the fence — He wants you standing on solid ground. Decide today to get on the hot side — and be a fire in your church for Him!

Plus Or Minus?

"The light of the eyes rejoiceth the heart: and a good report maketh the bones fat."
— *Proverbs 15:30*

Do you know the Negative family? They may live in your neighborhood or even next door. They might even live in your own house! Everything about Mr. and Mrs. Negative is wrong. Their kids are sick all the time, their dog tries to bite the mailman, and their cat snarls and hisses at everybody. Their yard is full of cars, and not one of them runs! Why? Because they have what they confess — they think and talk negative, so everything around them is negative.

Negative thoughts bring negative results, as we see in the story of a little old man who came to America from a foreign country. He was hard of hearing and his eyesight was poor. But, he made a great hot dog! He opened a hot dog stand on the side of the road and told the people, "I have the best hot dog in the whole world." He was so positive that he sold hot dogs to thousands and became king of the hot dog vendors.

He didn't keep up with the news because he could hardly see a newspaper or hear a radio. One day, his son came home from college and said, "Dad, don't you know we're in a recession? You'd better cut back — make less hot dogs and reduce your advertising costs!" Ashamed at his ignorance, the father did as his son advised. He cut back and soon lost his enthusiasm. Business fell off drastically, and he said to his son, "You were right — things really are bad!" He'd begun to think negative, so sure enough, things became negative.

If you want to prosper and enjoy good health, you've got to think and talk positive. Meditate on and live in the Word of God. Act positive, and your business will prosper, your whole body will prosper, and you'll have victory in your life. Be positive today, and bring a little heaven to earth.

Our Lawyer

"My little children these things write I unto you, that ye sin not. And if any man sin, we have an advocate with the Father, Jesus Christ the righteous."

— 1 John 2:1

Unless you're a lawyer yourself, you'll have a mighty rough time if you go to court these days without one. The average man trying to defend himself in court would hardly stand a chance. Our system of laws is so complex and its language is so specialized that most people can barely understand much of what is happening in a courtroom.

God holds court up in heaven, too, you know. He's the Judge of all the earth, the Bible tells us. You might think that the only time your case will be argued will be on Judgment Day, but there's evidence in Scripture that legal battles are going on up there all the time.

Our accuser is Satan. He's the accuser of the brethren (Revelation 12:10), and he's trying to build an airtight case against you right now. If you think you know the Bible, you don't know it half as well as the devil knows it. He can quote chapter and verse, he knows the Greek and Hebrew. You may never have been able to read through Leviticus and Numbers, but the devil has, and he knows every "jot and tittle" of every law. If you had to defend yourself against him, you wouldn't have a chance.

But I want to tell you something: You're not defenseless today in that great courtroom on high! You've got a Lawyer up there — and His name is Jesus! He fulfilled the Law. That's what the word "advocate" means in the Greek — a lawyer. For every one of the devil's accusations, Jesus has an answer: "Yes, that saint did commit that sin. But I shed My blood and covered it. I'm in that saint's heart, and devil, you can't have him!" And the Father says, "I declare that saint righteous. Case closed!" The devil screams, "Objection! Objection!" to no avail. Your Lawyer Jesus has just won another case — and He's even paid your legal fee, too! Praise God!

Get Rid Of What You Don't Need

"Wherefore if thy hand or thy foot offend thee, cut them off, and cast them from thee: it is better for thee to enter into life halt or maimed, rather than having two hands or two feet to be cast into everlasting fire."

— *Matthew 18:8*

In my home state of Michigan, a teenage boy some years ago actually cut off his own leg with a jacknife! A farm boy, he got it mangled in a corn-picking machine he'd been driving that suddenly lurched. Both his left foot and hand were trapped, and he was losing a great quantity of blood.

He took his hunting knife from his belt and cut until he had severed his leg below the knee. Then he pulled his left hand free, crawled to a tractor and drove to the nearest house. He knocked on the door — no one was home! Desperate, he found a phone and called his mother, who sent an ambulance that carried him to a hospital, where his life was saved.

What lengths people will go to, even cutting off a limb, in saving a physical life! But how much do we protect ourselves when it comes to avoiding spiritual death? We're being bled dry by envy or greed or any of the other sins that seem to beset us.

Do we cut those sins out of our lives? All too often, we hang onto them, somehow dulling ourselves to the truth we know in our hearts — that these are death to our life with God and need to be "lopped off" before they destroy us. What Jesus is asking in this verse is that we prefer even death to offending God in any way.

What are those things in your life today that you know are grieving God? Are there any secret sins or unwholesome habits that you have kept inside you? Do you want to live a life that's pure unto the Lord? Ask God right now to give you the strength and courage to cut away the things that don't please Him, and the grace to walk rightly before Him.

Whitewashed Tombs

"Woe unto you, scribes and Pharisees, hypocrites! for ye are like unto whited sepulchres, which indeed appear beautiful outward, but are within full of dead men's bones, and full of all uncleanness."

— *Matthew 23:27*

There's a very popular television series about a large city in Texas that's become very popular in recent years. Every actor and actress in it is a beautiful looking person. But each of them plays a character worse than the other one. Behind their handsome and pretty faces, they're constantly scheming someone's downfall or planning some other wickedness, all the while looking so neat and glamorous.

Jesus recognized the same types among the scribes and Pharisees of His day. But He looked past their outward righteousness and saw the rottenness of their hearts.

Someone has said, "People are like buckets. It's sometimes difficult to know what's in the bucket until it spills out." If you were walking along, carrying a bucket of water, and somebody bumped you, the only thing that could spill out would be water. But if you had a bucket of garbage, you would spill garbage on someone if they ran into you.

You carry a heartful of feelings and motives around with you wherever you go, and you "bump into" people along the way. If you're full of jealousy, hate, or bitterness, those things are going to spill out. If you're filled with the Spirit of God and His love, you'll spill out that love if someone collides with you. But, you will spill out whatever's in you.

Regardless of how you look on the outside, what are you carrying within you today? If you know you're carrying "garbage" around, why don't you "dump" it right now and let Jesus take it away? Ask God to fill you to overflowing with the Holy Spirit — and get ready to spill some life and love all around you today!

Lessons

"A wise man will hear, and will increase learning, and a man of understanding shall attain unto wise counsels."

— *Proverbs 1:5*

"School days, school days, dear old Golden Rule days . . . " Who can forget them: the jammed lockers, crowded hallways, the smell of chalk dust? I can't! I wasn't a very good student in grammar school. In fact, I was tagged a "slow learner" by most of my teachers. By the time I'd reached junior high, I had no faith in myself or my abilities.

One day in the eighth grade, my photography teacher Mr. Harrison surprised me. "Jim," he said, "I believe you've got the natural instincts to become a good photographer." He offered me a job cleaning up the darkroom. In exchange, he spend many hours teaching me the in's and out's of good photography. I was amazed that this man would take a personal interest in me. He showed me he cared for me as an individual. Then he helped me channel my abilities, emphasizing my good points.

Do you know what the result was? My overall grades began to improve. I signed up for journalism and found I enjoyed writing. By the time I reached senior high, I was named editor of the school paper. My success can easily be traced to that teacher. He saw something in me no one else had recognized and took time to personally instruct me, so I could see my worth.

That's just the way the Lord works. He'll take you under His arm and show you your worth to Him as an individual. Then He'll give you direction so your life can bear fruit.

God has a lot of "lessons" to teach you, if you'll allow Him. If you haven't found that out yet, you soon will. He's the Principal of the biggest "school system" in existence. If you'll open your heart to His instruction right now, He'll equip you to handle today and every day's "exams."

The Lesson Of Failure

". . . Forsake me not when my strength faileth."

— Psalm 71:9

There's a wonderful thing about failure. I think it can be the best thing that ever happens to anyone. Failure prepares you for success.

I have never yet met a successful person who hasn't failed at some time. If you make decisions, you'll fail with some of them. I've had to start over several times.

I left the Christian Broadcasting Network after starting the 700 Club, which I had hosted for almost seven years. One morning, the Holy Spirit spoke to me to resign. That same morning, I walked into Pat Robertson's office and told him I had to leave. When he asked where I would go, I didn't know what to tell him because I didn't know myself!

The Lord had spoken to me that it was time to leave CBN, but He didn't tell me where He wanted us to go. We felt like the children of Israel going out into a land they didn't know.

We went to California and started another ministry. I was the president of an organization and helped pioneer a Christian television station there. But that wasn't where God wanted us to settle, either. I resigned once more.

I had nothing left but faith in God. And you know what? That was the greatest moment in my life. That was the beginning of what is now the worldwide outreach of PTL.

You see, sometimes you can hold onto something that you think is so good, and the entire time God wants to give you something even better. You may hold onto one little business when God wants you to have a string of businesses. Because you hold on so tight, you don't understand that with God you have everything. With God, you can always start over — with more fun and excitement. With God, never be afraid of losing it all. Look forward to gaining everything. There's no such thing as being "washed up" with God!

Growing In Grace

"But grow in grace, and in the knowledge of our Lord and Savior Jesus Christ..."
— *2 Peter 3:18*

Have you ever had a "dry spell" in your walk with God? I have had them, and they're not much fun. You just don't seem to be in touch with God. You don't seem to be growing. Your Spirit seems dull, like it's marking time.

These times have a way of coming right on the heels of seasons of great blessing. You've heard some great teaching. You've gotten an important insight from the Word of God. God has used you in a mighty way. You think you've really got a foothold on a new plateau, and suddenly — you're in a spiritual desert, or so it seems.

But don't lose hope! You haven't really stopped growing. Let me tell you a little story that might help explain what's going on.

A man wanted to plant a flower garden, and he went down to the store and looked over the display of seed packets. He picked out the seeds with the most beautiful pictures of the flowers on the outside and took them home. He planted those seeds and then threw away the packets. He was excited about the garden and the wonderful vision of the garden he'd seen while looking at those pictures. But after awhile, he'd just look out his window and see that bare dirt out there. He forgot the thrill he'd felt, and the vision faded. But then, after a while, little seedlings started to come up, and gradually the whole garden sprang to life and bloomed even more beautifully than he'd imagined!

That's how it is with God's Word and teaching. You get excited when you first receive it, but it needs to sink in and take root in your life. Remember — the thrill isn't the fulfillment! If you're in a "dry place," take heart. God is still "growing" you — and the "blooming" will be better than the "planting!"

Confessing Your Faults

"Confess your faults to one another, and pray for one another, that ye may be healed."
— *James 5:16*

Have you ever confessed your faults to a friend — just sat down with a friend and told about that rumor you spread or whatever? It's a hard thing to do. We all have faults, and it seems only natural to try to cover them up and hide them from our friends.

It's so much easier to keep those things to ourselves. But then, the guilt of them grows and gnaws at our very being. I know, I've been there. I've kept things to myself, thinking that if anyone knew them, I couldn't minister any more. Then God led me to this verse and made it real to me.

Here's how it works: If you confess your faults to a friend, and he does the same to you, you in your area of weakness can understand him in his area of weakness. The result will be greater love for one another. What about the "rumor mill" getting hold of your story? Well, if you confess *to each other,* you'll be no more likely to spread his story than he will yours — there's little risk.

There's healing in this verse. Doctors say that a great number of illnesses, emotional and physical, are caused by one thing — guilt. It surfaces one way or another — and God has given the right relief for it in this one verse!

Remember, God's promised to forgive your sins: "If we confess our sins, He is faithful and just to forgive us our sins, and cleanse us from all unrighteousness" (1 John 1:9). Do yourself a favor and find a close friend and learn to practice this simple but important truth of God. You'll feel beter for it!

Ladies — Look Your Best

"She looketh well to the ways of her household, and eateth not the bread of idleness."

— Proverbs 31:27

TAMMY: I always laugh at C.M. Ward's saying, "That any old barn looks better with a little paint."

So it is with us gals!

I think a woman should do the very best with what she has. And no one ought to try to make her feel guilty for doing it!

Some Christian women don't think it's right to dress up and wear make-up just because women have gone around looking dowdy for so long. They think that's the thing to do!

But, I think it is time that we Christian women started looking better than the women of the world. We don't have to settle for looking like them — we can look so much better!

We need to put our make-up on as soon as we get out of bed every morning. Don't go around in an old housedress or a gunny sack all day, but put on something that makes you feel pretty and lady-like.

A little while back, John Wesley Fletcher was staying at the house with us, and he said to me, "Tam, you walk around all day long looking like you just stepped out of a bandbox."

I think that's the way Christian homemakers should be — and don't think your husband won't notice! It keeps your husband excited and noticing you when he can't predict how you'll look when he gets home.

One of the reasons he married you, ladies, is because you were attractive to him when you were dating. So, keep him interested. Don't meet him at the door in curlers and a bath robe — look your best and it'll make his day!

And by the way, it'll help your self-esteem, too! So, practice good grooming for the both of you!

The Peril Of The Occult

"Many of them also which used curious arts brought their books together, and burned them before all men . . . "

— *Acts 19:19*

Our country today seems to be fascinated with astrology — Charting your future by plotting the path of the stars has become a new fad in the hands of thrill-seeking people.

Classes in astrology are offered at many major universities — and the desks are filled with curious young people. In New York, not only can you "dial-a-prayer," but you can now "dial-a-horoscope." At the check-out counters in busy grocery stores across the country, pocket-sized astrology books are conveniently displayed for easy browsing while you wait in line. Even some Christians read their daily horoscopes in the paper every morning — "just for fun."

Dear friend, if you're one of those "just for fun" readers, I caution you not to get even that involved with astrology, because there's a master sorcerer behind it and every other form of the occult — Satan!

The word "occult" means dark, secret, and hidden. That's the lure of all wicked practices like astrology — some hidden power or knowledge that, if acquired, will make life better for the person who has them. The occult appeals to people because it seems to offer power to influence events from behind the scenes. But, the real hidden power is the influence of Satan. For rather than getting power to "pull life's strings," a dabbler in the occult puts his hands into Satan's harnesses — and then the devil starts to pull the strings!

That's why the new believers in the passage above got rid of everything they had that smacked of the occult. I urge you today, if you have any books or objects that are connected with astrology, please get rid of them. Trusting God means giving up trying to wield power on our own — it means placing the key to our future into God's hands for Him to reveal as He chooses.

Drawing Near To God

"Draw near to God, and He will draw near to you."

— *James 4:8*

Have you ever wanted to get to know a person, but felt afraid to meet them because you thought you wouldn't be interesting or good enough for them? I've felt like that. I'm really a shy person, and I've been afraid at times that people wouldn't like me.

I think a lot of people feel that way about God. They've never gotten close to Him because they see Him so high and great that they don't think they can ever measure up. They don't believe that God will accept them if they approach Him.

However, this verse says that God *will* accept you if you'll come to Him. Imagine that! The great God who made all things is willing to draw close to you if you'll just come to Him! Jesus said, "He that cometh to Me, I will in no wise cast out" (John 6:37). You don't have to be afraid of rejection by God.

God has truly given you the privilege of knowing Him! When you come to Him, He meets you in a way that's precious beyond words: He sends His own Holy Spirit. The Holy Spirit takes you past the fearful stage and even the "just friends" part of knowing God. He leads you by the hand right to the heavenly Father and says something wonderful to you: He "speaks to us deep in our hearts, and tells us that we really are God's children . . . that all God gives to His Son Jesus is now ours, too." (Romans 8:16-17)

Now, you can talk to God, person to person. Let Him know all about you. Make Him part of your lifestyle as you do your daily tasks. Learn to listen to Him and learn to love Him as He cares for you.

Draw close to God right now and feel Him accept you. He loves you so much. He's just a prayer away. Reach out to Him: He's ready to meet you, right where you are.

Weight-Lifting

"Come unto Me, all ye that labor and are heavy laden, and I will give you rest."
— *Matthew 11:28*

Many people, men and women alike, now lift weights to get in shape. After losing thirty pounds two years ago, I decided to give weight-lifting a try myself. Well, there was no way I could lift the same amount of weight as a lot of the muscle men around me, who'd been lifting those barbells for months with a lot of coaching. I had to use some common sense.

The first thing I learned about lifting weights was that if you try to lift too big a load, you'll break your back! It would be silly for me to try to hoist two hundred pounds my first day at the gym. Even if I managed to get the barbells off the floor, I couldn't carry them any distance. I had to start with light weights and work my way up.

Carrying a strenuous load, physical or mental, will get you nowhere. I know, because I broke down once trying to handle too much stress. Doctors have linked stress and strain to heart trouble and high blood pressure that can slow you down or shorten your life.

People are just not made to continually carry the kinds of heavy burdens today's fast living puts on them. You try to shoulder the proverbial "weight of the world," and you'll be headed for a sure nervous breakdown or total exhaustion.

I'm glad I shifted a big part of my load onto Jesus' back. Folks, it was just too heavy for me! Now, I've got just about as much "weight" as I can handle and grow, and I let Jesus carry the stuff that takes the muscles.

What about you? Jesus can help you carry the load of life, too. Be honest — are you struggling to prove how much you can bear — and going under? Give it all to Jesus right now, and let Him give you rest for your Spirit and just the right amount of weight your faith can lift safely.

True and False Prophets

"Balaam also the son of Beor they slew with the sword."

— *Numbers 31:8*

This scripture is a sad and ironic footnote to the story of the prophet Balaam, found earlier in Numbers. It seems that Balaam tried to sell his prophecy for money to a foreign king. He tried to curse the people of Israel to gain the favor of the pagan king of Moab and a few shekels.

But try as he might, every time Balaam opened his mouth, nothing but blessings would come out! The enemy king became very angry.

Balaam did not stop trying to curse Israel until God opened the mouth of his donkey, who rebuked him! Then Balaam faded out of sight for a while. But without the verse above, his story and its lesson is incomplete.

So often, I hear people criticize preachers for "being in the ministry for the money." I laugh to myself, because I've been told that I could make much, much more money in secular work. This is true of many of the great men and women of God that I know.

A few preachers may be trying to make money from the gospel. Some are ministering for other reasons, such as power and influence over people. Many of them started out well, with the anointing of God on their lives, but became corrupt at a certain point in their ministry. These false prophets and shepherds have done a lot of harm to needy people. The Bible indicates, in the story of Balaam, that they won't get away with it forever.

Balaam was killed because he consorted with the enemies of God. All those who seek to serve God should abandon such companions as lust, greed, and falsehood, lest when these sins are dealt with by God, they don't perish along with them.

Support great servants of God with confidence. God is in control, and He won't be mocked. Pray today that God will bless and keep pure all those who minister for Him.

A Last Choice

" . . . Choose you this day whom ye shall serve . . . "

— *Joshua 24:15*

I hear a lot of people saying that the United States of America has one last chance. One last chance to solve unemployment, one last chance to whip inflation, one last chance to renew our respect in the world community.

I believe that our nation and its people don't have one last chance — we have one last choice! God never talks about chance, He talks about choice.

Our ancestors were very much concerned with their right to make a choice. Religious choice was a major reason the Pilgrims first came to America. Choices about representation and taxation were basic factors in the American Revolution. The right to choose was so important our forefathers risked their very lives for it. Their victory is our heritage.

Today, we are suffering as a nation. In recent years, even our military has sustained defeats and failures unthinkable only a few decades ago. We seem to have turned our backs on God and His will. We've failed to make Him and His righteousness our choice. In fact, in many areas, we've come to identify sin as a modern lifestyle: Greed, selfishness, and homosexuality have become all too acceptable. How can we, any more than Israel of old, expect God's blessings when there is sin in the camp? The answer is, we can't.

There is one, and only one, true foundation for us to build on as a nation: the Rock of Ages, Jesus Christ. Upon that Rock, God can and will heal our land. The future of this country depends on whether or not we will turn from our sins.

Individually, you can help strengthen that foundation by placing God first in your life. Choose to serve Him. From this moment on, pray for the leaders of our country. God has a plan for America. Choose to honor it today. Remember Psalm 33:12 — "Blessed is the nation whose God is the Lord."

A Lord Who Dances?

"The Lord thy God in the midst of thee is mighty; He will save, He will rejoice over thee with joy; He will rest in His love, He will joy over thee with singing."

— *Zephaniah 3:17*

Every time we have those dancing Scots, the Camerons, on the PTL Club, a few eyebrows are raised. It's because they're almost sure to sing a song called "The Holy Ghost Will Set Your Feet A-Dancing" — and dance it, too! There are believers who just don't think dancing has any place in worship. I know they're sincere and they have their reasons to exclude dancing. But the Bible has a lot to say about dancing, and even commands it in places as a part of worship, so I've chosen to keep an open mind on the subject.

You may remember that Miriam led the daughters of Israel in a dance of praise to the Lord after the crossing of the Red Sea (Exodus 15). And David danced before the Lord after a victory in battle (2 Samuel 6:16). In Psalms 149 and 150, we're told to praise the Lord with dancing. In all, there are over twenty-five references to dancing in Scripture, all positive in tone.

Then there's our verse for today. The King James doesn't reveal it, but many scholars believe this scripture gives us a picture of God dancing. That word "joy" at the end of the verse can be translated "dance," and "singing," means "loud singing." Several commentators say that here God is depicted as singing loudly while doing a triumphant war-dance in the midst of His people. If this is true, it's no wonder God saw David as a man after His own heart, in his dancing, too!

So I'll stay with the Camerons on the subject of dancing. I'm not a great dancer by any means, but I give it a try. And at times when I'm just full of the joy of the Lord, I can't keep my feet still! Maybe the Lord would like to teach you a few steps, too. You can keep it dignified. But when you feel that urge, let it happen. I believe it'll lighten your spirit, as it does mine!

_____

Passing Through

"And it came to pass..."

— Acts 9:32

Have you ever noticed that a lot of words dealing with travel have in them the word *"pass?"* A *pass*enger traveling from the United States to a foreign country needs a *pass*port to enter another country and *pass* through it. Time and distance *pass* while you're traveling. And on the way, you *pass* by many varied and interesting sights.

Just as a traveler passes different places before reaching a destination, so your life keeps on changing as time passes, doesn't it? You've probably had good times, such as a family reunion, when time seems to pass by quickly. Then, too, you may have passed through difficult circumstances that seemed to last almost forever.

My good friend, evangelist C. M. Ward, once pointed out the above verse to me. He grinned and said, "Jim, aren't you glad your troubles and problems don't come to stay? They come to *pass!"* I got a chuckle from that bit of insight, but it has a powerful meaning. For hardships always pass, even though they are not pleasant while you're going through them.

Thank God you and I have got a *pass*port to help us through troubled days and give us peaceful passages to better times. For your personal relationship with Jesus Christ, through Bible reading and prayer, can see you through any situation and provide a map for everyday living.

Travel the road of life with Jesus today. Remember that old Gospel song that says, "This world is not my home; I'm just a-passin' through." Pass your day with Jesus close by your side, and you'll find steady direction on your passage to heaven.

God Will Take Care Of You

"Show thy marvelous loving-kindness, O thou that savest by thy right hand them which put their trust in thee from those that rise up against them. Keep me as the apple of thy eye; hide me under the shadow of thy wings, from the wicked that oppress me, from my deadly enemies, who compass me."

— *Psalm 17:7-9*

The Lord is well able to care for His people! Maynard Ketcham, one of our Elders here at PTL and one of the great pioneering missionaries living today, tells many exciting stories about how God has intervened for His children's safety in other countries.

Dr. Ketcham remembers one little church in Indonesia whose pastor was once a bandit who threatened the Christians instead of shepherding them! His name was Runtu, and he and his band of two hundred men held a remote area of Indonesia in terror before the bandit met the Lord.

Once Runtu and his men decided they would "have a little adventure" with the local church. They swaggered in during a service and demanded valuables. As the people cringed and began to hand over jewelry and money, the power of the Holy Spirit came on the pastor. He called Runtu a sinner, and told him to get out!

The bandit couldn't believe someone would talk to him like that and tried to raise his pistols, but his arms were limp. When he tried to move his feet, he couldn't. Slowly he turned and walked out of the church with his men.

The next Sunday, Runtu and one of his men sat quietly in the back of the church, and they returned the next Sunday, and the next. One Sunday Runtu made his way to the altar in tears, and accepted the Lord as his Savior. He attended Bible school and this bandit, who had once terrorized Christians, became a pastor!

Today, take comfort in knowing we serve a God who is able to keep His children safe under the attack of the wicked.

Don't Bow To The Negative

"Beloved, I wish above all things that thou mayest prosper and be in health, even as thy soul prospereth."

— 3 John 2

Recession. It's a word that's striking fear into the hearts of people all over the world today. But as Christians, I don't believe we have to fear that word, its meaning, or its consequences. I believe we can have the greatest prosperity in spite of a recession, depression, or any other problem — because God wants us to prosper.

Yet so many of God's people tend to think in negative terms about their material needs. To them, the cup is always half *empty* rather than half *full*. People always say, "Go down to the *stop* light and turn right." They never say, "Go down to the *go* light and turn right."

Then there's the expression "poor as Job's turkey" — when in reality, Job was one of the most blessed men in all history. After his trial of faith, when he faced many problems but still refused to give in to the negative, God restored his family, his land, and his riches. He even had seven more sons and three more daughters and one hundred forty more years of abundant living — long enough to see his grandchildren and great-grandchildren.

If we, too, will refuse to bow to the negative side of life, God will bless us with prosperity. God's promises are just as true in bad times as good times. So today, we can decide if we are going to let the world and its conditions control our destiny or if we're going to let God's Word be the deciding factor.

What controls your day? Do you latch on to the television or radio report or newspaper headlines first thing in the morning — or do you take time to reflect on the Good News in God's Word? Keep starting your day in the Bible, and you'll develop that positive attitude that'll bring victory to your life.

Strength For Each Day

"... As thy days, so shall thy strength be."
— Deuteronomy 33:25

During the Israelites forty years in the wilderness, God provided food for them every day. Every morning, a sweet wafer called manna fell all over the ground. Later God sent quails as well. Now, God told the people to gather just enough food for each day, except during the day before the Sabbath, when they were to collect enough for two days.

If they gathered more than they needed for the day, a strange thing happened: The extra just rotted away. God only supplied just what they needed, and no more.

It's easy to feel like you need to store up extra strength in God for hard times that you think might come along. You start thinking sometimes, "What'll I do if I go broke?" "What if I lose my health?" "How will I bear up when my husband passes on?" We want God to give us the courage and strength to carry on.

We want to have the need supplied, so God won't "forget" when the right time comes. But God doesn't work that way. He's promised that He'll see to that need — we have to learn to trust His promises.

Corrie Ten Boom, that great woman of God, once shared how she told her father that she was afraid of persecution or death at the hands of the Nazis during Hitler's regime. Her father said to young Corrie, "When I send you to your grandmother's to visit, when do I give you the train ticket?" "Why, when I'm about to get on the train, Father!" "Just so! And when you will need strength for a trial, God will give you the grace as you need it."

God has everything in your life under control today. You can trust that He will give you whatever kind of "food" or "ticket" you need — when you need it most — already paid for by Jesus.

An Honest Doubt

"And the disciples of John showed him of all these things. And John calling unto him two of his disciples sent them to Jesus, saying, Art thou he that should come? or look we for another?"
— *Luke 7:18-19*

One thing that's precious about the Bible is its honesty when it comes to people. Scripture never tries to hide anything under the rug.

Poor John the Baptist! I can understand how he felt. Early in the Gospel accounts, he stands out as a heroic figure. Jesus Himself said that there was "not a greater prophet than John the Baptist" (Luke 7:28). Yet, John was in prison, seemingly abandoned by the Lord.

What seemed to make it even worse for John were some of the great promises that Jesus had made, including one about releasing the captives. That must have hurt. Why wasn't He getting John out of jail?

Even though John had heard the voice of God Himself proclaim Jesus as the Son of God, the great prophet began to doubt. He began to think he'd backed the wrong man.

You almost can't blame him, can you? You and I both have known dark times when, in spite of the faithfulness and mighty revelation of God in our lives, we've succumbed to doubt. We've said to ourselves, is Jesus really real?

Jesus had an answer for John, and He has the same answer for you and me today. He didn't condemn John for his doubt. He just said to the two men, "Just tell John that the blind see, and the lame walk, and the lepers are cleansed, and the Gospel is preached — and happy is the person who doesn't give up on Me!" (Luke 7:22-23) John never got out of jail alive. But he stuck with Jesus and died a joyful man. If you stick with Jesus, you'll live joyful today — and forever.

Two Wings To Fly

"Let my cry come near before thee, O Lord:
give me understanding according to thy Word."
— *Psalm 119:169*

A lady came up to a preacher after a Sunday service and asked, "Reverend, which do you think is more important: Bible study or private prayer?" The man of God replied, "Madam, which do you think is more important to a bird: the right wing or the left?"

Just as God was smart enough not to create birds with only one wing, He knew better than to launch us out into the Christian life without the "wings" of Bible study and prayer.

I said "study" because there's a difference between just reading the Bible and *studying* it. Some people say, "Jim, I read my three chapters every day, but I just don't get anything out of it." Well, you've got to do more than just read it. Lady, if you're doing some complicated crochet work and want to get it right, you pay close attention to the directions. Mister, if you're trying to replace an engine part, you read that parts handbook carefully before you head for the auto store for a new part.

Likewise, you've got to meditate, or "chew over" (that's what it means) God's Word. What does it mean for your life? How does it fit in with other verses? Is there a special fact or piece of insight that stands out? To do otherwise is like trying to swallow a big meal whole!

And prayer — you wouldn't dare start a million dollar job without your boss' say so, would you? I don't know why so many Christians think they can live their life, which is eternally priceless, without hearing from God.

If you're going to "straighten up and fly right" with God, make sure you've got both wings working today. Meditate on His Word. Ask Him to make it real to you. Tell Him your needs. Give Him some praise from your lips. You'll start to soar!

Rejoice In The Lord

"Be careful for nothing; but in every thing by prayer and supplication with thanksgiving let your requests be made known unto God. And the peace of God, which passeth all understanding, shall keep your hearts and minds through Christ Jesus."

— Philippians 4:6-7

November, 1973, was an important month in the lives of some of the members of my staff from California. For the twenty people who left the Christian television network in California with us, the situation looked desperate. All of us were out of work and broke. We gathered together and asked the Lord to guide us through this time and lift the burden of worry from our hearts.

I remember telling everyone that we had to hear God to survive the situation we were in. Worry is a negative force, and we had to keep our guard up against worry or we wouldn't be able to hear God.

As the first of December approached, I realized we had a sizable house payment to meet. I was praying over the problem when Tammy ran in the room and told me the bank in Virginia had made a $1,500 error in our favor! For the next two months, miracle after miracle took place in our lives, as well as in the lives of the other twenty people.

Friends all across the state sent contributions to us daily when they learned we were no longer associated with the station. We received cards and letters with over a $1,000 a day in contributions, and we were able to pay each staff member their usual paycheck. Herter Backland, a Christian woman who owned three restaurants, gave us and our staff a standing invitation to eat at her delicious smorgasbord, and boy did we eat!

As Christmas approached, the Lord provided all of us with presents, food, rent, and mortgage payments.

We had been in a desperate situation, but by committing our needs to the Lord he carried us through!

It Is Finished!

"... He said, It is finished: and He bowed His head, and gave up the ghost."
— *John 19:30*

This is one of the most thrilling verses in all the Bible! You may have heard preachers from time to time talk about "the finished work of Jesus Christ." Well, today, I want to make sure that you know the exact meaning of that. It's so glorious it can change your life!

In the Roman world, every convicted criminal was sent to jail or his place of execution with a scroll on which his crimes and his sentence were written. The jailer or executioner kept this scroll until the punishment was complete. Jesus had a scroll like this at Calvary. It said that His crime was claiming to be king of the Jews, and it was nailed to His cross.

The very moment a criminal's sentence was completed, his scroll was taken and the words were written across it, "IT IS FINISHED." Then the scroll was handed to the criminal, for him to carry as evidence that his sentence had been served, or to the authorities to prove that the execution had been completed. Once that piece of paper was signed, never again could punishment be administed for that criminal act — even if the wrong person had been put to death.

When Jesus cried from the cross "IT IS FINISHED!" He paid once and for all for every sin of every person who would come to Him and accept that full payment. To those who accept Jesus by faith, God hands a scroll with every past, present, and future sin of theirs on it, and the words "IT IS FINISHED!" written across it in Jesus' precious blood!

That means, beloved, that if you hold fast to Jesus Christ — nobody, not the devil himself, can make you pay for a single sin of your life. IT IS FINISHED! Act like it, and live holy for God today.

From The Depths

"Out of the depths have I cried unto thee, O Lord."

— *Psalm 130:1*

After a PTL Club telecast, I was talking with a well-known Christian singer-songwriter. I had really appreciated the anointed song he'd just sung. He looked at me and confided that this song was written at one of the lowest moments of his Christian experience, when he was nearly at his wit's end. "I was ready to give up," he shared. I replied, "I'm glad you told me that. Now I can feel for you and with you as never before."

Folks, great songs are very seldom written at the peaks in life, when times and feelings are good. The great Christian songs have been written when people have been grieving in their souls. Just look at the Psalms. They were written from grief many times. I can relate to Psalms, sometimes, more than anything else in Scripture. They're so honest and unpretentious.

In Psalm 130, we hear from a man who's seen some trouble. That word "depths" means in Hebrew the deep places of sin and the toughest problems. How wonderful it is that the Bible doesn't leave out the testimony of the tough times.

I've noticed something interesting about these Psalms that begin in despair — once the hurt has been told to God, they almost always end in praise. God really wants to know about the things that are causing us pain, He wants us to cry out to Him from the depths of our souls, He wants us to call out to Him when the fiery darts of Satan are speeding towards us. All too often, we think that we can only come to Him when we're victorious. But I know that He loves us just as much, and is waiting to meet us just as much, when we're in the depths.

Today, you may have a hurt so deep in your heart that no man knows of it. You may think that no one cares. But I tell you that my God and David's God cares. Cry out to God right now. Lay your head on His mighty shoulder. He'll meet you and lead you to a place of peace, comfort, and praise.

Give Up!

" . . . Shall we not much rather be in subjec-
tion unto the Father of spirits and live?"
— Hebrews 12:9

I almost entitled my life story "I Give Up!" The night I received the Baptism in the Holy Spirit, I'd been seeking God for years, struggling and crying out in my heart to get to the right place with Him. I had done everything I could to get His presence into my life and failed.

Finally, I just looked up into the face of God and said, "God, I have tried everything. I don't know what else to do — I give up!" At that moment, the supernatural took over, and I cried, laughed, and praised God in a heavenly language for hours!

You see, God really doesn't want big ability. He really doesn't want a person with a big head or a high I.Q. — He wants us to say, "God, I'm available — I'm usable. God, such as I am, here I am, I'm all yours!"

I remember when Tammy started to sing, she'd say, "No, Jim, I just can't do it!" I said, "Honey you've got to sing! We have been holding revivals for fifty dollars a week, and this church is paying us two hundred dollars — you've got to sing, we have to have music!" Then the organist wouldn't show up, and she would have to play the organ. Tammy would say, "But I have never played the organ." I'd say, "Well, ask God to help you!" And believe it or not, God helped her. One day she talked to the Lord about an accordion, and not many days later, somebody walked up and gave her one.

Little miracles like that lead to big miracles. You know why God has used Jim and Tammy Bakker — the most unlikely people on earth? It's because we took everything we had and gave it to God, and little is much in God's hands. It's the truth.

If God can use a couple of scared, small-town kids, He can use you, too. When you give up and give God your "all," even if your "all" doesn't seem like much, the Lord can do big things with you.

Love — And You'll Get It Back

"And if the house be worthy, let your peace come upon it: but if it be not worthy, let your peace return to you."

— *Matthew 10:13*

Jesus gave this instruction to His disciples when he sent them out to minister to nearby towns. When they visited a home, they were to bestow God's peace on it if it was worthy. But even if it wasn't, that peace was going to return to them.

Many people say to me, "Jim, you worry me when you pray for sinners. I've heard you pray for murderers and prostitutes. These are awful people and you're praying for them. Why are you asking God to bless such terrible people?"

Well, I'll tell you. My Bible says that if I pray that God will help somebody, God will bless them. And if they don't deserve the blessing, the blessing will come back on me. You see, God gives that promise because He wants so to bless everybody. If He's got to promise people something in it for them, He'll do it, if it'll get them to pray.

God has made loving and praying and doing good a "can't lose" proposition. The loving or caring thing that you do will come back to you — even if the person you do it to doesn't respond. I'll buy that, won't you?

There's an old song that has words like these: "Love is something, if you give it away, you end up having more. Love is like a shiny penny — hold it tight, and you won't have any, spend it, spend it, and you'll have so many, they'll roll all over the floor!" It works something like this: If the person you're loving returns your love, then you've got it back from him. If he doesn't return it, God will get it back to you some other way. Either way, you can never waste love.

Have you ever held back on loving someone or doing a good deed because you've thought the recipient would be unworthy? I guess we all have. Let us, with God's encouragement, step out and bring love and peace into the lives of others. God's promised that we've got nothing to lose!

He Won't Give Up On You

"How shall I give thee up, Ephraim? How shall I deliver thee, Israel? . . . Mine heart is turned within me, my repentings are kindled together."

— *Hosea 11:8*

A father had a son who robbed a store and spent a year in prison. Almost as soon as he got out, the boy broke parole and was arrested again. The father went down to the police station to bail him out.

There, a police officer told the father, "Sir, I'm sorry to say it, but your boy has a bad streak in him. For all the trouble he's given, if he were my son, I'd forget him."

"Yes," the father answered, "I'd forget him, too, if he were your son. But you see, he's my son, and I can't forget him."

That's just the way God feels about all of us — no matter how rotten or bad we are, when we fall into sin, or lose faith in Him, or even forget all about Him, He always takes us back, because we're His chosen children, and nothing can separate us from His love.

In the Old Testament days God chose the Israelites to be His people, and they were constantly being unfaithful to Him. Yet, as great as God's sorrow was over their forsaking Him, He never gave them up.

Today, God's heart still grieves when His people stray and are unfaithful to Him. And yet, He still comes to take us back every time. God loves us so much!

Today, if you've strayed from God, and you think He doesn't care anymore, then feel His heart cry out in this verse! God will keep on loving you until you love Him enough in return to be obedient and faithful to Him.

Go Forward!

"And when the Lord said unto Moses, Wherefore criest thou unto me? Speak unto the children of Israel, that they go forward."
— *Exodus 14:15*

TAMMY: We must go forward. How often have I heard Jim Bakker say that? He feels, you have to continue growing or you die. To stand still is to do nothing.

Of course, moving forward has its price. A dear price! Ever since God called Jim into a full-time ministry, early in our marriage, Jim has put everything into it.

At CBN, he worked day and night on radio shows, talk shows and our children's puppet shows. He built sets, he helped with the lighting. He did everything in his power to make each production better than the last.

When God moved us to Charlotte and we began the PTL Club, we had no idea that it would ever get this big. But when we were on one station, broadcasting from the furniture store, Jim pushed for more stations. When we outgrew the building, Jim pushed for building Heritage Village. When we outgrew that, Jim began believing God for Heritage USA.

The easiest thing in the world would have been to stand still, but Jim wouldn't do it. Now we are broadcasting in forty-two nations!

God wants to bless all of us, but first we have to make the effort to move forward. Like the old saying goes, you can't steer a ship until it's moving!

Get moving today! Put your faith in action and believe God for your needs and desires to be met today. Believe me, I've seen it happen, just get moving!

A Torment to the Devil

"And behold, they cried out, saying, What have we to do with thee, Jesus, thou Son of God? Art thou come hither to torment us before the time?"

— Matthew 8:29

In His travels one day, Jesus encountered two demon-possessed men who lived in a cemetery. The men were known to be so fierce that no one would go near them.

Jesus, however, didn't know the meaning of fear. He went right into the area, and the men came out to scream at Him, using the voices of the demons within them. Jesus cast those demons out and sent them into a herd of swine, which plunged down a cliff into the sea.

Notice the words above, which the demons cried out to Jesus. First, they recognized that He was the Son of God. Yes, demons know Jesus only too well, and they tremble at the very mention of His name. Jesus came "to destroy the works of the devil" (1 John 3:8), and He had already begun. He finished the job at Calvary and went to Hell to take the keys of Hell and death right out of Satan's hands.

That's why Jesus was a torment to those demons. They could not stand to have Him around. They tried all they could to defeat Him, but He became victor forever at His glorious resurrection! Hallelujah!

Since He ascended into heaven, He has given us the same power over the devil and his wicked demons that He had, through the Holy Spirit. Did you know that? Right now, you're a torment to the devil. He can't stand you. He's afraid of you! He tries to bluff you into thinking he has you overpowered — but if you'll just take authority over him, you can give him a whipping, just like Jesus did.

Be a torment to the devil today, will you? Give him a hard time. In the strength of Jesus Christ, do the work of God and send the devil packing.

All on the Altar

"And He said, Take now thy son, thine only son Isaac, whom thou lovest ... and offer him there as a burnt offering ..."

— *Genesis 22:2*

The fulfillment of God's promises has to go onto the altar before the Lord. All too often we think that once we've sacrificed in obedience to God, the things He rewards us with are ours. Not so: These belong to God, too, and we have to offer them up to Him, and ask Him what He wants us to do with them.

Abraham had waited long years for the fulfillment of God's promise of a son. Isaac's birth was the result of a miracle. But, Abraham was willing to give up his son. Hebrews 11 tells us that he believed God would raise Isaac up from the dead if necessary. We need to have that willingness, too, to give up anything to God — or for Him.

I can't tell you what it meant for me to lay Heritage USA on the altar. God had given me a powerful vision for a city dedicated to soul-winning, where old and young alike could strive together to win the world for Jesus. Putting it up for sale was like raising the knife over my child's heart. But I had to do it, to learn that nothing, not even a work being done for God, was more important to me than He Himself.

Heritage USA went on the altar, but God did not let the knife plunge down. Negotiations for its sale fell through. And finally, God restored it to my keeping. Today, that vision is nearing total, glorious fulfillment.

Now I know that once finished, Heritage USA will be totally God's, not Jim Bakker's. I'd like to ask you: Has God richly blessed you recently? Have you experienced answered prayer, or the fulfillment of God's promise? If you haven't yet done so, lift that answer or fulfillment up to God right now. Give him total charge of it. It will never be more yours than when it is totally given over to God.

A Listening Heart

*"I will hear what God the Lord will speak:
for He will speak peace unto His people, and His
saints: but let them not turn again to folly."*
— *Psalms 85:8*

In order to survive in today's world, we Christians must learn to discriminate between two voices — God's and Satan's. We know from experience, as children of God, that Satan is a great impersonator. He's always trying to trick us into believing his voice is really that of our Lord's. So we have to be extra careful who we're listening to when we ask for help with a decision.

There are several ways the devil gives himself away, though, if you'll listen carefully. If the voice that you're hearing is a "tinny," rather shrill, persistent voice, constantly urging you to act hastily, then recognize it as Satan's. Also, when the devil talks to you, he'll perch on your shoulder, and speak in your ear.

God, however, speaks to His people in just the opposite manner — He talks to us with peace, in a still small voice, directly to our hearts! He'll never try and rush us into committing some foolish or sinful action *RIGHT NOW*, the way Satan will. Instead we will hear gentle words our Spirits can bear witness with!

Only when we learn to develop a "listening heart" will we be able to determine whose voice is speaking to us. By seeking God and obeying what He tells us, even when it's not what we would prefer to do, we can have that "listening heart" that is sensitive to the voice of God. Begin today to listen with your heart, and you will never mistake Satan's voice for God's again!

No Dark Corners

"If you are filled with light within, with no dark corners, then the outside will be radiant too, as though a floodlight is beamed upon you."

— *Luke 11:36 (LB)*

If you've got the light of Christ inside of you, you'll never have to put on an artificial smile. You'll smile for real, and people will know you've got something special. The best kind of beauty you can have is inner beauty. Years of your life will pass, and wrinkles may line your brow, but you'll get more and more lovely with each year, if Jesus is shining out of you.

In the heart of one of America's great cities stands a church. Its architecture is strikingly modern. Inside, a huge stainless steel figure of Christ draws in the eye first. Then, high in a balcony above the sanctuary, stand row upon row of gleaming pipes, of various shapes and sizes. These form a beautiful design that reflects the light in all directions.

Visitors are surprised to be told that this lovely design is the mechanism of a splendid pipe organ. A guide explains, "We felt that the instrument is so beautiful inside that we wanted all of it to be seen by everyone."

Jesus wants us to be so pure and beautiful on the inside that we, too, wouldn't mind having anyone see a single corner of our lives. Jesus said we were the light of the world. But how clearly does that light shine forth from your life. Have you ever seen an overhead light covered with a fixture that was full of bugs? Not very pretty, was it?

Use the light of God to search out any dark corners that may be spoiling the way you shine for Him today. Ask God to expose them, one by one, and pray right now that He will rid your life of them, so you can radiate God's presence daily.

A True Friend

"And there is a friend that sticketh closer than a brother."

— *Proverbs 18:24*

TAMMY: Remember the song I used to sing a lot, "There's No Shortage?"

Well, there were a few lines in there about, "There's a shortage of friends, yet there's millions (of people) for miles."

People, I know what that songwriter meant, and I'm sure you do, too. A true friend is a hard thing to find; and a hard thing to keep.

It's so easy to get burned with friends. I know once I had a really close friend betray me. I had really cared about her, loved her, and shared with her like us gals do. But she betrayed me. And I got afraid of making friends.

But, God began to deal with me, and I began to see that I had to get over that lack of trust and allow myself to trust a good friend again. Because, even though I forgave my friend, I still had to overcome this trust.

Ladies, it's a terrible terrible thing to let a beautiful friendship be ruined — and to see a part of a friend broken just because of idle talk or rumors.

If God has blessed you with a dear friend, thank God for her. But more than that, work to show that friend the kind of love you want shown to you.

Don't talk about her behind her back, don't tell her secrets — because there is always a high price to be paid for gossip.

Be a friend today. Laugh with your friend when she's happy, and cry with her when she's sad. And above all, stick close to her — never betray a friend.

The Playful Lord

"Then I was by him, as one brought up with him: and I was daily his delight, rejoicing always before him."

— *Proverbs 8:30*

In some circles, Christians have gotten reputations as sour-pusses and killjoys. Even among some believers, acting solemn is necessary to keeping your seat in church. A laugh, a shout, or even a hallelujah in some churches would bring an usher with an undertaker's smile to tap on your shoulder and motion you to the door.

I'm not against being quiet in the church. There are times when silence before the Lord is the proper response to what the Spirit is doing. But at other times, light-hearted laughter and clapping hands and shouting out praises to God are all very much in order. You could be saying right now, "Of course you feel that way, Jim, you're a Pentecostal!" That's true, but I've got other reasons, too, such as our verse for today.

This verse is part of a long passage in which Wisdom speaks as a character. We know from elsewhere in Scripture (1 Corinthians 1:24) that the wisdom of God is Jesus Christ. So this scripture is saying that Jesus was with the Father at the time of creation and was the delight of God the Father. And it says that Jesus was "rejoicing" always before the Father. The Hebrew word used there means "laughingly playing," and is translated that way in some versions. The picture it gives is of Jesus enjoying His role in creation, playfully revelling in His power and imagination, as He created the heavens and earth and man.

If God Himself can be joyous and playful, why shouldn't we be also? That's why on the PTL Club, we encourage laughter and gaiety, bright music and playful fun. So today, if you feel joyous about God, let yourself go a little bit. Say a hallelujah or two. Put on some music and do a little "two-step" before the Lord. Some people might think you're a bit strange, but the Lord won't. He's been playful since before the world was made!

The Uniqueness Of Jesus And You

"I am the good shepherd, and know my sheep, and am known of mine.""
— *John 10:14*

Perfume manufacturers have on their staffs experienced "sniffers" who can distinguish between more than thirty thousand different shades of scent! Most of us can tell the difference between a rose and a lily of the valley, but if you're a professional sniffer, you have to do a lot better than that!

Such "sniffers" sound pretty phenomenal, but a highly trained tracking dog has the potential to tell the scent of every living human being from another. For no two people, not even identical twins, have the same scent. Each person's body chemistry is unique and gives off a particular odor. Scent is a foolproof means of identification, as individual as fingerprints.

God has never confused one of His children with another. He knows the makeup of every human being who ever lived. He knows where each one of them has stood with Him. The Bible says He knows how many hairs are on your head right now (Matthew 10:30) — or even how many have fallen out, in case you're bald. In an age where all too often we think in millions, and individuality gets blurred, Jesus knows His sheep in every way.

And His sheep know Him! There are many "ways" to God, the devil tells people, and many false religions and cults in the world today. But Jesus' sheep aren't fooled by them. When you really get to know the Lord, there's no mistaking Him for anyone else. He's given us a "nose" for Him that will find Him out, in spite of all the devil's counterfeits, if we'll keep seeking Him.

If you truly *know* Jesus, and He knows you, if you keep on the lookout for Him today, I doubt if you'll miss Him. And if there's a chance you'll run into Him, make every effort to do so. You'll never enjoy better company.

A New Creature

"Therefore if any man be in Christ, he is a new creature: old things are passed away; behold, all things are become new. And all things are of God, who hath reconciled us to himself by Jesus Christ, and hath given to us the ministry of reconciliation."
— *2 Corinthians 5:17-18*

When we accepted Jesus Christ as our Saviour and Lord, we were "reborn." Jesus died and was resurrected so we could be redeemed, acquitted, declared righteous, and put in the right standing with God, our Father.

We begin to act as new creatures when we accept this as our life. We have new emotions, desires, thoughts, morals, and attitudes — we are new people.

Don't let the "old you" come through in your daily life. Your old feelings, desires, fears, and attitudes will try to break through and claim victory over you, but the devil won't win if you concentrate on your new self and on Christ.

Whenever Satan tempted Jesus, he couldn't find any ground to stand on. Jesus was a man, just as human as you and I, but Satan couldn't possess any part of him. Do you realize that Jesus, as a man, defeated Satan through his human qualities? If you understand this, then you know that you, too, can defeat Satan when we begin to function totally dependent upon Jesus as our source.

Christians must also reject all that is false. When the old attitudes and thoughts begin to creep in on you, refuse to accept them because it isn't part of the nature of God and it has no place within you. When you do this, you find a new strength in the Lord. You become free of the opinions of others and free from the need to have approval of others. We become truly one with God!

Truth And Facade

"Love not the world, neither the things that are in the world. If any man love the world, the love of the Father is not in him."
— *1 John 2:15*

This verse has been misunderstood by many. Some think that it means that we should have nothing to do with the world around us. Rocks, trees, birds, fish, and animals are all part of the beauty of nature. Some Christians have made themselves hate God's creation. But that's not what this verse is about at all. God doesn't want to take all the joy and beauty out of life. When He made the world of nature, He declared it "good!" That's not the "world" God means.

Someone told me that when the New Testament talks about the "world," it uses a particular Greek word — "kosmos." Our modern-day word "cosmetics" is taken from this term, which means, among other things, a kind of makeup, such as a woman uses on her face. It is used to mean a false front, a facade, that is added to make something look different.

What this scripture says is that the devil has put a false front on what God made good. He's created a sort of makeup to cover over the good that God's done. Pornography, for example, is the devil's false front over sex, which God made good. Corrupt government is the devil's facade over true authority, which God has ordained. Cheating to win is the devil's substitute for winning honestly, by merit. Flattery is Satan's phony version of sincere encouragement. A Christian is not to love those things. We're to love what's true and pure in God's sight.

The devil's like an undertaker, who's dressed and made up a corpse. He tries to make his phony lifestyle look like fun. But it's really dead as a doornail and rotten. Don't love it. Don't be fooled by it. Pray right now for God to give you eyes to see the reality of His love and ways. Don't settle today for the devil's cold substitute.

Be Still

"Be still, and know that I am God . . ."
— *Psalm 46:10*

A lot of people never hear from God because they never get quiet enough before Him to listen. You might call these people "spiritual chatterboxes." And they come in several varieties.

First, there are the know-it-alls. They've got God and everybody else figured out, and they're ready to let God and the whole world know it. They're busy talking about the latest "revelation" they had or giving unasked for advice for every situation. They're just too busy telling all they "know" about God to listen to Him. They secretly hope *He's* listening to *them* — and learning!

Then there are the blow-it-alls. They're constantly giving God and everyone around them a rundown on the latest failures in their lives. "Oh, I've really fouled everything up this time! How can God ever love me? How can I face the world again after the mistakes I've made! I'll never be anything at all for God!" To listen to them, you'd almost think they were beyond salvation, the way they put themselves "beneath" God's love.

Then we have the woe-it-alls. They never stop moaning to everyone about the aches and pains and problems they have. "Oh, God, there's just no hope for me in this situation. Oh, how my head hurts. Oh, these back pains. Oh, these bills. Woe is me, O God!" They're too busy telling God how hopeless things are to listen to His precious promises of help and cheer.

To all of these, God says, "Be still!" In a modern translation, that means, "Keep quiet! Don't you know that I'm God? Don't you know that I'm the one who has all knowledge at My fingertips, and if you'll only listen, I'll teach you things of which you never dreamed? Don't you know that My grace is sufficient for you, even in your weakness, and I'll comfort and give you strength if you'll let me? Don't you know that there's always hope in Me, no matter how bad the situation looks? Be quiet a minute and listen to Me — I'm your God!"

Rejection

"But God, who is rich in mercy, for his great love wherewith he loved us . . ."
— *Ephesians 2:4*

There's no more painful experience than being rejected. Being willing to love means being willing to get hurt. That kind of readiness to be vulnerable takes a love that can only originate in God.

Jesus understood rejection. After He'd been arrested, He looked into the eyes of Simon Peter, who had been His close companion for three years. Peter had just denied their friendship to bystanders who were sure they remembered him as one of Jesus' followers. The memory of this denial was to sting the conscience of that big, bluff man for some time.

Yet Jesus, in His love, hardly noticed. When He went to the cross but a few hours later, He went for Peter, too. And one day, not long thereafter, that same big fisherman, transformed by the love of the man he'd rejected, stood before a vast crowd and shared the news of eternal life through Jesus, his Savior.

Though Peter and his companions were arrested for preaching Christ and beaten, love hardly noticed. Peter couldn't stop preaching the saving power of his Jesus. And later, he followed his Lord into death because of his love for God and men.

If Jesus' love could take the rejection of a close friend just when He needed him most, and remake that man into a mighty preacher of God's Word, that love can transform you also. You may feel you've let the Lord down one time too many, that your rejection of Him is greater than His love for you. But you're wrong. His love never fails (1 Corinthians 13:8), and if you lift up your heart towards Him, He will meet and restore you. He will never cast you out or reject you.

Instead, His love will transform you, just as it did Peter. It doesn't matter if you've rejected Jesus before — Love's hardly noticed. That love is available for you today — accept it, as Jesus accepts you.

What Is A Disciple?

"Then said Jesus to those Jews which believed on him, If ye continue in my word, then are ye my disciples indeed."

— *John 8:31*

In the Greek, the word for "disciple" means "one who is taught or trained." Jesus indicates in the verse for today that a true disciple is more than one who merely "believes" — a true disciple is one who keeps on doing God's will.

James always had a way of cutting the nonsense out of people's "spirituality." In his Epistle, he says this: "Thou believest that there is one God; thou doest well: the devils also believe, and tremble" (James 2:19). Jesus meant the same thing above — unless believing leads to obedience to the Word of God through training and discipline, a person is not really a disciple of His.

The training of Arabian horses for warfare and transportation in the desert was very severe. Each horse was conditioned to be obedient to his master's slightest command. But the last test of the training was the most demanding of all.

All of the horses going through training at one time were taken out into the desert for several days and given no food or water. As they neared death from exposure and lack of sustenance, they were slowly led towards an oasis. Just as they seemed to have no strength left, they would near the oasis and begin to sniff the water in the wind. Their ears would perk up and they would begin to stagger toward the water. They would be allowed to approach to within a few yards of it. Then the master's whistle would call them to a halt. The ones that stopped, in spite of their burning thirst, were worthy for riding use.

God can teach you to be well trained enough to hear His voice also. Let Him begin to teach and train you completely — be a "disciple indeed."

Two Words

" . . . There is no man who has left house or brethren . . . for my sake and the gospel's, but he shall receive an hundredfold now in this time . . . with persecutions . . . "

— Mark 10:29-30

I think we all have the ability to blank words out of the Bible. Sometimes we do that because we're reading King James and it's old-fashioned. But a lot of us want to pick out parts we like and sort of "flow over" those other ones that say, "Get right, repent," or something else that makes us uncomfortable. Take those last two words of today's verses!

Here Jesus was answering a question of His disciples: "Well, Jesus, we've given up all to follow you; what is this going to get us — in the now? You told a rich man to give up everything to the poor — now tell us what's in it for us."

Now, Jesus' answer pleased them — up to a point. No matter what you give to God, He'll give back a hundred times! I'll accept that, won't you? God is going to bless the socks off of you! But here are those two words — Oh, dear me! **"With persecutions!"** Now, why did He have to put those in there?

Before, when I read that verse, I'd see all the "goodies," but believe me, during the last couple of years, I had to get it out and reread it. Now that God has given me victory after victory, I can accept them, and I know why they're there. God made my faith stronger, because I realized that with all the attacks of the enemy and his cohorts, that God was going to keep right on blessing me. I came to know that prospering in God always brings persecutions — the world doesn't understand it, they can't explain it, and every time you stick your head above the crowd, you'll get tomatoes pitched at it.

If you want God's best, you might get the world's worst. But don't let that hold you back — even God's "worst" is better than the world's best!

God Cares About *Everything!*

"Casting all your cares upon Him; for He careth for you."
— 1 Peter 5:7

God cares so much for us that He's willing to shoulder every one of our concerns, no matter how big or small. Many Christians hate to "bother" God with anything less than an earth-shaking matter, though, because they feel they shouldn't "waste God's time" with little things. But I take God literally — when He tells me in His Word to cast *all* my cares on Him, I do it! I know Uncle Henry and Aunt Susan do, too!

On the day they were packing up to move from Virginia to PTL here in Charlotte, it was threatening to rain. Well, Aunt Susan could just see the rain ruining her furniture while they were trying to load it, so she simply asked the Lord to take care of it.

Some people may think Aunt Susan shouldn't have bothered the Lord with something like that, but I tell you, not a single drop of rain fell while the furniture was being loaded on the truck, but the minute it was safely packed away, it started to pour, and it didn't stop until the next day!

When the furniture arrived in Charlotte by truck a few days later, Uncle Henry and Aunt Susan were waiting for it at their new house — but it was raining there, too.

Aunt Susan just gave the problem to the Lord again, and the rain stopped the minute the truck pulled up in the driveway. It didn't rain for three solid hours while the men unloaded the furniture, but when they had finished, and were closing up the back of the truck, it suddenly started to pour! Uncle Henry and Aunt Susan praised God for the beautiful way He cares. They've learned God really means it when He tells us to cast *all* our concerns and worries on Him!

Today, you can give the Lord any cares you may be carrying around, too, and He'll gladly lift them off your shoulders, because He loves us so very much! Praise God!

A Lesson From Grandma

"And there came a certain poor widow and she threw in two mites, which make a farthing. And he called unto him his disciples, and saith unto them, "Verily I say unto you, That this poor widow hath cast more in, than all they which have cast into the treasury."

— Mark 12:43,44

One of my employees was telling me about her grandmother the other day. The little lady lives in the tiny town of Mississippi and loves the Lord with all of her heart.

Every Sunday, she gets up and walks to church, a near mile uphill climb. At eighty-five years of age, she does admit to "setting down half way for a spell."

This little grandmother lives in an old, redone church building next to the jail house. And every month, out of her pension, she gives her tithe to the church, and whatever extra she can to PTL. Now sometimes it's only two dollars or five dollars. But she faithfully gives to God all she can.

I know God smiles and is pleased with that. And I'm equally sure that some of her friends think she is foolish. After all, she's a widow and her income is very limited.

You know something though? That little lady will never be without. God promises that. You can't out give God. And I'll bet that little Grandma would be the first to back me up on that.

It's easy to give out of plenty, but the real test of love is when you give out of your need. In spite of your bleak looking finances.

Learn a lesson from Grandma today . . . and from God's Word.

Who's In Charge?

"Then the Lord said to Satan, Behold, all that he has is in your power; only do not put forth your hand on him. So Satan departed from the presence of the Lord."

— Job 1:12

Many people seem to think that God is sitting up in heaven "twiddling His thumbs" while the devil has a field day down here on earth. It can appear that way at times from our perspective, can't it? But the Bible tells us that God is in control of all things, and no scripture demonstrates this better than the story of Job.

The opening of this book reveals the character of Job, a very wealthy man who was righteous and God-fearing. Job was a man who cared deeply about his family; he sacrificed and interceded for them daily (as all parents ought to do for their children). He was the kind of man who avoided evil, and God Himself acknowledged that there was no one like Job in all the earth.

Then the scene shifts to the courts of heaven. It's interesting to note that among the angels who had to give an account to God up there was Satan. And God, when He questioned Satan about what mischief he was up to, brought up the subject of Job. In a flash, Satan was furious. I don't think he wanted the subject brought up! Job had given the devil too many black eyes!

Satan proposed a theory about Job — that Job served God because he was well-fixed materially. So God let Satan put his theory to a test. God let Satan have a go at Job — with limitations! Satan did not have a completely free hand. Even at his worst, he was subject to God's ultimate control!

God knew the strength of Job's faith. And when His purposes were completed, God broke in and ended the whole story of Job Himself. I can assure you that no matter what you're going through today, God hasn't forgotten you. He's still in charge, and Satan still has to answer to Him. You have to answer to Him, too, so trust Him today, no matter what!

You Can't Bribe God!

"A bribe works like magic. Whoever uses it will prosper."

— *Proverbs 17:8 (LB)*

If you looked at the verse for today, you may be saying, "Jim Bakker, that's the last straw! Do you mean to tell me you're advocating bribery now?" No, I'm not saying that any child of God should ever resort to bribery. But this scripture is a part of the Bible, believe it or not, and God's got a lesson in it for us, if we'll search it out.

It's a fact that bribery works in this sinful world. It seems like every day you read about some public official or government contractor who's gotten caught making or receiving a bribe. Bribery is one of the only ways people without the love of God in their hearts know how to "give!" It's almost like a "negative" reflection of God's "positive" desire for people to have a giving nature.

Over in India, one town some years ago stopped trying to fight bribery, it was so rampant. What they did was to open an office just for bribes at city hall. If the government had to contract a job, the prospective contractors would bring their estimates to one office — and register their bribes at another!

Yes, a bribe does work like magic, and it will bring a short-lived prosperity to anyone who uses it. But you know, there's one place where a bribe won't have a bit of influence whatsoever. That's before the Judgment Seat of God. There, no amount of money that could ever change hands on this earth will make a dent in a soul's chances to get to heaven. Only faith in Jesus Christ and His shed blood will open the door to heaven.

God's people don't need magic, nor do they need the false prosperity that bribery brings. But we should always be a giving people — as unto the Lord. We don't need to try to buy our way into heaven — but we can sure "buy" a lot of blessings of people who need them down here. Be a giver — and prosper eternally in God.

The Blessed Meek

"Blessed are the meek: for they shall inherit the earth."

— *Matthew 5:5*

If you visit the catacombs in Rome, those underground hideaways where the early Christians fled from persecution to worship Jesus, you will find abundant evidences of these believers' love and loyalty to the Lord, and also of their lowliness and humility. In many of the burial places of the saints, the inscriptions are misspelled, some have mixed Greek and Roman letters, and the grammar of most of the epitaphs is poor.

Many of Jesus' early followers were not well-educated people, wealthy, or prominently positioned in the world. And yet, they confounded the wisdom of the ages and destroyed the gods and philosophies of powerful kingdoms.

How much chance would political analysts, at the time, have given this small band of undistinguished people? With no earthly resources to commend them, with nothing to add to worldly knowledge of science, the victims of brutal persecution, how did they survive?

Jesus had promised, "The meek shall inherit the earth." Within a few centuries, the Roman empire had crumbled, and that ragged group of lowly people had become a tremendous power.

I know of many people who feel God has passed them by because they have had fewer advantages in education and upbringing than others in the Body of Christ. But as God blessed the simple testimonies of Jesus' early followers, He can bless your word of testimony to someone's heart today.

Jesus' promises are just as true today as when He first gave them. Believe me, were it not for the love and care and testimonies and encouragement of even the lowliest of our Partners, PTL wouldn't even exist and I wouldn't be PTL President! Act like an inheritor today, for that's what you are, as a faithful follower of Jesus.

How To Control Your Tongue

"If any man among you seem to be religious, and bridleth not his tongue, but deceiveth his own heart, this man's religion is vain."

— James 1:26

Have you ever thought about how little words spoken by you can harm others? Your tongue seems like such a small part of your body, but think of the damage it can do. Even though your arms and legs are bigger and stronger and your brain is smarter, your tongue has a bigger influence in your life.

Many times you say things before you think. I know this has happened to almost everyone. Can't you remember a time when you were really in a panic to get something done and a friend or co-worker came up to you to ask you a question. You probably snapped his head off because you had more important things on your mind. You may not have realized you said anything at all to hurt the person, but he was hurt by your remarks. But, you didn't have the time to take to say a few kind words to help your friend with his problem.

James referred to the tongue as the rudder of the whole ship of a "person." When you realize all spoken words are controlled by your tongue, you can see why James referred to it as a rudder.

God doesn't want our tongues to take part in idle words that may hurt our friends, but only God can help us tame them. When you turn your life over to the Lord, your tongue will stop wagging. God made your tongue to praise Him, make peace, and to tell your brothers and sisters how much God loves them. If your tongue has been used for other purposes that don't glorify God and lift people up, ask God to put a guard on your tongue today. Ask Him to tame it so you can use it to His glory.

Don't speak before you think — let God control your speaking for you!

_____

Restoration

"And I will restore to you the years that the locust hath eaten, the cankerworm, and the caterpillar, and the palmerworm, my great army which I sent among you."

— *Joel 2:25*

Can there be a more precious promise in the Bible than this? Few can mean so much, for there are few regrets that cause the soul more heartaches than grief over wasted years.

An elderly man once said, "We grow too soon old — and too late smart!" How true that seems at times! How often I've wished that I could undo something that's been done in my life — or do something I've left undone.

You may have had a great many "locusts" and "cankerworms" and "caterpillars" in your life. You may have had illness or heartache far beyond anything I've ever known. You may have felt some cruel blows.

But I'll tell you something on the authority of God's Word: it doesn't matter how many blows life has dealt you! It doesn't matter how many years of your life may have been wasted — God can restore them and turn all that's been destroyed into abundance.

A certain man had lived a life of violence and crime in the Mafia in New York City. But as an elderly man, though still a "tough guy," he was led to the Lord by an evangelist. He got so on fire for God and made such an impression for Jesus that when he died a few years later, his son told the tombstone carver to put this epitaph on his headstone: "Vito A. — Born Again!" God wiped out years of sin and did mighty works through this man.

He wants and can do the same for you. I want you, right now, to claim this promise of God. I want you to lay hold of what God has for you. He loves you so much — He wants to heal those wounds the years have brought. Let Him do it!

What It Takes To Be A Fool

"The fool hath said in his heart, There is no God. Corrupt are they, and have done abominable iniquity: there is none that doeth good."

— *Psalm 53:1*

David, who wrote this Psalm, was no fool, but he knew one when he saw one! When the Bible talks about fools, it doesn't mean people who walk around in clown suits and do funny things. It means someone who is completely wicked and thoroughly rejects God. That kind of person gets that way with the help of some fouled-up thinking.

Think, for example, about the statement in today's verse: "There is no God." Who can say such a thing that's got an ounce of real sense? I mean, a person who doesn't know God might say, "I don't know God, and I don't know if there is one, because I've never met Him or seen Him." Someone else might say, "You can't prove there's a God, and I can't prove there's not a God." I might respect someone like that, because he's at least got an open mind.

But anyone who says, flat out, "There is no God," hasn't thought out what he's saying. Because to say for sure that no God exists anywhere, you'd have to be everywhere, know everything, and be perfect! In other words, you'd have to be God yourself! And I don't know that anyone in his right mind would claim that much for himself.

Any person who thought he knew enough to say there was no God would have to think he was a God unto himself. And a person like that would probably be capable of just about anything.

It's better to be a little bit humble and a whole lot smarter, isn't it? I'm glad I know there's a God in heaven and that I can depend on Him today. I don't have to know all the mysteries of the universe to live well. And if He's firmly enthroned at the center of your life, you'll never make the most stupid mistake of all — thinking He doesn't exist!

Freedom For All

*"If the Son therefore shall make you free, ye
shall be free indeed."*

— John 8:36

Not long ago on the PTL Club, I prophesied that soon Christians
would no longer be in the minority in this country. Christians would
be the majority. According to the latest Gallup poll, over 52 percent
of the people in the United States profess to be born again. If we're
the majority, we shouldn't accept minority "tokenism" any more in
government. We should let our voices be heard in a nation under
God — with freedom and liberty for all.

But just as we enjoy freedom to express ourselves, we must
recognize that in our form of government, all others, including
atheists and homosexuals, have the same freedom of expression.
We can't want freedom for our group and deny it to others. It just
won't work that way in the United States.

I'm not afraid of those who disagree with me. I'm not afraid of
the enemies of the Gospel. If the atheists want to have a television
show, and they can raise enough money, let them buy their own air
time. But don't give it to them free — that's not fair.

The reason I believe in freedom is because I believe in the
Gospel of Jesus Christ. I know that my God can conquer all sin, and
I don't have to take freedom from anybody to have my freedom.
Freedom for all — that's what our founding fathers had in mind at
our country's beginning. In fact, the only fear that creeps into my
heart is when people try to destroy the freedoms of others. Look
what happens to any nation that has taken freedom away from any
group — Slavery!

We have a great system in America, and we must let it work by
standing up and making our voices heard — and not denying that
right to anyone. As a born-again majority, we can change America
— change the world. Let freedom ring!

Real Manhood

"Let your manhood be a blessing; rejoice in the wife of your youth."
— *Proverbs 5:18 (LB)*

It's an old and sad story: A middle-aged husband leaving the wife of his youth. You've heard it before: How she worked to put him through school, helped him get started in business, bore his children, and took care of his home. And now that he's made it in life, he just discards her and runs off with someone new.

God meant manhood to be a blessing, but a man like this turns it into a curse. He becomes guilty of tearing his wife's and children's lives apart — and then he makes someone else guilty of adultery. Then perhaps a divorce follows, adding the curse of something that God has stated He hates — "I hate divorce," He says in Malachi 2:16 (NIV).

God's people need, as never before, to uphold the husbands in the body of Christ. The moral standards of the world are fast decaying. Many so-called "experts" are saying that the family is a dead institution. They're talking about "temporary or provisional marriage contracts" and the like.

But the Bible doesn't say "Have yourself a series of young wives, and you'll keep rejoicing." It says that true joy comes in keeping happy the same wife you married when you were young.

Actor Ricardo Montalban has long been famous for his romantic roles. Once he was asked for his definition of a great lover. Mr. Montalban, who has enjoyed over thirty-five years of happy marriage to one wife, answered, "A great lover is a man who can make one woman happy for her whole lifetime." That's the kind of definition God agrees with!

You husbands, keep romance alive in your marriage. Bring your wife some flowers and tell her you love her often. She needs to hear it. Your wife can always be "the wife of your youth" — if you'll keep treating her the way you did when you were courting her. She'll keep you feeling younger, too!

The Great Teacher

"But the Comforter, which is the Holy Ghost, whom the Father will send in my name, he shall teach you all things, and bring all things to your remembrance, whatsoever I have said unto you."

— *John 14:26*

When Jesus returned to heaven, He sent the Holy Spirit, just as He had promised in this verse. One of the "jobs" the Spirit was sent to do was to teach. I think that all too often we don't avail ourselves of this important ministry of the Spirit in our daily lives.

It reminds me of a little child who's having trouble learning his times tables in school. He puzzles over them in class and tries his best to do his homework every night. He even asks his father to help him, but he just can't seem to figure it all out. At night when he goes to bed, he can't get to sleep for thinking he's going to fail. He creeps into his desk at school one morning, his head down. His teacher, seeing his sad face, and taking pity on him, says quietly, "If there is ever anything you don't understand, you can ask me, and I'll help you. That's what I'm here for, you know." Suddenly, the little boy looks up. The teacher's there to help him. Why didn't he ever ask her? He had thought she would condemn him for not knowing the times tables and the answers, so he always avoided her — when she wanted so much to be of help!

We're like that little boy, and the Holy Spirit is the teacher. He's trying to teach us lessons about life with God and other people, and sometimes we don't understand. But do we ask Him for help to make it plain? No, for all too often we feel that He'll think we're stupid and send us away.

A schoolteacher used to say, "The only stupid question is one that you don't ask." Are you confused about anything in your life or in the Word of God? Ask the Holy Spirit right now to make it plain to you. He will — that's why He's here!

Sheer Laziness

"The slothful man roasteth not that which he took in hunting..."

— *Proverbs 12:27*

Here is real laziness! What if a man went out for a walk in the woods with his dog and a rifle, and seeing a rabbit, took a potshot at it and brought it down. His dog trotted off and got the rabbit. Then the man took it home, threw it on the counter, yawned, and settled back in his easy chair, too lazy to cook it! He wouldn't get much nourishment from that rabbit, would he?

He reminds me of some Christians of the jolly, go-to-meeting variety. They'll hear that some well-known teacher is in town, and off they'll go to hear him. The preacher will go through his sermon, and they'll take notes and "shoot down" every fine point while playing it back on their tape recorder. But then, when they've got the whole message "in the bag," they'll just throw the cassette in a drawer with a lot of others, and never put the message to work in their own lives.

They "bag the game," but they don't "cook" it. They enjoy the hunt, and they feel great about getting hold of the truth, but they never let it sink in and really change their lives.

There is a "cooking" method that you can use for a message from God that I'll give you. First, if you're going to "hunt" to begin with, go after a good message. Then, when you get it, go through it and "clean" it. There may be things in any message that are just the preacher's opinion that won't nourish your soul. Don't hang onto them. But the rest — take it into your mind and turn it over and over the fire of a warm heart. Wait until it's really "tasty" in your spirit, delight in every bite of the truth. Then live it out, to the glory of God.

Don't be lazy about the truth of God. Make sure you "cook" it and digest it well. Start with this Word for today!

Faith Worketh Love

". . . for in Jesus Christ neither circumcision availeth anything, nor uncircumcision; but faith which worketh by love."
— *Galatians 5:6*

Mark Buntain, the great missionary to India, has helped to feed literally millions of starving children in that poverty-stricken country. He simply loves people, and he tries to help people anyway he can.

One day he was driving down the street and there was a man standing in the pouring rain waiting for a cab. So Mark pulled to the side of the road and offered the man a ride. "No," said the man, "I'll wait here for a cab." "No," said Mark, "I want to take you where you are going, please get in the car." The man saw the deep compassion Mark had for him, and gratefully got in his car.

A year or two after that, Mark was trying to build the hospital in Calcutta, and he needed one more permit. He walked into the room of the government official who could grant that needed permit and guess who was sitting behind the desk? The man in the rain!

God honors it when you reach out to others. A lot of people think they are really serving God because they attend church every Sunday and know how to pray at prayer meetings. But serving God is more than just lip service — it's reaching out to others in need with love.

And remember these words of Jesus in Matthew 25:40 "Verily I say unto you, inasmuch as ye have done it unto one of the least of these, my brethren, ye have done it unto me."

Do something for God today, and yourself — reach out, in love, to someone.

Rx For America

"If my people, which are called by my name, shall humble themselves, and seek my face, and turn from their wicked ways, then will I hear from heaven, and will forgive their sin, and will heal their land."

— *2 Chronicles 7:14*

America is in trouble. There is no doubt about it. Crime is on the rise. Legislation is currently being discussed in Congress that could alter our rights and freedoms and virtually destroy the family unit as we know it today.

It's a sad, sad thing. But, who is to blame?

I've heard preachers, Bible teachers, and laymen blame it on everybody from the communists, to the atheists, to one minority group or the other. We don't seem to have any trouble finding someone to point the finger of blame toward.

But that's not what the Bible says. The Bible says that He is looking at the Body of Christ; that the responsibility for our country lies totally on our shoulders.

He outlines, in this verse, how to change the nation. First, we have to humble ourselves to Him, to admit to Him that only God Almighty can redeem this land. Second, we must seek his face . . . his will. Third, we have to turn from our wicked ways.

Wicked ways? Yes, the sin in the church must be cleansed in the blood of Jesus.

When we do these things, God has said that He will hear our prayers, and forgive us of our sins. Then, He will heal our land.

The bottom line is this: We Christians must repent of our sins before God can save America.

God Uses Everything!

"A man's heart deviseth his way: but the Lord directeth his steps."

— *Proverbs 16:9*

I don't know about you, but over the years I've found myself doing some unlikely things every now and then, wondering what they've had to do with my "ministry," if anything. But while we sometimes get trapped into seeing one task before us with tunnel vision, God sees our whole lives and directs our steps accordingly.

The Lord never wastes anything — He is perfectly capable of taking any experience we've ever had and using it for His glory and to further His purpose.

I remember one time Tammy and I went home to Michigan to visit my folks, right before we went to work at CBN. We had been traveling as an evangelistic team, and seeing souls saved was our burning desire.

While we were home, Dad decided to rebuild the porch — now I didn't know a thing about building, but Dad had some knowledge, so we rolled up our sleeves and went at it. When we were finished, we'd done a pretty good job, and I knew an awful lot about porch building I never knew before! Of course, as an evangelist, I didn't figure knowing how to build a porch was something I'd have a whole lot of use for, but God knew differently!

A short time later, when we found ourselves at CBN, one of the first things I had to do was build a porch to use as our set on the "Jim and Tammy Show!"

If I hadn't had that experience with Dad at home, the set I built at CBN wouldn't have been as good, nor could I have finished it as quickly.

But God knew what was before me, and to this day, He's constantly leading me into "unlikely" experiences I'm going to need down the road. Today, if you find yourself involved in something unusual, don't count it as a waste of time — instead praise God for the experience. You'll never know when you might need it some day. God always prepares His people!

Enrichment

"That in everything you are enriched by Him, in all utterance, and in all knowledge."
— 1 Corinthians 1:5

When you go to the store to buy something, you don't always get what you think you're getting. "Enriched." You often read that on bread labels, don't you? That sounds really great, doesn't it? Makes you think, "Wow! This bread must be just packed with vitamins and minerals. If I eat a few slices of this, I'll soon be sailing on clouds, talking to eagles!"

Well, the truth isn't quite so wonderful. For what "enriched" really means on a label is that the manufacturer has taken some good food, stripped it of almost all its nourishment, and then put a few nutrients back. The final product is about as enriched as you'd be if you got held up by some mugger and the thief gave you back a few cents to make a phone call!

Words can be very deceiving. Nobody uses words falsely more than the devil. He's got a million get rich quick schemes. He'll tell you your life will be richer if you commit adultery. He'll tell you how much spice a little bit of sin here and there will add to your life. You take his word for it and try his goodies. He takes away your joy and your peace and tells you how much your life is improved. What a liar!

When God says you're "enriched," He really means it. He doesn't take all the good things out of your life and then give you back a few crumbs. He gives you every good thing on top of what you've got. He gives you good things to say, good things to think about, good fellowship, a clean heart, love, joy, peace, patience, self-control. In every part of your life He pours in all His riches, as much as you want to hold.

If you'd like to really "get rich," take a taste of the Bread of Life today. Don't be fooled — and don't settle for less than the "richest"—Jesus!

The Solution Giver

"A double-minded man is unstable in all his ways."

— James 1:8

Have you ever listened to someone tell you about a problem they've been wrestling with, unsuccessfully trying solution after solution? They wonder why God hasn't helped them, yet, actually He's already given His answer — He's just waiting for them to use it!

A professor I heard of assigned his class a very difficult math problem as homework one afternoon. The next day he asked his students for the solution to the puzzle. One young man gave his answer, only to have the professor tell him it was wrong. After several more students tried unsuccessfully to solve the problem, the young man who first volunteered his solution spoke up again: "I sat up all of last night figuring out this problem and I know my answer has to be the correct one!"

"Yes," the professor agreed, "Yours is the correct solution." "Then why did you tell me it wasn't?" questioned the bewildered student. Slowly choosing his words, the professor explained, "It's not enough to have the right answer — you have to believe it's right, too!"

That's where we Christians get so bound up many times. God gives us the answer to a prayer, but we flounder around trying to decide if we really heard from God, or if we heard Him exactly right.

When I first began building Heritage USA, I knew it was God's answer to my strong desire to minister Jesus through a soul-winning city. When a recession came, people began to tell me I had heard the wrong answer to my prayer. But at the very core of my soul, I knew Heritage USA was God's answer for me, and we kept building. Now, even those who told me I was wrong are beginning to see just how right Heritage USA — a soul-winning city is.

When you ask God for an answer today, believe He'll provide one. Then, when He does, trust the solution enough to act on it, because that really means you're trusting in the Solution Giver.

The Mad Bomber

"Therefore thou art inexcusable, O man, whosoever thou art that judgest: for wherein thou judgest another, thou condemnest thyself; for thou that judgest doest the same thing."
— *Romans 2:1*

Did you ever think that when you judge others, you're writing your own list of charges against yourself? That's what this verse is saying. Judging another, in God's eyes, is like entering a guilty plea in whatever you're accusing them.

Whew, that's a hard Scripture! A lot of folks would like to edit that one out of Holy Writ. But even if you've never read it, the principle holds true, because God's laws don't change. A little scary, isn't it, when you think of all the different kinds of people you have judged.

If you judge an alcoholic, God will condemn *you* for being an alcoholic. If you judge an immoral person, you'll find yourself standing before God trying to answer a charge of immorality. If you judge a liar or a thief, you'll have to defend yourself against lying and stealing charges before God's throne.

Some of you may remember a man called the Mad Bomber who haunted New York City back in the late 1950's. This man set off explosions from bombs he had made, all over the city, injuring many people and damaging much property. He was finally caught because police found a pattern in his bombings: Every place he bombed was in some way connected with a former employer of his, whom he resented. Well, I'll tell you something: When you judge, you become a Mad Bomber of the very bridge of redemption you have to cross yourself to get to heaven. If you want to keep that bridge intact, you'd better learn to forgive others!

"If you don't forgive others their sins, God won't forgive your sins" (Matthew 6:14). I pray that the Lord will bring this to all our minds before we are so bold as to do another bit of judging. Build bridges, don't bomb them!

Master Designer

"Now when Jesus was born in Bethlehem of Judea in the days of Herod the king, behold, there came wise men from the east to Jerusalem. Saying, Where is he that is born King of the Jews? For we have seen his star in the east, and are come to worship him."

— Matthew 2:1, 2

Have you ever heard someone say, "I'd like to believe in God, but there is no proof that He exists."

The problem is not the lack of proof of his existence, but the lack of their willingness to make an effort to find Him for themselves.

No one came and tapped the three wise men on the shoulders and told them that if they followed the star, they would find the Christ child. No, they were in tune with God's creation enough to recognize a supernatural event in the stars. They knew God had a purpose for that fabulous star, and they knew it had to be the coming of their Messiah.

We have the same obligation to be in tune with God's creation enough to realize the realness of Him. A popular gospel song in the early seventies, "Master Designer" ministers this message:

"Cotton candy clouds so fluffy and white, Who put you there in a sky of deep blue? Or do you just happen to float along, pretty and white in a sky so blue? Master Designer, whoever you are, all of this beauty both near and afar, can't just have happened, the odds are too great. Help me to simply believe now in You."

Yes, the odds are too great that the masterpieces of creation we see every day could have just happened. The rainbows, the glittering waterfalls, the majestic mountains, the mighty oceans — God is the Master Designer. Follow the example of the three wise men, find Jesus and worship Him today.

God Takes Care Of Details

"Then Joseph, her fiance, being a man of stern principle, decided to break the engagement but to do it quietly, as he didn't want to publicly disgrace her. As he lay awake considering this, he fell into a dream, and saw an angel standing beside him. Joseph, son of David, the angel said, don't hesitate to take Mary as your wife!"

— *Matthew 1:29, 20 (LB)*

How would you have felt, if a few months before you married your wife, you got a message from a "third party" that your fiance was pregnant! And you hadn't been near her!

When this happened to Joseph, he was torn apart inside. He couldn't marry her, and yet he loved her too much to have her bear the shame of his breaking the engagement. The townspeople might even stone his lovely Mary.

Yet, what else could he do? One lesson we can learn from this story is that God takes care of all the details. He sent an angel to assure Joseph, in a dream, that the child was of the Holy Ghost.

God had already spoken, through the scriptures, that Christ would be born of a virgin (Is. 7:14), which confirmed the angel's message in the young man's mind.

God also works out the details in our lives. Maybe He hasn't sent an angel to whisper something to you in your sleep, but if you are a child of His, your every step is ordered by the Lord.

The key is trust. Joseph had to trust God that this child was His through a dream and the Word of God. If he had listened to the doubts Satan surely tried to put in his heart, he would have walked away from Mary forever.

Trust in God today. No matter what problem looms before you, you can be assured that God has worked out the details, just like He did for Joseph.

Leave Christ In Christmas

"And she shall bring forth a son, and thou shalt call his name Jesus: for he shall save his people from their sins."

— *Matthew 1:21*

TAMMY: Everytime I see the words "Merry Xmas" in a store window, it almost makes my skin crawl.

I think what bothers me the most about that spelling is that it is deeper than "Xmas" being abbreviated — it's a reflection of the attitude.

In recent years, fights have ensued in the courts that threaten the rights of our children to sing "Away In A Manger" in public schools. The atheists are fighting to keep the message of the Christ Child out of the pageants. It's a serious, serious thing.

Nonbelievers have taken our celebration of the coming of our King, and turned it into a commercial facade . . . a mockery of the true message of Christmas. And every year it gets worse.

But, hallelujah, we are the salt of the earth. We can make a difference.

By refusing to let this commercial spirit creep into our own families, by fighting the demands of the atheists, by showing more and more love to nonbelievers — we can make a difference.

People, let's leave Christ in our Christmas, in all phases of the holiday. Read the Christmas story to your children and make sure they understand the meaning of the precious gift of the Christ child.

Sure, there is a place for "Jingle Bells" and holly berries, but keep it in prospective to the beautiful Christmas hymns, "O Holy Night," "Away in the Manger" and all the others.

Our children need to know the real meaning of Christmas; and thank God, we live in a country where we are free to share the Bible truths with them!

Joseph or Jonah

*"Then Joseph being raised from sleep did as
the angel of the Lord had bidden him, and took
unto him his wife."*

— *Matthew 2:24*

He did what God told him to do. Now, that might not sound like
such a big deal, but I wonder just how many of us always respond
that way when God says something to us.

My good friend, Mike Warnke, tells a delightful version of how
another man in the Bible didn't do so well when God spoke to him to
do something.

To hear him tell it, God told Jonah to go somewhere he did not
want to go, so he boogied down the beach in the opposite direction.
So he hopped aboard this boat and took off. Well, the Lord doesn't
take "no" for an answer, so, as Jonah found out, it is always easier if
we listen to Him the first time.

A big storm came up and the boat was "fixin'" to go down. Then
Jonah 'fessed up to the skipper, "I'm not doing what God told me to
do." So they laid hands on Jonah suddenly and threw him overboard.

Now, waiting for him was a great, big fish that gulped down
Jonah in one swallow. Three days later, the fish spit him out and he
found himself right where God told him to go.

Every time the Lord tells us to do something, we can either be
like Joseph, and do as the Lord asked right away, or we can reject
the Lord's pleas and take off in the other direction and suffer the
consequences.

In all honesty, I haven't heard of anybody being swallowed by a
fish in recent days, but I do know this: God will perform His will at
any cost.

Be a Joseph. Do what God asks you to do.

_____

Give Yourself This Christmas

"And when they were come into the house, they saw the young child with Mary his mother, and fell down, and worshipped him: and when they had opened their treasures, they presented unto him gifts; gold, and frankencense, and myrrh."

— *Matthew 2:11*

TAMMY: I love this time of year! I love to see the children so excited, whispering secrets, and planning for Christmas Day.

Choosing each special gift for the loved ones on my list is a lot of fun. And sometimes I can hardly wait for Christmas morning to come so that I can see the expression on their faces when they open the gaily wrapped presents.

But there is a much more important gift that we should give this Christmas. It has nothing to do with your Christmas budget, and you don't have to find a box to wrap it in.

It's the gift of yourself to the Christ Child.

No matter what your relationship is with God, just like any other relationship, with a little extra effort and love, it can be so much better.

Remember, man was created to fellowship with God, to talk to Him, and share with Him. But it's so easy for all of us to get busy with "important" things and let our quiet time with Him slip by the wayside.

The only way to get to know God better is to spend more time with Him — just like any other friend! He is there for us to talk to all day long, and He wants to fellowship with us more than we'll ever know.

Draw closer to Him this holiday season, praise Him more, serve Him more, talk to others of His love.

God gave to you and me the most precious gift of all — His Son, Jesus Christ. Without Jesus, there would be no love, no salvation, no hope.

Give Him yourself in a fresh new way. It's the greatest gift you will give anyone this Christmas.

Is There A Vacancy?

"And so it was that, while they were there, the days were accomplished that she should be delivered. And she brought forth her first born son, and wrapped him in swaddling clothes, and laid him in a manger, because there was no room for them in the inn."

— Luke 2:6-7

"No Vacancy." Tammy and I have traveled enough to know the sick feeling it gives you to see that sign in window after window when you need a motel room.

Oh, we've driven miles and miles in search of a room, from little town to little town, until both of us were so on edge that we almost started to bicker at each other.

I can imagine the helplessness Mary and Joseph must have felt as they slowly moved from inn to inn with Mary groaning in labor every step of the way. But there was no room.

While, that was a terrible thing, it has gotten worse over the years. People are still telling the Christ child that there is "no room" in their lives for Him. Not now, anyway.

Over the years, I've had hundreds of people say to me, "Jim, I'm going to accept the Lord . . . one day. But, not now, I've got my wild oats to sow first."

That's a sad thing, because so often that day for repentance never comes, and the Holy Spirit stops tugging at their hearts.

If God is calling you today, and you've never accepted the Lord in your heart, do so now. Just pray, "Dear Lord, I'm sorry for my sins and I'm asking you to forgive me. I do believe that Jesus Christ is the Son of God, and that He died on the cross and shed his blood to wash away my sins. I accept Him into my heart today as Savior. In Jesus' name, Amen."

Now, tell somebody you've asked Jesus into your heart. Call us at 704-554-6000, or write to us, or call a Christian friend. This is a day of rejoicing! You have received the *best gift* of all! *Jesus!*

See Your Salvation

"Mine eyes have seen thy salvation."
— Luke 2:30

The Bible tells us that there was a man in Jerusalem whose name was Simeon. And he was a very just and devout man who loved the Lord with all of his heart.

Luke 2:25 says, "The Holy Spirit was upon him," and the Spirit of God revealed to him that he would not die before he had seen the Lord's Christ.

Now, I'm sure there were some "good ole boys" in the neighborhood that kind of made fun of Simeon. They probably thought he had lost his mind going around saying that he would see the Messiah before he died. He was an old man and all of Israel had been awaiting their King for years and years.

But eight days after Jesus was born, Mary and Joseph took the child to Jerusalem to be circumcised, according to the law of Moses. And it "just so happened" that Simeon was at the temple that day.

When he saw Mary and Joseph and the child, he hugged them and "blessed God saying,Lord, now lettest thou thy servant depart in peace, according to thy word: For mine eyes have seen thy salvation . . . A light to lighten the Gentiles, and the glory of thy people Israel. Behold, this child is set for the fall and rising again of many in Israel . . . " (Luke 2:28, 29, 30, 31, 34).

A dear friend of mine and a member of the PTL Board of Directors, A. T. Lawing, had a word of prophecy spoken to him from a noted man of God when he was just a teenager. He was given several prophetic promises concerning his future. One of them was that he would be in the rapture of the church when Jesus comes back in the clouds. Of all the prophesies that the late Dr. Alfred G. Garr, Sr. gave to A. T., that is the only one that has not happened yet and he is now a grandfather. But I'll tell you something, my spirit bears witness to that Word from God.

A. T. is a devout Christian and worker for the Lord and I believe, with all of my heart, that he will be in the rapture.

Jesus *is* coming soon, Praise God. Now is the time to get ready, before it is too late.

Worth More Than Gold

"The judgments of the Lord are true and righteous altogether. More to be desired are they than gold, yea, than much fine gold . . . "
— Psalm 19:9-10

It takes a tremendous amount of equipment and money just to get a few ounces of gold out of the ground. How many lives have been lost in the pursuit of gold, in the form of ore, buried treasure, and art works?

Did you know that, with all the millions spent on finding it, only two thousand tons of gold are mined every year in the whole world? And if all the gold that's above ground — worth about $65 billion! — were melted into a single block, it would only be about as big as a large barn.

Men have killed and stolen for gold. They've hoarded it. Today, men are frantically buying and selling gold, as paper money continues to lose value. Bright and beautiful, gold is just as much an obsession now as it was when today's scripture was written.

Yet, God's Word says that His judgments and commandments are more desirable than gold. For all the glitter of gold cannot enlighten the eyes of a spiritually blind man. Nor can the possession of great wealth lessen the worries or increase the inner security of a person who doesn't have Christ in his heart. In my experience, no one worries more about money than wealthy people without God. Does that seem strange? It isn't, when you consider that without the Lord's blessing, gold is merely another burden, secure only as long as its possessor is strong enough to hold onto it.

But God's Word will last when money fails, gold is stolen, when friends desert you. His promises never fail — you can take it from me. I've lost it all, and I know. You can have a roomful of gold and be lost — but with God, you're never lost, no matter what!

Judge Not . . . Like It Or Not

"Judge not, and ye shall not be judged: condemn not, and ye shall not be condemned: forgive, and ye shall be forgiven."
— *Luke 6:37*

The greatest deterrent to fellowship among the body of Christ is the Christians trying to figure out who is right and who is wrong.

I literally almost lost my mind one time because of believers judging each other. When I was hosting the 700 Club years ago, people would come up to me and say, "Did you know who you had on the program?" I would say, "No, who?" and they would say, "Well, 'So-and-So,' and he is not right with God." I almost got a case of ulcers worrying about who was right and who was wrong.

I was so frustrated by this, that I became very ill. And one day, as I was driving down the road, God spoke to me and what He said changed my whole life.

While I sat at a traffic light, God said to me, "Jim, you love them, and I'll judge them." And I said, "God, that's the best deal I have ever heard!" I took that Word from Him and I don't have ulcers anymore.

Judging people will make your life miserable. But worse than that, by judging and condemning others, you set yourself up for the same treatment.

Reading the above passage backwards, it tells you if you judge, you will be judged and if you condemn you will be condemned. We all realize that we are not perfect, yet we expect others to be; especially in the Body of Christ.

The answer is in forgiveness. If we forgive others, God will forgive us of our imperfections. That's a great feeling!

How Many Times?

"Then came Peter to him, and said, Lord, how oft shall my brother sin against me and I forgive him? till seven times? Jesus saith unto him, I say not unto thee, Until seven times: but Until seventy times seven."
— Matthew 18:21-22

How many of you have ever had a good friend cheat off your test paper? I don't care if you were in grade school, high school, or college, some people don't think they can get through the course without a little help from a friend. If you ever had this happen to you, you know your friend was stealing from you. They had stolen your thoughts just as if they had taken money out of your pocket.

As Jesus told Peter, no matter how many times your friend sins against you, you are to forgive him. Many times guilt will cause your friend to come up and ask you to forgive him for what he did. But, whether they come and ask you to forgive them or if they run around the campus gloating over stealing the right answer off your paper, you are to forgive him in your heart.

Christians aren't supposed to harbor grudges and resentments in their hearts against their brothers and sisters. By acting as Jesus told us, we are to open our hearts up and forgive those who have sinned against us.

Aren't we blessed that we have Jesus' power in us to forgive others? You may need to call on Him today to help you forgive someone. If you do, before you start praying for the person who sinned against you, count all the times Jesus has forgiven you for your sins. When you realize how often He has forgiven you, it won't take you long to forgive your friend.

Old Testament Grace

"Therefore take unto you now seven bullocks and seven rams, and go to my servant Job, and offer up for yourselves a burnt offering; and my servant Job shall pray for you: for him will I accept: lest I deal with you after your folly, in that ye have not spoken of me the thing which is right, like my servant Job.."

— *Job 42:8*

Some people say there's no grace in the Old Testament, that before Jesus came, God was just an old ogre in the sky with a bat in His hand. If that were true, today's verse wouldn't be in the Bible.

God is speaking here to the three friends who troubled poor Job in the middle of all his trouble. They had harangued Job, accused him of all kinds of sin, spoken falsely about God, and done everything but given that stricken man any comfort. They were almost as bad as the FCC lawyers when I was on the witness stand in Washington! If anyone ever deserved a swift kick from God, it was these friends of Job.

But notice how gracious God was to them. He promised to accept their sacrifice for the way they'd sinned. He told them that He would have Job pray for them, and that He would accept Job's prayer and not punish them for their folly. God knew what they had done wrong and told them clearly. But in His love, He made a way for these foolish men to be restored to Him.

Notice, also, how God made Job a part of this reconciliation. He told Job to intercede on their behalf. What an opportunity for Job to cast aside any bitterness he may have felt towards his friends! What love, grace, and wisdom God showed, even in His handling of this delicate situation.

If even before Jesus' birth, the Father bestowed such tenderness upon these unworthy men, how much more through the reconciliation of Jesus, will He make a way for us, when we've been foolish or let Him down. Thank God right now for being so loving and good, even though we don't deserve it.

Blackmail

" . . . For I will forgive their iniquity, and I will remember their sin no more."
— Jeremiah 31:34

Satan is the inventor of blackmail. He thinks he has the "goods" on everyone and he really enjoys reminding Christians of the "skeletons in their closets." I don't care if it is night or day, winter or spring, every chance he has he will try to tell you what a rotten Christian you are. Satan wants you to think you have been a failure to God, but he won't ever remind you that God has already forgiven you of all your sins and has forgotten them completely!

When I see Christians who have so much fear in their hearts, I want to sit down and cry. They live in real fear that lightening is going to strike them or their children are going to die or God is going to take all their money away to get even with them for their past sins or present weaknesses.

Well, the devil is a liar! God's Word says that Jesus died on the cross at Calvary so our sins would be totally wiped away. The devil wants you to think God is mad with you, but don't listen to him! As long as you claim that Jesus shed His blood to cleanse your sins, He never will be angry with you. Praise the Lord! The devil doesn't want you to know that, but today you need to know that God loves you and Jesus died for your sins once and for all. You need to have this in your heart.

Remember, the devil never forgets a wrongdoing, but praise God, the Lord never remembers them. The Lord has forgiven all your sins and remembers only how much He loves you. If you remember God's love when the devil begins shaking your "skeletons" at you, then you'll be free the way God wants you to be!